Classical
Music Criticism

PERSPECTIVES IN MUSIC CRITICISM AND THEORY
VOLUME 2
GARLAND REFERENCE LIBRARY OF THE HUMANITIES
VOLUME 1879

Classical Music Criticism

With a Chapter on Reviewing Ethnic Music

Robert D. Schick

Garland Publishing, Inc.
New York and London
1996

Library of Congress Cataloging-in-Publication Data

Schick, Robert D.
    Classical music criticism / Robert D. Schick.
        p.   cm. — (Perspectives in music criticism and theory ; v. 2)
(Garland reference library of the humanities ; v. 1879)
    Includes bibliographical references and index.
    ISBN 0-8153-1895-2 (alk. paper)
    1. Musical criticism.   I. Title.   II. Series: Perspectives in music criticism
and theory ; vol. 2.   III. Series: Garland reference library of the
humanities ; vol. 1879.
    ML3880.S3   1996
    781.1'7—dc20   96–5797
                                                      CIP
                                                       MN

Printed on acid-free, 250-year-life paper
Manufactured in the United States of America

Contents

Preface

One of the fascinations of the music criticism found in newspapers and popular journals is its ability to appeal to the imagination of both lay people and professional musicians while still providing solid information. It may seem strange that any writing which caters to such an odd mixture of readers could flourish but it does, and the reasons for that success will be explored in these pages.

Everything that is called music criticism isn't directed toward that audience, however, since the term "music criticism" has another meaning. When a musicologist writes a study of the music of Josquin or Palestrina or Bach and publishes it in a journal meant for a scholarly audience, that kind of writing may also be called music criticism. Occasionally someone tries to avoid confusion by calling what appears in newspapers and popular journals "journalistic music criticism" or "music journalism." Neither term will do, however, for the first one is awkward and the second offensive to the writers for those publications. They think of themselves as music critics writing music criticism, not as music journalists writing music journalism. The public also would be puzzled by any change in name.

The music criticism appearing in newspapers and popular (non-technical) journals is the subject of this book, *not* the writing directed toward a more scholarly audience. By popular journals I mean magazines like the *Atlantic Monthly* and *The New Yorker* (each of which has a music critic), the *Musical Times*, the various record magazines (like *Gramophone, Fanfare*, and the *American Record Guide)* and those magazines primarily about stereo equipment which also contain record reviews.

The time is ripe for a new book on this subject since the last survey, Oscar Thompson's *Practical Musical Criticism*, appeared back in 1934 and is now out of date.[1] Although many of Thompson's points remain valid, music criticism has changed greatly since he wrote, largely in response to the new types of music, the improved technology of recordings, the growth of radio and television as media for transmitting music and music criticism, and to alterations in the sociology of music making and listening. Developments in journalism have also had a vast impact on music criticism.

This book emphasizes the reviewing of Western classical (art) music, but other kinds of music are mentioned when an example casts light on a problem of criticism. The reviewing of ethnic music even receives a chapter of its own, because the critic who reviews *Tosca* today might have to discuss an Indian *raga* tomorrow.

Still, except for that chapter, when these pages talk about music criticism, they usually mean the criticism of classical music, unless the context indicates otherwise. Jazz, popular music, and rock receive little attention, even though some newspapers make that same critic review a pop singer too. So many articles have already been printed about jazz, pop, and rock, articles often written in a style very different from that for classical music, that a separate volume would be required to do justice to the criticism of those musics. One or two chapters would not be enough.

Even though this book emphasizes current practice, examples abound from the past twenty, thirty, fifty, and even one hundred years. Many older examples are quoted because they are still fresh and useful—something readers should assume unless told otherwise—and because they reveal a long tradition behind the point being made. Some other examples are less benign, however, and illustrate practices that are questionable or clearly bad.

These pages concentrate on the practice of criticism in English-speaking lands, but frequent mention is also made to what happens on the Continent, since the activities of music criticism cut across national boundaries.

Incidentally, the title *Classical Music Criticism* is short for "The Criticism of Classical Music," *not* for "Writing from the Classic (Golden) Age of Music Criticism." I don't believe there ever was such a period.

SOURCES OF INFORMATION

In addition to my own thoughts and knowledge of music, the information for this book comes from six main kinds of sources. The most important one is probably the criticism found in newspapers and journals, past and present, since a good review teaches worlds about what to do and a bad review shows what to avoid. Still, the order in which these sources appear here isn't crucial, since they are hard to rank in importance.

The books and articles about music criticism make up a second significant group. Writings about aesthetics—a field often defined today as the philosophy of criticism[2]—form a third category. Insights from aesthetics appear throughout the book and dominate chapters five and eight. Philosophers aren't the only ones contributing to aesthetic theory, for many critics ponder the principles behind their work and express their thoughts in print. Often their ideas are condensed into a paragraph or two in a review, but at other times their ideas expand into an essay or even a book.

A fourth helpful source is the growing body of scholarly research into the history of music criticism. The conferences I attended on music criticism—an important fifth group—provided information about the latest developments within the profession.[3]

A questionnaire to music critics provided a sixth valuable source of information. (The appendix to this book contains that document and a summary of the responses.) I sent the questionnaire to members of the Music Critics Association in 1980 to learn more about the thoughts and feelings of critics and about the current practice of the profession. Had I realized how much the pressure of other work would delay completion of this book, I would have sent out the questionnaire later, but the information it provided remains valuable and is often impossible to find elsewhere. These pages, particularly chapter four on music criticism and journalism, frequently refer to the replies.

SOME DIFFICULTIES IN STUDYING MUSIC CRITICISM

Those studying music criticism encounter several major problems. First, too much is printed daily in English, to say nothing of foreign languages, for any one person to read. A related difficulty is that the sheer quantity of writing makes it hard to collect accurate statistics about music criticism and to make generalizations which are more than impressions without firm evidence.

In addition, evaluating a critic's work is difficult unless one hears some of the same programs and recordings as the critic. Granted, the task becomes easier if the writing violates a basic principle of criticism—I hope this book helps readers spot when that happens—but elegant and convincing writing can disguise poor ears and questionable taste.

For these reasons, preparing a report card naming today's best and worst critics would be a formidable task. Another consideration also kept me from trying to prepare one: Readers might gain little from it. Not only would the verdicts soon become dated as critics retire or pass their peak, but the report might be tainted by my likes and idiosyncracies. Although I have tried hard to eliminate my prejudices, nobody can eliminate them completely.

The difficulties associated with biases are central to the problems of criticism. Although David Hume recognizes that he expects a lot, he asserts that the critic "must preserve his mind free from all *prejudice*, and allow nothing to enter into his consideration but the very object which is submitted for his examination."[4] Yet this seemingly admirable goal is unobtainable, as chapter five will show. Those who forget this today are either naive or conceited.

ACKNOWLEDGMENTS

I am grateful to the many people who helped me with this book. The responsibility for any mistakes is mine, however, because I am the author and because the final draft often differs greatly from what readers saw earlier.

First, my thanks to my colleagues at West Chester University, both past and present. Peter Kent and Patricia Taylor Lee read the first half of the book and suggested many improvements. The library staff, particularly Ruth Weidner, the former music librarian, was invaluable. Walter Fox helped sharpen chapters four and twelve, and Neil Fitzgerald aided with the preparation of my questionnaire to critics. Sue Taylor was also of great assistance.

The cooperation of the 140 music critics who completed that questionnaire is truly appreciated.

Sandra Grilikhes of the University of Pennsylvania's Annenberg Library provided useful advice, as did other librarians at that university, the Philadelphia Free Library, the Music and Theatre Research Divisions at Lincoln Center in New York, and that city's Television Information Office.

Chapter five on the principles behind value judgments profited from the comments of my philosophy teacher, the late Monroe C.

Beardsley, and from the ideas of Jerrold Levinson, who also read chapters one and eight.

The chapter on radio and television criticism gained from the observations of Terry Peyton of radio station WFLN in Philadelphia, and from television producer Clemente D'Alessio. Stations WGMS-AM and FM in Rockville, Maryland, also provided me with useful information.

Judith Lynne Hanna, another writer interested in criticism, directed me to several useful sources. The late Lois Ibsen al Faruqi helped improve chapter ten on reviewing ethnic concerts. The comments of John Rockwell on the entire book are also appreciated, along with those of Patrick J. Smith. My son Joseph also offered some useful suggestions, particularly in regard to chapter three.

The Association of Pennsylvania State College and University Faculties (APSCUF) assisted with a small grant to cover the distribution of my questionnaire to critics.

In addition, I wish to thank the following for permission to reproduce the newspaper articles mentioned below:

Michael Kennedy, for "Roaring Brawl and Lyric Musing: Michael Kennedy on two extraordinary new compositions," from the *Sunday Telegraph* (London), 26 November 1989

The Financial Times (London) for "Le Grand Macabre: Festival Hall," by Rodney Milnes, 3 November 1989

The Observer (London) for "Terror Town on the Downs: Music: Peter Heyworth on Tippett's new opera and serious Rossini," by Peter Heyworth, 8 July 1990

The Times (London) for:
- (a) "Nihon Ongaku Shudan: Queen Elizabeth Hall," by Paul Griffiths, 16 September 1978
- (b) "CONCERT, Noel Goodwin, LPO/Tennstedt, Festival Hall," by Noel Goodwin, 15 December 1989

The Irish Times (Dublin) for "Ferenc Liszt Chamber Orchestra at RHK," by Michael Dervan, 9 November 1989

CBS News for "Vladimir Horowitz plays benefit concert in London," CBS Evening News with Bob Schieffer, 22 May 1982

I.H.T. Corporation for two articles by Virgil Thomson from the *New York Herald Tribune:*
(a) *"Die Meistersinger,"* 13 January 1945
(b) *"Aïda,"* 27 March 1949

The Boston Globe for "Harbison Debuts 'Five Songs,' " by Michael Steinberg, 2 March 1973

The New York Times for:
(a) "Miss Darré Brings Vivacity and Power to Liszt Program," by Allen Hughes, 2 November 1967
(b) "Graffman Heard in a New Concerto," by Donal Henahan, 4 April 1968
(c) "He Calls the Shots on Those 'Live From' Programs," by Lucy A. Kraus, 29 April 1979
(d) "Disks: 'Pathetique' In Furtwängler's Interpretation," by Joseph Horowitz, 17 July 1980
(e) "Recital: ——— Piano Debut," by Bernard Holland, 1 March 1982
(f) "11 Opera-Audition Finalists in Concert at the Met," by Will Crutchfield, 17 April 1985
(g) "Schiff's Central European Assortment," by John Rockwell, 22 October 1989
(h) "A Glimpse of Azerbaijan," by Jon Pareles, 15 January 1990
(i) "The World of Richard Strauss Murky and Not So Honorable," by Allan Kozinn, 25 August 1992
(j) "When France Goes into a Straussian Trance," by John Rockwell, 21 April 1994

CLASSICAL MUSIC CRITICISM

Part I: The Background

Chapter One

Some Basic Issues

Music criticism in the popular press is generally defined as writing about music for a lay audience or for a group of both lay people and professional musicians. There are at least three reasons for music criticism's success in attracting such a broad public with its interesting mix of readers.

In the first place, music criticism in newspapers and (to a lesser extent) music journals provides a day-by-day account of events in the music world. Reading it helps one keep up to date about the latest concerts, operas, recordings, radio programs, personalities, and trends that dominate the musical scene. Another reason for reading music criticism is that it discusses and summarizes the musical experience more clearly than other professional writing about music. This clarity is refreshing and contrasts with the many technical analyses which miss the spirit, poetry, and excitement of the art. A third and related reason is that its language and style are usually simpler than those of more specialized journals. Granted, some topics in these journals are difficult, but an experience described without their thickness of style and technical jargon seems fresher and more comprehensible.

Admittedly, the degree of restriction against terminology varies with the style of a newspaper or journal and the segment of the public toward which it aims. Writing in the *New York Times*, for example, differs from that in a tabloid or *U.S.A. Today*. Nevertheless, most technical language is out of place in a general newspaper or journal and always was.

Bizet had that point in mind in 1867 when he thought he was becoming a newspaper critic. Although a dispute with the paper's

management then caused the plan to fall through, consider what he
had already told the public about his approach to criticism:

> One further word. I have a horror of pedantry and
> false erudition. Certain critics of the third and fourth
> rank use and abuse a so-called technical jargon which is
> as unintelligible to themselves as to the public. I shall
> take care to avoid this absurd error. You will find here
> no information about octaves, fifths, tritones, false
> fifths,   dissonances,   consonances,   preparations,
> resolutions, suspensions, inversions, cadences broken,
> interrupted or avoided, canons in cancrizans or other
> refinements.[1]

Prior to 1766, when Johann Adam Hiller began in Germany one of
the first music periodicals addressed to the general public, the kind of
music criticism discussed here did not exist. Earlier writing about
music had been directed toward a different and usually more formally
learned audience.[2] That kind of criticism is still being written, as was
described in the preface, but it's not the subject of this work.

The distinction between the two kinds of criticism isn't always
clear cut, however. Some kinds of criticism are found only in the
scholarly press (for instance, theoretical analyses which use the
terminology mentioned by Bizet), and some kinds appear almost
exclusively in the popular press (interviews and profiles), but the
content of other writing might fit into either category. Usually, though,
there will be a difference in tone, and the scholarly example might use
more terminology and include details inappropriate for the popular
press.

Even if it appears in the popular press and is directed toward that
newer and broader audience, writing about music must meet two
further requirements to qualify as the kind of music criticism described
here. The first is that the criticism must tie in with something taking
place now, a quality described by the French term *actualité*.[3] An
article about the different versions of a Bruckner symphony isn't music
criticism unless related to something current, such as a performance of
the work. *Actualité*, or timeliness, helps differentiate music criticism
from music history. For example, when historians consider Clementi's
piano sonatas important but inferior to Beethoven's or claim that
Schubert's operas are weakened by their poor libretti, they are making
critical judgments. Still, such remarks aren't music criticism by this

definition, even if written in a popular style, unless they relate to something happening now, to a performance of a Clementi sonata or Schubert opera. This distinction is significant, for a newspaper or magazine editor probably wouldn't let an article on Clementi sonatas or Schubert operas appear if it lacked *actualité*.

The quality of *actualité* explains why music criticism appears in journals and newspapers and to a lesser extent on radio and television but not in books unless they reprint articles originally found elsewhere. By the time a book is printed, its words aren't sufficiently current. This may change, though, now that new technologies for printing make possible the "instant" book.

The last requirement for a definition of music criticism is that critics shouldn't be paid by anyone connected with the music they are writing about. Otherwise they might be restricted in what they could say. (This point may seem obvious, but to the best of my knowledge, it has never been made before.) I make it largely to show why program notes, as well as record jacket and liner notes, aren't music criticism, even if a moonlighting critic writes them. The producer pays the bills, and no sensible producer would let a writer say that the soloist is second rate or the concerto not worth reviving for fear of chasing prospective listeners away.

The same concern about who pays the bills affects the status of public-relations writing. If a writer is paid directly by the group being described, the result isn't music criticism, but if a critic reports in a paper about next season's concerts, the situation is different, since the critic isn't paid directly by a program's sponsor. (It's true that the sponsor might advertise in the paper, but a discussion of the headaches that can create is best deferred until chapter four.) In any case, a simple description of the coming events in a music series probably isn't music criticism, because the article merely rewrites a commercial press release. If, however, a critic adds an opinion and describes the strengths and weaknesses of the series, then the article becomes music criticism. Still, the entire question may be academic, since music critics must often turn out both kinds of articles regardless of how they are classified.

As one might expect from such a controversial subject, some misconceptions exist about music criticism which need correction. For example, despite the common belief that criticism implies saying something negative, music criticism often says positive things. Indeed, in its broadest sense, criticism comments about works of art without necessarily attacking or complaining about them. Although it can be disapproving, it need not be. Second, although many believe that music criticism must evaluate either the music or the performance, this isn't always true. An essay in a Sunday paper, for example, could report on a current trend and contain little or no evaluation. Third, one doesn't have to be a professional to be a critic. Indeed, anyone who says that a concert is good or bad is a kind of critic, though not necessarily a good one. Granted, this book emphasizes the work of professionals—those who express their ideas in print or on radio or television—but the remarks of amateurs are criticism, too, and can be judged by the same standards.

Another misconception is that music criticism always involves the printed word. Radio and television, however, have long broadcast music criticism but not to the extent they should. Indeed, these media remain the new frontiers of music criticism (though the Internet may soon take over the title). Both radio and television offer interesting possibilities for criticism, including supplementing words with music, having specialists interact on panel discussions and combining sound and visual effects with spoken comments in a seemingly endless number of ways. Unfortunately, music criticism underutilizes these resources.

In order to avoid repeating "the printed press, radio and television," which would soon become tiresome, this book usually mentions only the printed press. Most points, however, apply also to radio and television. In any case, these media get their due in chapter eleven, which is devoted solely to their concerns.

Comparing the criticism of music with that of dance and theatre, as well as with the latest darling of the American and Canadian press, restaurant reviewing, may yield some interesting insights into music criticism as practiced in the popular press. Many bonds link the reviewing of these arts together, among them the common desire of impresarios, restaurateurs, composers, playwrights, choreographers, and performers for reviews. Although they may all complain about a bad one, they are still willing to take the chance.

Including restaurant reviewing with music, drama, and dance criticism might puzzle those who question whether cooking is an art. After all, we must eat to survive—though, admittedly, simple food will do—and the other arts are less essential biologically. Besides, if cooking is an art, it's curious that its artists (chefs) expect their work to be destroyed (eaten) shortly after creation. Yet musical performances don't last long, either, if we exclude recordings. Perhaps the recipe resembles the score and the food, the performance. In any case, regardless of the status of cooking, including it in the discussion may prove fruitful.

The criticism of these arts will be compared but usually not the artworks themselves. For instance, these pages make no claim that a lobster dish can be the equal of a Beethoven symphony, though a gastronome might make one. Nor is it implied that the critical processes are identical for each kind of reviewing. Indeed, they are often very different, but studying the differences can be revealing.

Restaurant critics, unlike their colleagues, must be hungry to the right degree. Even the most elegant repast could repel one without appetite, and a mediocre meal would taste marvelous to the starving. In contrast to this, our responses to the performing arts aren't controlled by our stomachs and the levels of our blood sugar. As a result it's easier for critics of the performing arts to respond at any time, though they, too, can become satiated.

All kinds of critics must be selective even before beginning work, since a major metropolitan area has too many concerts, plays, dance programs, and restaurants for them to review everything. As a result, music critics usually ignore school programs, band concerts, church choirs, and amateur recitals or give them low priority when busy. Similarly, food critics skip fast food places, pizzerias, and coffee and donut shops unless writing a special feature about them.

Often, reviews of the performing arts say little about where performances take place, for the same halls are used again and again, since most cities have only a limited number of rooms with good acoustics and sight lines and a decent stage and seating capacity. Food critics, though, pay more attention to the surroundings, since an unattractive decor, bad ventilation, and excessive noise could spoil any meal. Patrons of higher-priced restaurants in particular often consider the surroundings as important as the food.

The situation is different for the performing arts, however, since the least pretentious productions may be the ones which call attention to their surroundings. Off-off-Broadway plays and evenings of experimental music or dance frequently take place in small rooms that were never intended to be theatres or concert halls. The way the production adapts to the available space—perhaps theatre in the round—is of interest.

Since critics of the performing arts generally have good seats—often the same ones again and again in the chief halls—they don't experience the discomforts of the less fortunate. At times, though, it makes sense for them to try other seats, as most critics do when reviewing a new building, in order to check the acoustics and sight lines throughout. And when hearing, say, a string quartet in a large auditorium, some critics try to learn whether the tone which sounds well in the best seats remains appealing in the cheaper ones.

Restaurant reviewers generally try not to be recognized, since that could lead to their getting better food, tables, and service than the rest of the public, which might render their reviews worthless as a buying guide. Critics of the performing arts, however, needn't seek anonymity since they hear the same program as everyone else.

Although a drama critic can return for a second look if the play survives opening night, a music critic can't unless the concert is repeated. Under these circumstances one might ask how valid can a music review be? Musicians often complain that it's not, since the pressures of giving a major recital keep them from playing their best. Yet the ability to stand up to pressure is a major requirement for being a good performer.

Judging a restaurant from a single meal is even less valid, since a restaurant's quality may vary from lunch to dinner, from a slow night to a busy one, or could drop on the chef's night off. To avoid this problem many papers send their reviewers to a place more than once, and frequently with at least one guest so that the diners can sample a variety of dishes.

A review of a restaurant may keep its validity only briefly, for a change of chef or management or an increase in popularity beyond the point a restaurant can handle may cause it to go downhill quickly. Long-run theatrical productions also suffer when the players become bored or the cast changes and the replacements are inferior. Although drama critics frequently report when this happens, such observations receive less publicity than the initial review. An acclaimed pianist or violinist, however, is likely to be good year after year.

Critics usually review a new play or concert immediately—indeed, many performances, particularly concerts, are heard only once—though some plays and musicals postpone the New York reviews by calling the first performances "previews." Restaurant critics may also defer a review until a new place has settled down.

Sometimes what a review says is suggested rather than stated overtly. If we learn, for example, that the steak was tough, the vegetables overcooked, and the hollandaise sauce curdled, or that the violinist was out of tune, had a scratchy tone, and continually dragged the tempo, we can get the point quickly without an overall generalization.

In some ways restaurant reviewers have an advantage over music critics. For instance, they can talk about new dishes and print recipes for them, even complicated ones at times, but music critics can seldom print scores in newspapers. (When one does appear, it's likely to be only a photograph of the first page, because scores take up too much space and most readers can't follow them.) In addition, a major city usually shows more interest in exotic cuisine than in the exotic performing arts. In music only Indian ragas and African drumming have begun to acquire a following comparable to ethnic restaurants. As a result, the criticism of ethnic music remains primitive compared to that of ethnic food, if only because many critics don't see enough performances to sharpen their skills. Of course, reviewing ethnic music is also challenging because it requires a knowledge of dance, ritual, and theatre in addition to music.

As this suggests, love of the subject alone isn't enough to make a good critic, even for cooking. Although many non-professionals might suspect, for example, that the fish tasted inferior because it was frozen or not today's catch, few would have the experience to risk stating that in print. Most would protect themselves by merely saying the fish didn't taste quite right. And if reviewing, say, a Hungarian restaurant, how many would know whether the dishes were made in the traditional style? The same situation holds for music. Although some dilettantes are sharp listeners, they usually lack the scope and depth of knowledge needed to make a good critic.

In smaller communities some newspapers make the critic's job even harder by making the same person review music, dance, theatre, and sometimes even film. But if that person is to say anything worthwhile about music, he or she must begin with a strong music background. Music is too complex a subject to learn on the job. Dance can also be difficult to review, particularly for types based on lengthy traditions. A critic needs training, at least as an observer, to know whether ballet steps are properly done or what the hand gestures mean in South Indian dance.

Many critics also talk about more than the artistic aspects of the performance and include a range of sociologic and economic topics. For instance, theatre critics sometimes complain about the high price of tickets, though I know of only one music critic who has.[4] Restaurant reviewers, though, probably grumble the most when something is overpriced, for diners expect different things from a $50 meal than from a $5 one. Inevitably, standards in restaurant reviewing adjust to the price, since the public wants to know whether it's getting good value for its money.

This variability of standards is one way that criticism reflects the needs and wishes of a democratic society. Because the public wants to know whether a meal is worth the cost, critics usually tell them. They can only do this, however, with a free press independent of outside control. Indeed, the criticism described in this book depends on such a press.

In other societies, though, a different relationship holds. Often, the concern is not about what the public wants but what the govenment thinks it should want, which produces a different and inferior kind of criticism. Consider what Joseph Goebbels, the German Minister of Propaganda, stated in November 1936:

> As the year 1936 has passed without any satisfactory improvement in art criticism, I herewith forbid the practice of art criticism as it has been practiced to date. From today on, the art report will replace art criticism. During the period of Jewish domination of art, art critics violated the concept of 'criticism' and assumed the role of judges of art. The art critic will now be replaced by the art editor. . . . In [the] future only those art editors will be allowed to report on art who approach the task with an undefiled heart and National Socialist convictions.[5]

In a review of *Art in the Third Reich* by Berthold Hinz, John Russell reports the appalling effects this had on German art of the time:

> The official art of the period 1933-45 in Germany was not regimented. . . . [But] of the momentous and terrible events that occurred in Germany between 1933 and 1945, there is hardly a trace in the hundreds of illustrations that Mr. Hinz has mustered. A perennial petit-bourgeois taste prevails throughout. Young love is always wholesome,

> family life is an earthly paradise, manual labor is pleasant
> and redemptive, all battles end happily, nature functions
> as a friend and support.[6]

Until *glasnost*, Soviet Russia controlled its art more directly and officially than Nazi Germany, since Soviet administrators told artists what kinds of work to create. Although the system relaxed at times, the Soviets generally believed that the arts couldn't be politically neutral. A work was either for or against the Revolution's values and could not refrain from taking a stand. Even great works were not exempt, for a bureaucrat could reject them for failing to support and further the aims of the Communist revolution.

As a result, superficial art was often favored over profound because it appeared less elitist, and music for choruses and ensembles was preferred because it supposedly glorified and supported the Russian collective spirit. In such an atmosphere criticism of the arts was no freer than criticism of politics.[7]

Both the Soviet and Nazi positions reflect an extreme concern with the moral effects of art, that is, with the way it determines human behavior. Such moralist theories often rest on shaky foundations, however, since it's debatable how much art can influence the actions of humans. Nevertheless, the various forms of moralist theories, which generally hold that the possible influence of art on behavior is more important than its aesthetic qualities or beauty, have been important throughout the history of art.

Because music is basically non-representational, some moral issues arise less frequently with it than with the other arts. For instance, a statue is more likely to be considered pornographic than a piece of music, although some members of the public condemn rock music as immoral. Indeed, moral judgments about music are often based on what many musicians and music lovers consider peripheral aspects of the art, such as:

1. The texts of songs, whether sung or recollected by playing the tune alone.
2. The kinds of activities with which music is associated. (For example, anything connected with dance, including its music, is immoral to some.)
3. The number of instruments. (A large ensemble promoted the collective spirit better according to Russian dialectics.)

4.   The ability of music to imitate sounds, some possibly indecent.

The many controversies about music's place in ritual often center on conflicts between music's aesthetic and moral values. St. Augustine says:

> So often as I call to mind the tears I shed at the hearing of Thy church songs, in the beginning of my recovered faith, yea, and at this very time, whenas I am moved not with the singing, but with the thing sung (when namely they are set off with a clear voice and suitable modulation), I then acknowledge the great good use of this institution. . . . And yet again, so oft as it befalls me to be moved with the voice rather than with the ditty, I confess myself to have grievously offended: at which time I wish rather not to have heard the music.[8]

St. Augustine's moving description refers as much to his response to the music as to the music itself. He suggests, too, that the aesthetic qualities of religious music should reinforce the spiritual and not call attention to themselves. One might ask, though, whether that is a realistic expectation.

CARMEN

Many innovative and imaginative works, both sacred and secular, were condemned initially on moral grounds, though later generations found them harmless. As an illustration, consider what *Dwight's Journal of Music* said in 1879 after the first performance of *Carmen* in Boston. The vital issues it presents lead to an extended discussion of that sorry episode in the history of music criticism, *Carmen's* reception at its premiere in Paris four years earlier. Indeed, what happened then can teach us so much about the principles of music criticism and the questions to ask about them that a discussion of the premiere occupies the rest of this chapter.

> We can hardly trust ourselves to speak of *Carmen* (given on Friday evening, January 3), so disappointed were we and so little interested in the music, of which we had read and heard such glowing praise. It was the

romantic plot, the intense dramatic action, the picturesque local coloring, the Spanish scenes and tableaux, that made the principal appeal, and that mostly to the eye. Bizet's music has a certain piquancy, and charm of nationality; the instrumentation is brilliant, often rich, and sometimes overloaded; some of the melodies have a strange, peculiar beauty; but the resulting impression of the whole, in our mind, and we believe in most minds, was of a continual and rather tiresome succession of Spanish dance-tunes—many of them very pretty, but *so* many of them very cloying. The song of the hero of the bull-fight created some enthusiasm; but nearly every aria or song of any serious pretension seemed to be bedeviled by a restless struggle to get away from the key, right in the middle of a period sometimes, and then wriggle or jump back again; we cannot think it anything but willful, a desperate endeavor to appear original. Perhaps this is what some of the admirers mean by "traces of the Wagner style," which they discover in it. We will not hold Wagner responsible for anything so bad, although he did wage war upon the family relationship of keys. In Wagner's "unendliche Melodie," such restless confusion of all keys is one thing (*his* thing), but in set melodies, like those of Bizet, it is quite another. We cannot think it can be wholesome to become infatuated with such an opera, or such a drama.

Although he disliked the work, Dwight then gives high praise to the production. He concludes:

But the one redeeming element of innocence and purity, amid so much that is repulsive and depraved, was the small but gracious part of Micaëla, modeled apparently upon the Alice in *Robert le Diable*, which was most sweetly sung and impersonated by Mme. Sinico. But think of Meyerbeer's Alice music, and what is this to it in point of beauty, freshness, or originality! There were some graceful bits of ballet introduced. After listening to it all as well as we were able, we came away caring but little about *Carmen*, and many confessions to the same effect were whispered in our ear.[9]

Although Dwight's response seems quaint and prudish to us today, it was by no means unusual then. His moral disapproval shows most clearly at the end of the first paragraph as well as in these words from the opening of the last one, "But the one redeeming element of innocence and purity, amid so much that is repulsive and depraved. . . ." The lifelike qualities of *Carmen* were too much for him as they had been for many Parisians at its premiere four years earlier.

Even though *Carmen* was a realistic work for its day, it was not a naturalist or expressionist one. (Imagine what it would be like if Alban Berg had set the same story fifty years later.) The choruses, ensembles, duets and arias, the variety of dramatic action, and the second-act dances add color to the work and relieve the sordidness of the drama. Dwight was entitled to his opinion, but one must regret the narrowness of a vision which puritanically rejects a drama with lifelike passions.

His review also illustrates two dangers which all listeners face. The first is that of being disappointed in a work from which one expects too much. The second is that of being prejudiced by the opinions of others. Should a critic listen to others before writing a review? Dwight's remarks about the decadence of the story are also suspiciously close to those of some French critics and suggest that he was influenced by their writings.

This episode illustrates the difficulty of appreciating a work properly at first hearing. We may find *Carmen* simple and easy to understand, but the very qualities which keep it fresh and appealing may have been stumbling blocks to some in the 1870s. Often a listener needs familiarity with the music, or in its absence, familiarity with the style, to appreciate a work, even one as seemingly accessible as *Carmen*. The lack of this familiarity is an ever-present danger for critics who are confronted with new and surprising music. (Though some of *Carmen's* critics seemed to resent even being faced with the challenge.)[10]

Ludovic Halévy, one of the librettists for *Carmen*, gives a similar explanation for the work's failure:

> During rehearsals I went through a series of very different impressions of this piece. At first the music seemed distorted, complicated. . . . It took a little time for us to get to like and admire this score. At the outset we were more astonished than enchanted by it. Such was the evident impression on the audience the first evening.[11]

This lack of familiarity with the work may explain, too, Dwight's inability to comprehend or enjoy its imaginative modulations, though his response may be just the product of a conservative taste. He clearly has the right, however, to complain if he finds the music cloying.

Halévy's reasons, although perhaps valid, are only part of a complex story. In order to understand why *Carmen* was initially rejected by most critics, it's necessary to consider the circumstances surrounding its premiere in Paris in 1875. The reviews of *Carmen's* first performance are one of the great disasters of music criticism. Even though the initial verdict was soon reversed by the work's success in other countries, the negative response upset Bizet and may have helped bring about his death three months later. A study of what happened can tell us much about the problems of music criticism and will point out questions to explore in later chapters.

Carmen had its first performance on March 3, 1875, at the Opéra-Comique with many music critics in the audience. Of the fifteen mentioned by name in the biographies of Bizet by Mina Curtiss and Winton Dean, and in Nicolas Slonimsky's *Lexicon of Musical Invective,*[12] eleven reacted negatively and one was lukewarm, though three later softened their positions. Only two responded positively. (Curtiss and Dean disagree about the verdict of another, Blaze de Bury.) Here is a table summarizing the reactions of the critics:

Critical Reactions to the Premiere of *Carmen*

NAME	PAPER	SOURCE	VERDICT
Theodore de Banville	*Le National*	D:113	positive
Baoudouin	*La République Française*	D:111	negative
Ange-Henri Blaze de Bury	*Revue des Deux Mondes*	C:416 D:279	positive negative
Oscar Comettant	*Le Siècle*	D:111	negative
Léon Escudier	*L'Art Musical*	D:111	negative
Victorien Joncières	*La Liberté*	D:112-13 C:394	positive positive
Bénédict Jouvin	*Le Figaro*	D:113	negative*
Adolphe Jullien	*Le Français*	D:113	negative
Henry de Lapommeraye	*La France*	D:111	negative
Achille de Lauzières, Marquis de Thémines	*La Patrie*	C:399	negative
François Oswald	*Le Gaulois*	D:111	negative
Arthur Pougin	(name not given)	D:110	negative
Ernest Reyer	*Le Journal des Debáts*	D:113	lukewarm*

| Paul de Saint-Victor | *Moniteur Universel* | S:63-64 | negative |
| Johannès Weber | *Le Temps* | D:113 | negative* |

Code:

C=   Curtiss
D=   Dean
S =   Slonimsky
* =   Critic later softened his position

Some claim that the work was a success from the beginning because it ran for a total of forty-eight performances in its first year (March 3, 1875 to February 15, 1876) before the Opéra-Comique dropped it from its repertory, thirty-five of them in the opening season from March 3rd through June 13th.[13] The records indicate, though, that the house was never filled and the work consistently lost money.[14] It's possible that Antoines de Choudins subsidized the performances in the hope that if the work achieved fifty performances it would help the sale of the orchestral score which he was going to publish.[15]

Winton Dean places much of the blame on the generally poor quality of French critics at that time, most of whom were badly trained with little knowledge of music history and aesthetics.[16] They also had a curiously hostile attitude toward composers and new works. One of them, Théophile Gautier, the poet, novelist, and critic wrote in 1864:

> Our real duty—and it is a true kindness—is not to encourage them [young composers] but to discourage them. In art vocation is everything, and a vocation needs no one, for God aids. What use is it to encourage them and their efforts when the public obstinately refuses to pay any attention to them? If an act is ordered from one of them, it fails to go. Two or three years later the same thing is tried again with the same result.[17]

Instead of chiding the public for its lack of support, Gautier tries to dampen the enthusiasm of composers. Other critics were equally cold in practice, even though their philosophies may not have been as blatantly rejecting as Gautier's. This cruel discouragement of opera composers, at a time when opera was the chief Parisian musical interest, caused Bizet, Gounod, and others much grief.

Pierre Berton, an actor in the Comédie-Française and a friend of Bizet's,[18] had a different explanation for the disaster. He charged that Camille du Locle, the director of the Opéra-Comique, was at fault for not bribing the critics beforehand. Berton says:

> The great, the real culprit was du Locle. In Perrin's hands [the director of the Comédie Française] the success would have been unquestionable. He knows how to control an audience and how to handle the press. Among the most severe critics of *Carmen*, I could name those who are notoriously venal. I could say exactly how much it would have taken to transform their attacks into dithyrambic eulogies and even by what intermediaries these delicate negotiations could have been carried out.[19]

The very thought of bribing the critics would probably have repulsed Bizet.

Despite Berton's charge, it's still likely that most of *Carmen*'s critics believed what they said, for their opinions, while seemingly misguided and prejudiced, resemble the pattern of previous complaints about the music of Bizet and other progressive composers of the time. Some critics attacked both his earlier operas and *Carmen* for displaying "a certain tendency to sacrifice vocal interest to richness of accompaniment."[20] A composer as imaginative as Bizet, though, with skill as an orchestrator and a rich harmonic sense, would not write the superficial accompaniments and trivial music that many critics preferred. Hence, he was accused of being too learned, not spontaneous, insufficiently lyrical, with drowning out the voices, and, in short, of being a Wagnerian.

Some critics approved of these supposed leanings, such as Théophile Gautier in his remarks on an earlier Bizet opera, *La Jolie Fille de Perth*,[21] but many more deplored it. Here is an excerpt from the review of *Carmen* by Paul de Saint-Victor:

> M. Bizet belongs to that new sect whose doctrine is to vaporize a musical idea instead of compressing it within definite contours. For this school, of which M. Wagner is the oracle, themes are out of fashion, melody is obsolete; the voices, strangled and dominated by the orchestra, are but its enfeebled echo. Such a system must inevitably result in the production of ill-organized works. The orchestration of *Carmen* abounds in learned combinations,

in unusual and strange sonorities. But the exaggerated competition by the instruments against the voices is one of the errors of the new school.[22]

It seems absurd to complain about lack of melody in *Carmen*, of all works. That complaint may have come from those critics who called Bizet a Wagnerian and ignored the stylistic gulf separating the two men. The ears of these critics were too prejudiced to respond to the freshness of Bizet's melodies. The opening sentence of de Saint-Victor's review might also suggest that Bizet's forms were dissolved into one endless melody from the beginning of an act to its conclusion, without clear-cut cadences or set pieces, as in Wagner's mature operas. Nothing could be further from the truth. The sections are even separated by dialogue when *Carmen* is performed in its original form of an opéra-comique, without the recitatives that Guiraud wrote after Bizet's death to turn it into a grand opera.

Although Bizet uses a recurring theme to symbolize Carmen's fate and José's love, he does not develop it symphonically as Wagner would, and he restricts himself to one theme and not a series of leitmotifs. Bizet's technique was anticipated by Meyerbeer and the early Verdi.[23]

Still, classifying Bizet as a Wagnerian harmed him since Parisian critics were polarized into pro-Wagner and anti-Wagner camps. Some critics almost behaved like voters who cast their ballots according to the parties of the candidates and ignored other qualifications.

Bizet helped sow the seeds for the charge that he was a Wagnerian by a careless remark. In 1862, when he was still twenty-three, he said to the critic Jouvin, "You like Verdi's music. Well Wagner is Verdi with style." Jouvin relates the incident in his carping review of *The Pearl Fishers*.[24] Other stories, one clearly untrue, about similar remarks of Bizet did not help his cause.[25] Nevertheless, it is hard to assess their exact damage, for the charges of Wagnerianism were inevitable in view of the state of French criticism at that time.

This incident points out the dangers for musicians who associate with critics. A chance remark can cause a lifelong prejudice in a petty and vain individual.

To comprehend further what happened to *Carmen*, one must understand what Parisian opera houses were like at the time. Each of the two main centers, the Opéra and the Opéra-Comique, had its own rules about what was proper musically and dramatically and an audience that enforced them strictly. From 1847 to 1870 a more flexible company was in operation when its finances permitted, the Théâtre-Lyrique, but it was gone by the time of *Carmen*. It was at this house that Berlioz's *Les Troyens à Carthage* and Gounod's *Faust* were first performed. There were also the operetta theatres, where Offenbach presented his many works, and the Théâtre-Italien which performed chiefly second-rate Italian operas.[26]

In order to be an opéra-comique, a work had to meet some rigid requirements. One was that it use spoken dialogue, not recitative, to separate its chief musical sections. With this *Carmen* complied. Before *Carmen*, however, opéra-comiques always had a happy ending even if they weren't comic operas. A third requirement, which seems trivial and even laughable today, was that heroines belong "to the spotless and suffering soprano school."[27] Making the main figure a mezzo-soprano like Carmen was shocking, particularly since a suitable heroine, Micaëla, a soprano at that, was rejected by Don José in the opera. These matters were taken seriously, and one critic, Jullien, complained that Bizet had tampered with the "sacred forms" of the Opéra-Comique.[28]

Moreover, presenting such a story at this theatre, particularly one with such realistic details as Carmen's seduction of Don José, was unheard of and scandalous. An evening at the Opéra-Comique was commonly used for matchmaking or for completing arrangements for a wedding by families who purchased boxes for the occasion. Since *Carmen* seemed inappropriate for this, the director, Du Locle, frightened them off and none were present at opening night.[29] If *Carmen* had appeared elsewhere, many reviewers might have been less upset and puritanical. The disturbingly passionate working-class characters of *Carmen* seemed out of place to many in such a bourgeois theatre.[30]

Oscar Comettant, one of the most savage critics, was even distressed by the realism with which Galli-Marié, the first Carmen, played her part. He remarked, "At the Opéra-Comique, a subsidized theatre, a decent theatre if ever there was one, Mlle Carmen should temper her passion."[31]

Yet condemning a work because it appears at the wrong theatre seems provincial and inappropriate for a major center for music. Values are turned topsy-turvy when preserving the honor of a theatre is more important than evaluating a work fairly, particularly one with a claim to major stature. The critics wrote for too restricted an audience when they addressed themselves primarily to the patrons of the Opéra-Comique rather than to the music lovers of Paris and the world.

Bizet seems sadly prophetic of *Carmen's* reception in these lines written when he thought he was becoming a critic:

> Let us be unaffected and genuine, not demanding from a great artist the qualities he lacks, but learning to appreciate those he possesses. When a passionate, violent, even brutal personality like Verdi endows our art with a work that is vigorously alive and compounded of gold, mud, blood and gall, do not let us go up to him and say coldly: "But my dear sir, this lacks taste, it is not gentlemanly." *Gentlemanly!* Are Michelangelo, Dante, Homer, Shakespeare, Beethoven, Cervantes and Rabelais *gentlemanly?*[32]

What more can we learn from this pathetic episode? To find an answer, we must consider the unresolved issues in a broader context than *Carmen* alone, that of the entire field of music criticism. Four questions, or groups of questions, need to be answered. The first asks for whom critics write and to what audience they owe allegiance. (*Carmen's* attackers failed badly in this regard when they showed their chief loyalty to the Opéra-Comique and its patrons.) The second, and related, question asks about the proper functions of critics and criticism. The third asks what the training and qualifications of critics should be to avoid having another group as ill prepared as those who judged Bizet. The last and most difficult question asks what can justify a critic's claim that a work is good or bad, when history shows the many mistakes made in the past. Let us start by trying to answer the first two questions.

Chapter Two

The Function of Music Criticism

Although many readers of music criticism take its existence for granted and accept reading concert reviews in the morning paper with their breakfast coffee as part of their way of life, they seldom question why this should be so. They may gripe at length about a particular critic or review, but they rarely wonder why reviews deserve to be printed at all. Still, if we are to understand music criticism, we can't afford to be that superficial and must delve deeper to find its function.

Music criticism has never had a single, generally accepted role. No two critics ever agree in their concept of criticism and different reviews by the same critic may vary in emphasis. Besides, music criticism has changed throughout the years, though certain themes seem to run throughout.

For instance, one often-mentioned function of music criticism, perhaps the most basic of all, is to inform the public about what happens in music. The apparent innocence of that statement is perplexing, however, since it doesn't tell us who are the people making up the public nor what kinds of information they should receive nor which areas of music-making are worth reporting about. Answering these three difficult questions will take up much of this chapter.

One distinction is readily made, though, which partly addresses the last question. Music criticism in the popular press generally discusses the public aspect of music, the music-making open to everyone, whether it be a concert, opera, or recording. It usually prints only the thoughts of critics and not those of composers and performers, since these are private and not easily knowable, except at times through interviews.

Although Oscar Thompson, a critic for the *New York Sun*, wrote these words in 1934, they remain valuable today:

> Criticism, as practiced in the world of today, particularly with respect to the daily newspapers, has one clear function, so central and dominating that all others may be regarded as subsidiary or supplementary. That function is to *hold up a mirror* to what has been composed or performed and to the performance. The mirror is an intensifying one. It reflects the essentials, eliminates the unessentials. Its purpose is to

> present a clear picture of what the music is, with its good
> points and bad, or what the performance was, with its
> salient characteristics, meritorious or otherwise. It aims to
> be informative, to cut through confusions and distractions to
> the heart of things, to clarify and crystallize impressions for
> those who were listeners, to convey an intelligible report
> and analysis to those who were not present, so that the
> music or the performance has substantially the same
> meaning for them, so far as that is possible, that it had for
> those who attended.[1]

Thompson stresses the importance of giving a clear image of what happened, an image (the review) that focuses on the important and omits the trivial, so that readers who were not present can know what took place. Even though his remarks are primarily about concerts, his basic premise also applies to recordings.

The emphasis of Thompson's writing suggests that he perceives criticism as largely descriptive. Still, he casually includes a place for evaluation when he says the picture of the music should include "its good points and bad." For many readers this is the heart of the review. They want to know whether the music was good, the recording worth buying, or whether to go to the next performance of the opera. Unfortunately, deciding what "good" or its many synonyms mean in this context is far from easy. Indeed, the problems associated with this question are so difficult that an answer must wait until chapter five, which considers the principles behind value judgments.

In practice, most criticism includes value judgments, though the emphasis given them varies from review to review. One writer on criticism, M. D. Calvocoressi, even holds that critics who pretend not to judge but only to describe and interpret really include implied evaluations in their reviews.[2]

As Calvocoressi indicates, a third kind of statement, the interpretative statement (interpretation), also exists. Interpretations frequently, though not always, explain something about the meaning of a work.[3] Many examples are about program music, such as "Beethoven's *Pastoral* Symphony is a picture of nature"; "Debussy's *Feux d'artifice* depicts a fireworks display on Bastille Day"; and "Liszt's *Waldesrauschen* reproduces the sound of trees murmuring in the forest."

Some interpretations are more problematic than others. For instance, "Beethoven's Fifth Symphony shows courage in the heat of battle," is a debatable one that seems to lack supporting evidence. Although some passages in the work might appear courageous, such as those when one section of the orchestra answers (fights with?) another, this probably isn't enough to prove that the work shows "courage in the heat of battle." Indeed, partly because they are hard to verify, a defining characteristic of interpretative statements may be that they are based on evidence that is less than clear cut.[4]

Though harder to prove than descriptive statements, interpretations are still important, since criticism would dry up if critics couldn't speculate about pieces of music. Besides, outlawing interpretations would be impractical, if only because the boundary between description and interpretation is often unclear.

THE AUDIENCE FOR CRITICISM

People follow the music page for many reasons, including a love and interest in music and a curiosity about the daily happenings of music. Sometimes this curiosity also has a practical basis, for people read reviews for advice about which recordings and tickets to buy. A column may also be read for entertainment, which in this sense doesn't mean empty frivolity. A dull column finds few readers, a lively one, many. Being well liked is fine for a critic, provided popularity isn't attained by favoring style over content, elegance over profundity, and glittering but superficial subjects over difficult but important ones. Yet a popular and entertaining critic may still say something important, as George Bernard Shaw proved. (Although Shaw is best remembered today as a playwright, he was also a major music critic.)

Just as public speakers sometimes feel most comfortable addressing a particular member of the audience, music critics may direct their thoughts toward a specific person or group. Sometimes the object is an editor or other individual whose opinion they respect or fear, sometimes the audience and performers of last night's concert. But if a review disintegrates into a private conversation that is unintelligible to most readers, the critic is forgetting the main audience for criticism. Even so, V. Radanovic says:

> A critic sometimes, and in a certain sense, seems to
> be writing for himself. That is the case when he openly
> follows, and listens to, the world of associations started in

him by music, and is not reluctant to pour out even very
personal and completely individual opinions.[5]

Such an approach can yield interesting criticism provided the
writing still gives concrete information about the music. For it to
work, though, readers must identify with the critic's perspective and
be able to follow what is being said.

John Rockwell, who wrote until recently for the *New York Times,*
seems to share Radanovic's position to some extent, for he holds that
critics are narcissistic because they write for readers with the same
sensibilities as theirs.[6] Beneath the surface wit of this remark is the
serious suggestion that critics are egotistical, because they write
primarily about what interests them and assume this will excite their
readers.

Yet all readers can't have the same sensibility as a single critic. It
follows, therefore, that the public needs many critics of varied
backgrounds and interests to satisfy its needs, since no critic speaks
equally well to everybody.

CRITICISM AND NEW MUSIC

Some people claim that we are too close to new music to evaluate it
properly and should wait a while before beginning the job. As
evidence to support this position they point to the way history often
revises the standing of composers. For instance, Telemann and
Graupner were once ranked above Bach, since they were the first two
choices for the position at St. Thomas's Church in Leipzig which Bach
wanted. Bach received the post only because they were unavailable.[7]
Nevertheless, if professional critics won't evaluate new music, others
will, since the public wants to know right away which piece of
contemporary music is worth hearing. Indeed, if criticism ignored new
music, it would leave itself open to the charge that it was a useless
enterprise.[8]

There is no denying, though, that critics can make serious mistakes
about contemporary music. Barbara Mueser, writing about the
reactions of New York critics to contemporary music between 1919
and 1929, records their hostility and even insensibility toward it. One
of them, Henry Edward Krehbiel, wrote in 1920:

> The men who could not approve of all that Beethoven wrote were not dishonest fools; nor were they all imbeciles who objected to Schumann or Wagner or Brahms. It is not idiocy today to question the artistic validity of a phrase penned by R. Strauss, or Roger [Reger], or Debussy or Schoenberg. Honest antagonism to innovation is beneficial and necessary to sound progress. It provides the regulative flywheel without which the engine would go racing to destruction. . . . The things which shall be great in the future because they differ from the things that are great now can wait for the future. Better to fail now to hear the future's evangel of beauty than to proclaim that to be beautiful which shall not be recognized as such hereafter. We cannot wrong the future; we can wrong the present.[9]

Mueser comments:

> Krehbiel was actually discussing "progress" in terms of music almost two decades old. The future had already arrived for much of the music that he condemned. In reality, he paid lip service to progress while adhering to a belief in "unchangeable laws . . . inherent in the art of music."[10]

In fairness to the New York critics, Mueser points out that the 1920s presented them with problems because World War I delayed the orderly appearance of new music in that city. (Recordings of orchestral music and ensembles were still largely unsatisfactory in the early 1920s.) Critics often had little time to prepare themselves for the changes in musical style that had taken place. For instance, the *Rite of Spring*, first performed in 1913, didn't have its New York premiere until 1924, but Stravinsky's Symphony for Wind Instruments, written in 1920, also had its first New York performance in 1924, a week after the *Rite of Spring*.[11]

Mueser also notes that some critics wanted to protect their audiences and favored less difficult music.[12] It's not clear, though, that all audiences want to be isolated from demanding twentieth-century music. And even if they do, it's not the critic's job to shield them—a point some of *Carmen*'s judges failed to realize. A critic must inform the public about what is happening, and trying to guard an audience can interfere with that duty. If the public needs protection, which is debatable, that's a job for those presenting concerts.

In any case, other forces began to shelter the public from new music in the 1920s, for societies sprang up sponsoring new music in New York and elsewhere.[13] (Such groups are still around.) They helped get performances of new works at a time when radio and recordings were still relatively primitive and concerts remained the chief means for hearing music. But the existence of such groups symbolizes the growing estrangement between composers and the general public. Ironically, instead of helping the situation, in the long run, these groups may have furthered this separation. Not only did they reduce the pressure on mainstream organizations to perform new music, but they made it less urgent for composers to write music these organizations would perform.

THE CRITIC AS EDUCATOR AND TEACHER

Critics often remark that criticism helps bridge the gap between composer and listener. As Virgil Thomson wittily observes, "The function of criticism is to aid the public in digesting musical works. Not for nothing does it so often resemble bile."[14] Bridging that gap is particularly important in regard to new music and requires educating the public. Doing that is a tricky matter, however, for a light and almost inconspicuous touch is needed to do it well, since the public, like schoolboys, resists being educated when it realizes what is happening.

Although educating a large audience is fine, it's questionable whether criticism should try to teach individual performers and composers. (In this sense, an educator addresses many people; a teacher addresses a single person or small group.) Oscar Thompson says that critics should be fact finders and not super-teachers, since criticism is primarily for the general reader and not the artist.[15] Perhaps Thompson means that a critic shouldn't suggest specific ways for a performer or composer to make corrections. Not only would the critic be addressing too narrow an audience, but the lesson might be arbitrary, since there is often more than one way to correct a problem.

For these reasons Benjamin Britten's complaint that critics never pointed out the weak passages in his works or suggested how to improve them is out of line.[16] Not only does Britten expect too much of critics, but if they met his requests they would be addressing too restricted an audience.

Consider, though, what Harold C. Schonberg says about Gary Graffman's performance of the Prokofiev Third Piano Concerto. Couldn't Schonberg's remarks be interpreted as teaching Graffman how to improve his performance?

> About the only criticism one could make concerns Mr. Graffman's attitude toward melodic elements. He is, if anything, too melody-conscious, and he is so intent on singing out the right hand that the left-hand accompaniment can be all but inaudible. That happened in the fourth variation of the second movement.[17]

Perhaps the seeming disagreement is a semantic one which hinges on the meaning of "teaching." Lessons that are simple and indirect, as suggested by statements like "The left hand was too soft," "The tenor was flat," and "The pianist's octaves lacked the needed power," are clearly acceptable. Indeed, criticism would stop dead in its tracks if it couldn't say such things. But direct instructions giving details about how something should be done are another matter.

REVIEWING MUSIC INDEPENDENT OF PERFORMANCE

Although most critics of new music now report on what they hear in concert or on recordings, in the past there was a long tradition of reviewing music for the general public independent of its performance. For instance Schumann did it in the *Neue Zeitschrift für Musik* during the 1830s and 1840s,[18] and the practice flourished in Europe until World War II,[19] even though much twentieth-century music is hard to review without a live performance. Things have changed since the war, however. Discussions of printed music survive only in periodicals about musicology and music theory as well as in some for music instructors, but their subject matter is usually too technical or specialized to be considered here.

Why the custom of reviewing musical scores for the general public declined isn't completely clear. Perhaps it was so hard to do under the best of circumstances that the practice never recovered from its disruption by the war. A comparison between literary criticism and music criticism reveals some of the difficulties. A book reviewer can fill in space by summarizing the plot, but most music, except for opera and program music, doesn't have a plot. And though a reviewer of non-fiction can say the essay should have included certain topics, it's harder to tell the composer that his slow movement needs two more melodies.[20] Music is a non-verbal art that doesn't lend itself to that sort of criticism.

It appears that no magazine for amateur performers regularly reports on printed music today, though perhaps one should. The problems facing a publisher would be enormous, however, since readers at different levels of skill have varying needs, and each instrument might require its own journal, because the interests of violinists differ from those of pianists or flutists. Besides, performance by amateurs isn't as important today as in the past. Music lovers are more likely to listen to a CD of a Beethoven sonata than to play the sonata themselves. At one time, too, reviews of printed music inspired readers to rush to the music store to buy the new set of Chopin mazurkas or Brahms intermezzi about which they had just read. Unfortunately, that's less likely to happen now because the public is less interested in new music and because a smaller percentage of music lovers are performers.

Indeed, the decline in pianistic literacy of the public is a major part of the problem. Schumann expected readers to play at least some of the musical examples included in his articles, examples of both solo piano music and of orchestral music in piano reduction.[21] These many reasons help explain why the practice of reviewing scores for the general public disappeared.

ESSAYS

Reviews, of course, are not the only things critics write. In the essays that appear in magazines and the Sunday editions of newspapers, they explore various interests and ideas and expand on thoughts that the limited space of a review can't accommodate. Critics sometimes call essays "think pieces" or (less commonly) *feuilletons*, after the French fashion. That term is ambiguous, however, since it can also denote daily reviews.

Almost every conceivable topic related to music can be a fit subject of such articles: the proper behavior of an audience,[22] a description of an unusual concert hall used for experimental music,[23] an analysis of the programming for a concert series,[24] why singers have vocal problems,[25] the proper place to position a grand piano at a concert,[26] and a seemingly endless number of generalizations about the current concert season. Sometimes a critic functions as an aesthetician or sociologist and relates music to the main cultural and sociological trends of our time.[27]

Critics can try to determine the direction of the musical world by means of essays. For instance, in 1977 Daniel Webster of the *Philadelphia Inquirer* attempted (unsuccessfully) to influence the curriculum and goals of the Curtis Institute of Music during a crucial period in its history.[28] Alan Rich says, "As part of his community responsibility, the critic must guide the citizens of that community; he must set forth the guideposts for the establishment of good taste and standards in the community."[29] (Rich never defines, though, what he means by good taste and the proper standards.)

At such moments a critic functions as the musical conscience of society, just as a newspaper's editorials do on political and social issues and a minister's sermons on moral ones. Indeed, the challenge of writing a fresh essay each Sunday resembles the minister's burden of preparing a new sermon.

Much of the excitement of music criticism comes about because it is the crossroads through which all of the currents, trends, and ideas in the musical world must pass.[30] For instance, the public often learns of the latest work by scholars from a critic's essay on the subject, such as Harold C. Schonberg's description of Frederick Neumann's *Ornamentation in Baroque and Post-Baroque Music*. Schonberg explains the significance of Neumann's ideas on performing Baroque ornaments and makes the topic understandable and perhaps even enjoyable for readers.[31]

CRITICS AS CHRONICLERS, HISTORIANS, AND SEERS

Critics also provide data for future historians. Their concert reviews and essays, along with interviews, stories about coming concerts, and other features, provide a day-by-day chronicle of the life of the musical community.[32] Doing this gives an afterlife to a concert and preserves the memory of what took place. At times, too, critics go a step further and also function as historians. For instance, in 1978 Tom Johnson wrote in the *New York Village Voice* about the chief trends in experimental music, a field in which he specialized.[33]

Some reviewers, though, go beyond this point and try to predict the next wave of the future. One unnamed critic, who was quoted by Ernest Newman, wrote, "So-and-so will ere long be recognized as one of the leading composers of the present time. It is pleasing to me to reflect that I shall have been among the first to greet him as an outstanding figure, and to perceive in his works the touching and profound revelations of a great artist." Calvocoressi comments, "One can imagine writers of this type praising certain new works simply because they believe that the fact of having praised them early will contribute, later on, to their reputation."[34]

Although Newman made fun of the critic he quoted, Newman still believes "that the first business of the critic, in a time of change is to distinguish between the seminal forces and impotencies among the innovators."[35] At first glance this viewpoint sounds praiseworthy, but it could be a rationalization for issuing sweeping judgments on skimpy evidence. Or such a seemingly admirable devotion to the duty of weeding out the untalented might really be a conservative attempt to squelch new movements. (The reverse is possible, too, for the radicals could praise the revolutionary and damn the rest.)

John Rockwell had related concerns about the obligations of the rock and popular music critic when he wrote in 1979:

> Most rock critics who regard themselves as "serious" concentrate these days on new-wave rock. Critics who review for daily newspapers are more obligated to pay attention to what's popular; the "serious" ones ignore or slight what they consider to be a waste of time and devote reams of space to the latest obscure punk act.
>
> This state of affairs strikes some as paradoxical. What *is* popular music, anyhow, if it isn't popular? Has venturesome, underground rock become a new form of elite music, like jazz can be? And to whom does the rock critic owe his primary obligation, the audience or the art of music?[36]

The issues raised by Rockwell's last sentence extend beyond the realm of rock criticism. Critics who ignore the works which interest the public appear self-indulgent and negligent of their obligations, yet if they fail to report on the latest innovative pieces which may affect the art of music, they could miss an important new trend. In order to avoid these unpleasant extremes, many critics take the middle road and try to meet part of each responsibility.

(The paradox to which Rockwell refers can be explained away quickly. Although popular music consists of pieces in a group of styles that are popular with the public, every piece within each style does not have to be a hit nor must each sub-style attract a large following. The almost imperceptible shift between two meanings of "popular," one a style description and the other a statistical measure, causes the confusion.)

CRITICS AS SUPPORTERS AND ADVOCATES

Clearly, critics should help the music world, though how they should do this may not be obvious. In 1985, Robert Freeman, the director of the Eastman School of Music, charged that today's music critics fail to do enough and may even damage the musical life of a community by saying its music is not worth hearing.[37] Freeman may have a point, though he gave no evidence to support his claim. It would be absurd and destructive for critics to demand from most small-town musicians the standards of New York, London, Berlin, or Vienna at their best. A reasonably professional and musical performance should receive praise regardless of how it would fare in a major musical center. A critic who finds the local standards low should also try to raise them without demoralizing the community or eroding support for its musicians. (Though it may take the wisdom of Solomon to carry this off.)

A critic who strongly supports an organization, say, the local symphony, may seem biased, and one who champions the local conductor may later find it awkward to complain when that person hires mediocre soloists. Once again, experienced critics often assume the middle ground, that delicate position between being too warm or too cold to any individual or group.

A related concern is whether critics should become propagandists for a cause, since by doing so they might lose the seemingly objective stance that is the critic's great strength.[38] Still, a critic may occasionally feel morally obliged to take a stand and risk incurring the wrath of some readers and editors. At times, too, a cause may be so important that all critics must join the fight. If a flourishing concert hall is threatened with demolition to make way for an office building, as nearly happened to New York's Carnegie Hall some years back, the press would be derelict in its duty if it didn't contest that action.

Although critics may properly complain in print about an incompetent conductor or musical administrator, it's doubtful whether they should take part in removing that individual from office. Anyone who does that becomes a participant in the action and loses the observer status which is usually considered proper for a critic. Such considerations apparently don't hold in Vienna, however. In 1984 Lorin Maazel resigned as director of the Vienna State Opera after receiving a letter from Helmut Zilk, Austria's Minister for Arts and Education, citing problems with his administration. The letter was drafted at the home of Franz Endler, the music critic for *Die Presse*, who led the attack on Maazel, helped write the letter, and then had it published in his paper even though it was a private document.[39]

Alfred Frankenstein had his hands slapped when he became too involved in the welfare of a conductor and exceeded the prerogatives of a critic. Shirley Fleming's amusing account of this episode appeared in an obituary for Frankenstein.

> Frankenstein withdrew as music critic of the *San Francisco Chronicle* in 1965 to devote his full time to art, but his years on the music desk were pugnacious, thought provoking, and sometimes controversial. One of the sharpest local storms blew up over his championing of Enrique Jorda, conductor of the San Francisco Symphony from 1954 to 1963. Frankenstein, who was in correspondence with George Szell at the time, suggested to Szell in a personal letter that the Cleveland Orchestra invite Jorda to appear as a guest conductor. Szell fired the letter back to the rival *San Francisco Examiner* for publication (though legally letters remain the property of the sender) along with the accusation that the *Chronicle* critic was biased and subject to conflict of interest. The incident may have hastened Jorda's departure from San Francisco; it certainly added color to Alfred's vocabulary when he spoke of it in later years.[40]

THE INFLUENCE OF CRITICS

Although it would seem that critics must be highly influential since they receive so much attention, some people believe the opposite and claim that critics have so little power that they can be ignored. (As we have seen, the eventual success of *Carmen* despite the first reviews is an example supporting this last viewpoint.) Unfortunately, the debate is difficult to resolve because much of the evidence is nebulous. For instance, most polls that study public attitudes toward the arts are of little help because they usually cover all of the arts. Such inclusiveness clouds the results by making it difficult to say what applies to music and what does not. In addition, questions about the power of critics usually arise only in passing, if at all. (The notes give details about some of these studies.)[41]

At least one report about the influence of critics is restricted to music, however. About 1979, Hilda Baumol, William J. Baumol, and Edward Wolff surveyed audiences at four concerts, one at the University of Wisconsin in Madison, and three in New York City—one each at Carnegie Hall, Alice Tully Hall, and the 92d St. YMHA.[42] Though this group of concert-goers is hardly a representative sampling of the nation's audiences, much less that of the English-speaking world, the results are welcome since the survey was intelligently done. (Unfortunately, the report omits the dates of the concerts along with the names of pieces and performers.) Besides the poll of audiences the authors "examined 59 brochures for distribution to the public selected at random, including 4 complete press kits."[43] They also made a survey of those responsible for booking artists (presenters of performances) which elicited 147 responses,[44] and the authors interviewed four artist's agents (managers).[45] The conclusions support the claim that critics play an influential role in the music world, even though their power seems slight at first glance. Here are some examples:

> Audiences all judge the *direct* influence of criticism upon attendance to be *very* small, indeed, all but negligible. Reputation of the performer, word of mouth and even advertising far outdistance the critical reviews as reasons for attendance.
> However, the indirect influence of musical criticism, at least over the long run, seems to be very substantial. . . . This is confirmed by the extent of their [the artists's] efforts to arrange for performances in New York City, sometimes even on financial terms that are highly unattractive, in the hope that they will obtain a quotable review. . . . The flyers and brochures which serve

as publicity to both audience and presenters almost
universally contain quotations from critical reviews.[46]

Unfortunately, the preparers of such quotations often distort what a
critic said by taking words out of context. Even so, providing reviews
for use by performers and composers is an important part of a critic's
job. Although some critics grumble that they write for the entire public
and not the artists—a point which is generally true—when they claim
that providing reviews for performers and composers isn't a valid
function of criticism, their position is too extreme.

In her biography of Leonard Bernstein, Joan Peyser shows the
power that the chief critic of the *New York Times* can wield. Howard
Taubman, who took over the post in September 1955, wrote
extensively the following April about what was wrong with the New
York Philharmonic. His complaints started the process that led to the
appointment of Leonard Bernstein as its music director and the
"retirement" of its powerful general manager, Arthur Judson.
(Granted, Taubman's campaign was helped by support from the music
community.)[47] Taubman liked Bernstein's conducting, but Harold C.
Schonberg, who took over as chief critic in 1960, did not. Peyser
suggests that his carping reviews played a major part in getting
Bernstein to leave the orchestra.[48]

Anecdotes about the influence of critics, like the following one told
by Benjamin Britten, often yield useful insights:

> The reactions of the *Times* [London] to the first
> performance of one of my operas caused a foreign
> management who had booked the opera to try to cancel the
> contract. Luckily we found a favourable notice in the *Daily
> Mirror* or *News of the World* which reassured him, so off
> we went with our opera and had a great success.[49]

Sometimes critical power seems too great, as shown by this
humorous yet pathetic story told by Patrick J. Smith.[50] Two women
were overheard talking in the Metropolitan Opera House after a
performance. "What do you think of it?" asked one lady. The other
replied, uncomfortably, "I want to wait and see what Harold
Schonberg says in the *Times*."

One might wonder which reviews carry more weight, positive ones
or negative ones? A positive one probably has more influence, because
it can help secure engagements.[51] Besides, publicists and managers

only reprint what is favorable, and so positive reviews tend to be the ones remembered.

The power of critics is probably limited, though, when it comes to determining the pattern of a major historical change.[52] For instance, despite the support many critics gave to the original-instrument movement, their efforts probably counted for little in producing its popularity. What ensured the success of original instruments is the way that many performers, record companies, instrument makers, concert managements, radio stations, scholars, and, above all, listeners embraced the movement. Critics can no more alter the course of such trends than they can stem the flow of the tide. In the final analysis, the wishes of the public determine the direction and outcome of major historical changes.

One question, popular because of its romantic implications, is whether a great talent has ever been destroyed by bad reviews. Harold C. Schonberg asserts that no major talent has had a career destroyed by bad reviews.[53] Even if "the ability to resist bad reviews" is not part of the definition of a major talent, which would make his sentence logically impossible to disprove, it's difficult to find evidence one way or the other. For one thing, it's hard to tell exactly what Schonberg means by a major talent. If he means a performer who has already demonstrated the ability to perform an incandescent recital and to control the vast repertory that today's artists often need, then Schonberg is probably right. A person who has already accomplished that much could probably shrug off the critics. Someone, though, with the same potential but less accomplishment might become discouraged by bad reviews and quit.

Ernest Newman makes a somewhat similar claim about composers: "We can hold fast to the unshakable principles that no composer of genius has failed to be recognized as such in his own day."[54] Newman is considering composers whose ability was recognized at some time. Still, a composer of major talent, discouraged by what critics said, might quietly shift to another profession and leave little trace of what was lost. The debate seems impossible to resolve.

Perhaps, though, the remarks of Schonberg and Newman aren't empirical statements but metaphysical beliefs that criticism will reveal the truth when a great talent comes along. Like other metaphysical beliefs, however, these can't be proven to everyone's satisfaction.

If a great artist was ever destroyed by bad reviews, it was more likely to have happened in the past. Reviews have become less significant since World War II, partly because of the decline in the number of major newspapers. Winning an important competition is now a better way to launch a career than a well-praised debut recital, though even that approach has lost some value now that the number of contests has proliferated. Making recordings is another option for performers trying to get ahead. The resident conductors of orchestras are also key figures in building careers, because they decide which soloists to reengage to play concerti with their orchestras after the first appearances.[55]

Technological advances in communications, transportation, and recordings have further diluted the power of written criticism. Rather than rely only on what is in print, concert managers and conductors now telephone friends and colleagues for opinions, jet across continents and oceans to hear a concert, and listen to an artist's or composer's recordings.

Nevertheless, the influence of music critics remains considerable. If their words were unimportant, few would read what they say, regardless of how entertaining their writing might be, and a review could no longer raise the blood pressure of a performer, composer, or reader.

Chapter Three

The Qualifications and Training of a Critic

Although it seems curious and sad, few music critics are properly trained before beginning their work. Such a situation seems to fly in the face of logic, for with so few jobs available, one would expect that only the well qualified would fill them. But the psychology of young musicians is partly to blame for this crazy condition, since most want to become performers, teachers, or composers, indeed almost anything but critics. Music students are usually too involved in their own music to write about the music of others. Those who do write, the prospective theorists and historians, seldom meet critics and so lack the role models needed to picture themselves as critics. When musicians turn to criticism, it's usually later, often by chance, perhaps because they need work and a part-time opening appears.

John Ardoin, the music editor of the *Dallas Morning News*, writes:

> Ernest Newman, that ever-entertaining and enlightening man of musical letters, once remarked that "Young men sometimes come to me and ask how they can become music critics. I invariably try to persuade them to give up the idea; there are at least fifty other forms of crime that require less intelligence and less application, that have fewer working hours and longer holidays." I find it surprising that Newman even had an inquiry, for most of the music critics I have known fell into their profession by chance. No musician really plans or prepares to be a critic. In the flush of youth, he is either going to write the great American symphony, become another Heifetz, or devote himself to the ivy-walls of learning. But somehow the dreams of the young have a way of reshaping themselves in unsuspected ways.[1]

Ardoin, a composer, first worked at the magazine *Musical America* in 1959 when he needed money to pay for food and rent. For "rewriting press releases, filing pictures, and doing other busy work," he was paid $65 a week.[2] After a month, to his surprise, he was asked to write his first review. Gradually he wrote more and more of them and eventually became editor, a post he held until *Musical America* was sold in 1964.

Ardoin's belief that most music critics "fell into the profession by chance" seems plausible, though a lack of data makes it impossible to prove or disprove his claim. Still, his experience is probably atypical in one respect, because most critics probably work as free-lancers before getting a full-time job. At least one other critic besides Newman also disagrees with his basic position: Andrew Porter says that young people often approached him in New York asking how they can become music critics.[3]

Since generalizations about how critics enter the profession are educated guesses at best, a few brief biographical notes may be of interest showing how five important music critics began their careers. **Ernest Newman,** the leading British critic of the first half of the twentieth century, worked fourteen years as a bank clerk before devoting himself full time to music. The *Guardian* (Manchester) hired him a year later.[4] **George Bernard Shaw,** who is best remembered today as a playwright but was an important music critic before that, also slaved in an office (for four and a half years) before drifting into music criticism.[5] **Andrew Porter** (*The New Yorker*) was more decisive and started writing music criticism while an undergraduate at Oxford. Although he majored in English, many of his activities there involved music. He continued working as a critic after graduation, first part time and then full time.[6] The record for an early decision may rest with **Harold C. Schonberg** (*New York Times*) who resolved to become a music critic at the age of twelve and then strived to achieve his goal.[7] **Michael Steinberg** (*Boston Globe*) received the urge a little later—by his early twenties he "lusted" to become one—but several things sidetracked his wish, including teaching music history at the Manhattan School of Music for six and a half years. Steinberg didn't get a full-time position in criticism until he was about thirty-six.[8]

Various attempts have been made to improve the education of music critics including the workshops the Music Critics Association of North America runs for its members. Three academic institutions offered programs in the field, but unfortunately only one curriculum survives, that at McMaster University in Hamilton, Ontario, which provides a mixture of academic and journalistic criticism. The offerings at the

Peabody Conservatory of Music and the University of Southern California are now inactive.

Other factors besides training programs may be improving the quality of music critics, however. A shortage of university posts for musicologists is leading some knowledgeable individuals to music criticism, and the decline in the number of newspapers has increased the competition for the jobs. Since more people now want fewer positions, it would be disgraceful if the profession didn't get better candidates, though it may take a major educational campaign to show an editor how to choose a good one.

In order to introduce readers to the daily routine of a critic and to show the talents, training, and skills that individual must possess, the rest of this chapter describes a week in the life of an imaginary critic. These pages often suggest the qualities needed by critics instead of stating them directly, but readers can easily figure out what they are by observing the skills our imaginary critic and his colleagues must have to do their jobs well.

Graham Brinkley, who is thirty years old, has been writing for three years for a newspaper in Arcadia, a midwestern American city with a metropolitan area of about one million people. He considers himself fortunate to be there, for Arcadia has an active and varied musical life—although the quality is often lower than desirable—and has two newspapers which review music extensively. A number of small journals also have part-time music critics there. Not only does the competition help keep Graham sharp, but he sometimes learns from what the others say. In addition, his boss, the only other full-time music critic on his paper, prefers to review works from the standard repertoire, and so Graham covers most of the contemporary music and off-beat assignments, which he likes.

The down side to this arrangement, however, is that his boss usually reviews the chief orchestras, operas, and soloists. As a result, Graham can't hear them unless his time is free and he buys his own ticket. This week, though, his boss is on vacation and Graham attends what he wants. These seven days will be busy and without a day off, but knowing that it will be his turn to go on vacation afterwards cheers Graham up.

He was happy that his wife can accompany him to the first program of the week. Even though Martha is a music lover, they often see each other only during a hurried dinner, because she has to be at work by 7:00 A.M. and many concerts let out too late for her.

That Sunday evening the prominent Russian dramatic soprano, Maria Oblenskaya, was performing. Graham loved her voice, which was grand in size yet flexible, plush in quality, and effortlessly produced from top to bottom. Unfortunately, her phlegmatic temperment and disregard of the meanings of the texts made everything sound alike. (Graham reflected that his college voice teacher would have had fits when Oblenskaya made a revenge aria sound almost like a love song.) The French and German diction were also peculiar, though better than the English in some of the songs that Haydn wrote in London. Hearing "She Never Told Her Love" sung with a rich Russian accent almost gave Graham an attack of the giggles.

At intermission they encountered Graham's friend Peter and his new girlfriend Eva. When Peter introduced them, Graham immediately told Eva that he never discussed the program with anyone until after he wrote the review. Graham likes to express his opinions without the input of others in order to avoid being influenced by poor judges or those with axes to grind.[9]

He recalled, though, a time when he couldn't stop that from happening. A stranger, who somehow knew that Graham was a critic, approached him a few years back when they were leaving a concert and said, "I certainly hope you're going to write a good review of *that* program." Graham was too stunned to reply but resented being told what to say. [10]

While driving home after the program, Graham planned the beginning of his review because it saves time to have the opening in mind when starting to write. As usual, he began writing immediately when he reached home, because his memories were fresher and the work easier than if he waited until the morning. Although he always took notes at a program, he found they weren't enough. After completing the article, he faxed it to the paper.

Graham devoted part of Monday to writing an essay for the Sunday paper. This week Graham had chosen a major topic which was sure to generate much heat, the poor state of the local orchestra and what should be done about it. The immediate issue was the conductor's contract which was due to expire shortly. Graham strongly opposed renewing it because of the conductor's musical weaknesses, his failure to improve the mediocrity of the orchestra, and the sloppiness of his beat. (None of Graham's conducting teachers would have tolerated such vague motions.) Still, the board of directors was captivated by the conductor's charm and wanted to keep him on. For his article to be effective, Graham knew that that he must request changes in the makeup of the board. Most of its members came from a group of old Arcadia families who had traditionally controlled the orchestra. Unfortunately, they had little knowledge of music and were incompetent as directors. Indeed, any excuse for their position on the board had long vanished, since most were no longer wealthy and gave little money to the orchestra. Even so, the thought of a break with tradition upset many people.

At first his boss was nervous about the topic, but he relaxed when the publisher promised to support Graham even if his article created a furor. Before broaching the subject, however, Graham had searched his soul to decide whether he could bear up under the strain. He recalled that Michael Steinberg's first review for the *Boston Globe*—a less than enthusiastic evaluation of Leonard Bernstein's "Kaddish" Symphony—brought forth two hundred or so unsympathetic letters. Although nothing Steinberg wrote afterwards ever produced so much mail, other controversial reviews produced many responses, including obscene letters.[11] The enormous tensions critics face in such situations reminded Graham of Harry Truman's remark, "If you can't stand the heat, get out of the kitchen." Indeed, Graham knew that some critics can't and leave, as did Michael Nyman, a specialist in experimental and rock music, who quit the profession when the pressures, which included losing the friendship of two composers whose works he had reviewed unfavorably, became too much.[12] Fortunately for him, Graham concluded he could handle the stress. If he had felt otherwise, he would have had serious doubts about whether he should remain a critic.

Graham believed that all critics should have some understanding of the business side of music even if they usually describe matters more modest than the running of an orchestra.[13] The results can be unfortunate when that information is missing. He recalled a review of a community orchestra concert in which a critic wondered at great length why the soloist, a fine pianist, would play a concerto with such a terrible group. The critic failed to realize, however, that the pianist might not have heard the orchestra beforehand, needed the money, owed the conductor a favor, or needed practice in playing the piece with an orchestra, any orchestra. The lack of this information, or of the imagination to think of it, made the critic seem naive.

The invasion of Eastern European musicians continued on Monday evening with an orchestra from one of the Balkan countries. Although most Western orchestras of decent quality sound fairly similar these days, Graham noted that this one still had a flavor native to the region, which he enjoyed, particularly in the woodwind sounds. Unfortunately, the orchestra also had serious weaknesses, including winds and brass that were unbalanced in sound and whose chords didn't blend. Graham's experience as a cellist playing in orchestras from elementary school through college had trained his ear in this regard, though he had also learned from hearing performances, both live and on disks.

Before the program, Graham greeted Lucy Vecchione, a part-time reviewer for the rival newspaper and a teacher of violin and chamber music at a local university. Shortly after he arrived in Arcadia, Graham discovered to his chagrin that the content of her reviews of music from the Classic and Romantic periods was often better than his. (Her writing was worse, but that was another matter.) He first spotted his weakness when a visiting conductor performed the Brahms Second Symphony with the local symphony. Graham thought that all went well but Lucy complained that the conductor lacked the flexibility in rhythm and tempo needed to give the appropriate warmth and Romantic style to Brahms. When the concert was repeated two nights later, Graham went again and realized that Lucy was right. He recalled that his chamber music teachers had grumbled about his insensitivity to rubato and his reluctance to breathe between phrases in music from those periods, and this weakness seemed to fit in with that pattern. He resolved to remedy matters and tried to get help from Lucy, though subtly so as not to lose face. She seemed reluctant, however, to become more than a superficial acquaintance. And so he listened on his own to a variety of works from these periods by many performers. It appeared to help, too, for he noticed that his opinions and Lucy's were now closer for works from those eras.

Graham spent part of Tuesday at the office attending to correspondence and writing routine publicity announcements. Then he went to the library to prepare for the night's concert of contemporary and avant-garde music. In particular he was concerned about reviewing a new string quartet by Sarah Altschuler, a composer whose music was unknown to Graham but who was beginning to achieve some renown. Unfortunately, the available information about her was skimpy and there were no recordings of her music, but Graham found scores to her previous string quartet and piano sonata. In order to get some idea of their style, he then went home and read through the sonata and some passages from the string quartet at the piano.

As he entered the concert hall that evening, he met Lucy once again. "Hello," he said, "What are you doing here? I thought this kind of program wasn't your cup of tea." She laughed. "It's not, but John [the chief critic at her paper] took sick and I was the only one available." Graham wondered how well she would manage.

He knew that a full-time critic for a city newspaper like his needed to be a generalist able to review a great variety of music.[14] Many reviewers are not, of course, but usually such critics are part-timers who cover a limited range of assignments. For instance, Lucy's editor knew her strengths and tried to assign her to string programs or those concerts whose repertoire emphasized the Classic and Romantic periods.

Being a generalist can be difficult for a critic, though the variety is exciting. Not only does the strain of trying to do so many things well become wearing, but the critic may have to review a type of music he or she dislikes. Graham was thankful that his paper had a separate critic for jazz, popular, country and western, and rock music. If he had to review them, it would be carrying the role of generalist too far for him. Still he knew that some critics seem to thrive on any type of music, including the multi-faceted John Rockwell who wrote for many years for the *New York Times*.

That evening's concert was at a local university with an active music composition department. The lengthy program was a hodgepodge with chance music, mixed media, electronic music, a nude dance accompanied by minimalist music, and Sarah Altschuler's musical and sophisticated quartet which, though far from conservative, seemed out of place in this avant-garde evening. One of the chance works was accompanied by a pantomime or dance whose patterns were intriguing though the meaning was hard to grasp. The music consisted largely of brief noises followed by a long period of silence, then more noise followed by more silence, and so on. The spacing between notes varied, though, perhaps by chance. In his review Graham considered whether such a piece could even be called music. (He felt at home with the topic of what is music, since it had been debated at length in his college aesthetics class.)

When Lucy's review appeared later in the week, Graham was pleased that the content made sense, despite a gaffe regarding the technology of electronic instruments. (Graham rooted for his fellow critics and wished them well.) Her writing, though, was still clumsy. Some say that a music critic only needs a knowledge of music and the ability to write well, but Lucy proved them wrong. Although she had many sharp insights and could turn out a graceful sentence, she didn't know how to structure a review.[15] She even lacked the knack of knowing what to include and what to omit and would ramble on at length about something minor and then have no room left for something major. Graham wanted to help her but sensed that his advice wouldn't be welcome.

Later in the week Graham checked a journal of contemporary arts to see what another critic, Stefan Kalliganov, had said about the program. Stefan discussed the avant-garde works with insight and understanding but talked nonsense about Altschuler's string quartet. He apparently lacked the listening skills needed to follow the work's form and harmonic style. Graham wondered how much of his training was in music, since even a few of the theory and ear training courses provided by a standard music curriculum would have helped him comprehend the quartet better.

Wednesday, at lunchtime, Graham interviewed another dramatic soprano, Selena Shelbourne, in the dining room of her hotel. (Arcadia was fortunate to have two such stars appear that week.) Selena, who was in her mid-thirties, had come to town to rehearse for two weekend appearances with the symphony. She was one of Graham's idols and he had looked forward to meeting her, but her behavior sadly disillusioned him. She was nasty to the waitress, sent her food back twice, complained acidly about the hotel, orchestra, and Arcadia, and made catty remarks about her rival, Oblenskaya, who she knew had just been in town. Perhaps the five cocktails she had with lunch loosened her tongue. Graham hoped that her voice remained in good shape despite the drinking.

Although he seldom produced an unflattering interview, he felt so angry afterwards that he turned out one. This was easy to do by quoting from her remarks, which he had on tape, and by describing her actions including the alcoholic intake. By writing that way he didn't have to add his own opinions and could protect himself from a possible libel suit. Afterwards, though, he knew he had to run the article by the editor, and he wasn't surprised at being told to rewrite it. The editor pointed out that the orchestra relied on the publicity from an interview to sell last-minute seats and that such a report could turn people away. Although Graham generally wanted to help the orchestra, he felt that writing a dishonest story was going too far. Still, he kept quiet, perhaps because he was secretly relieved by the editor's action. Graham knew that his Sunday essay would create more than enough controversy for one week.

He felt irritated, though, and decided to leave the office and rewrite the interview at home. When he sat down, though, he soon discovered that he had little material with which to work. Instead of answering his questions, Selena usually yelled at the waitress or made a caustic remark which wasn't repeatable. Although he had some biographical data about her, Graham needed more to pad the report. Fortunately, he had a good selection of reference books at home, and he found some additional information by searching the computer for an appropriate data base.[16]

Graham felt grateful that afternoon to the kindly editor who taught him how to write interviews as well as features, profiles, news stories, publicity announcements, and even obituaries.[17] (Graham had never taken a journalism class, although that background would have been helpful during his early days as a critic.) He was also thankful that he was a quick typist and a fast writer, particularly under pressure, because he had to review another concert that night.

That event was a program of nineteenth-century American music honoring the Arcadia Historical Society on the hundredth anniversary of its founding. What a contrast it made to the previous evening! Tonight everything was genteel and proper to the point of boredom. The performances were professional and polished but almost too much so for music that was originally written for a minstrel show or for amateur performance at home. Particularly grating was a slow and sentimental rendition of Stephen Foster's *Old Folks at Home* which manipulated each word like taffy and destroyed the line. There was no attempt to recreate the original sound of the folk music of the period, and the Negro spirituals were heard in once-popular arrangements that imitated European art music. Graham was also disappointed that despite the "arty" tone of the evening nobody performed any art (classical) music, even though many examples were available by nineteenth-century American composers.

At the end of one dull piece, Graham glanced across the aisle and saw that another critic, Charlie Sempliss, was sound asleep.[18] That was no surprise since Charlie usually slept at least once during a concert, even when the music was livelier. Charlie was only a minor figure—he wrote for a local cultural arts newsletter—but Graham knew that some important critics also fell asleep in mid-performance. Even a respected person such as Virgil Thomson apparently nodded at times, particularly

after his first five or six years with the *New York Herald Tribune* when
reviewing began to interest him less.[19] Graham recalled how Thomson
knew that he had slipped but gave a different explanation for it in his
autobiography:

> When you are new to reviewing and still reacting
> passionately, you are not always led by wisdom. And later,
> when you have more control, you are not so passionate.
> Neither are you quite so interesting. Because the critical
> performance needs to be based on passion, even when
> journalism requires that you persuade.[20]

When he saw Charlie nodding, Graham promised himself that he
would retire when he could no longer stay awake at a concert or review
with enthusiasm. He knew some critics who had lost their love of music
and the desire to see the art prosper, and he never wanted to join that
embittered crowd. A moment later, after spotting Clifford Shanks, who
wrote about events in Arcadia for a national music magazine, he added
another reason to retire: "Or when I can no longer hear well." Poor
Clifford now had trouble understanding what people said.

The next day Graham largely devoted to preparing for that
evening's folk festival. The city government was sponsoring the
program in honor of the various ethnic groups that had moved to
Arcadia in recent years. The performers were mainly members of the
community, although a few were outside professionals. Graham loved
ethnic music and had taken several courses in it, including performance
classes in Indonesian gamelan and African drumming. Another class in
anthropology also helped him grasp the cultural contexts. But he still
had many holes in his background and had become upset two days
earlier when he learned that the concert would include works from
Vietnam, Cambodia, and Thailand. He knew little about their music
and had to spend much of Thursday trying to acquire the knowledge.
By evening time he felt more in control, particularly since the program
was varied, and his review could emphasize what he knew best and say
little about the rest.

After the concert Graham hurried to the classical music station
owned by his newspaper, where he wrote his review and then taped it
for broadcasting the next day. (Some reviewers did this weekly.) When
he began broadcasting shortly after coming to Arcadia, Graham was ill
at ease, but soon he relaxed and learned to color his words
dramatically. The few occasions when he appeared on television were

another matter, however. The camera made him nervous, and for some unknown reason he always felt compelled to scratch his nose, chin, or ear.

On Friday evening Graham finally heard Selena sing with the orchestra. Although her voice was fresher on recordings he was still thrilled, for the temperament which was so unpleasant during lunch made her an exciting performer. The review was easy to write, partly because the unique qualities which separated Selena from other performers were readily described, and he could contrast her to Oblenskaya, a singer with a better voice but a drab personality. (Graham always tried to indicate the traits which distinguish one performer from the others, even though this was often difficult to do. Instrumentalists in particular were a problem, since they tend to play in a more uniform manner than they did fifty or one hundred years ago.)[21]

The next morning a rather sleepy Graham reviewed a recording to meet a deadline for a record magazine. Although he received next to nothing for this bit of moonlighting, he did it to maintain his credentials as a record critic, since his boss covered all recordings for the paper.

At lunchtime he glanced at what Alice Sheehan, a part-timer for the other newspaper, had written about the folk festival. Alice's reviews were often good provided they weren't marred by her intolerance of any performer who was less than perfect. Today she told two unlucky Cambodians that they were so bad that they shouldn't have been allowed on stage. Although Graham also thought they were weak, he made the point more gently since they were amateurs who were past their prime and their duet was brief.

Still, there was one bizarre exception to Alice's usual acidity: She generally gave a young performer from Arcadia a good review, whether or not it was deserved. Although Graham also believed in supporting budding artists, her behavior upset him, because it was wrong to encourage anyone of limited talents to waste years pursuing an unattainable goal. Indeed, he believed that dispensing too much kindness could be as cruel as writing a damning review.

After learning what was on his mind, Martha said thoughtfully, "I wonder what makes her like that?"

Graham said, "Well, the way I heard it, she's a local girl who started out to be a concert pianist. Some critic panned her, though, when she gave a recital in Arcadia while still a conservatory student. That devastated her so much that she gave up her career. And now she goes out of her way to be kind to every would-be performer from Arcadia."

"And nasty to most of the others."

"You're right," said Graham. "Fortunately, most critics try to be fairer than she is. At least those that I know. Yet our prejudices still must surface at times. I hope mine are under better control than Alice's."

"It's lucky we don't fight much," said Martha. "People can't accuse you of writing a bad review just because you've had an argument with your wife."

Graham laughed. "If they want to they'll accuse me of anything. It doesn't have to be true. I'd never take it out on anybody because of what happened at home. Remember the night I got the phone call about my father's heart attack and had to review a singer afterwards? I was too upset to concentrate and listen properly. At the end I felt embarrassed because I could say little about her singing and had to pad the review with descriptions of the music. But I bent over backwards to be kind to her. Who knows, though, what other critics do under those circumstances?"

Martha thought a moment. "What about the composers?" she asked. "When they work as critics, are they any better at reining in their prejudices?"

"It depends," said Graham. "Some are, but not others. Look at the American composer Deems Taylor. He was both a conservative composer and a conservative critic.[22] But some composers did a good job. We certainly owe thanks to Schumann and Berlioz, Humperdinck, Debussy, and our own Aaron Copland."[23]

"Did a composer ever get into trouble by becoming a critic?"

After a pause Graham said, "Two that I know of, though there may be others. One was the Czech composer, Leos Janácek. Sometime, oh, about 1887, he reviewed an opera called *The Bridegrooms* by another Czech composer, Karel Kovarovic, who was all of twenty-one then. Janácek didn't like it and said so in his review."

Martha said, "That could make an enemy of a twenty-one year old."

Graham nodded. "Apparently it did. Kovarovic got his revenge some fifteen or sixteen years later. About 1903 Janácek asked the National Theatre in Prague to put on his opera, *Jenufa*. Kovarovic, however, was now the head of the opera program there and turned the work down. He didn't relent until 1916, although *Jenufa* had been successfully performed elsewhere in the country before then.[24] Since that time it's become an established part of the repertory throughout the world. They're even planning to put it on in Arcadia in two years."

Martha suddenly jumped. "It's time to get moving," she said. "We've got a long drive ahead. Save the next story for later."

"No, I'll tell it now and make it brief. Hugo Wolf, the great song writer, was the other composer who got into trouble. His mistake was that he attacked everyone he didn't agree with, including Brahms and the important Viennese critic Hanslick. And so by the time his songs appeared, he had already made enemies. Yet in spite of everything he prevailed as a musician. Still, he was one composer who shouldn't have been a critic. He was always ready for a fight and yet was naïve about the workings of society."[25]

Gordon and Martha were in a hurry because they had to drive one hundred miles to review the opening of an opera house in another city. His paper was covering the event because the new opera house, which had been created out of what had been an old movie theater, had received a great deal of publicity. Graham was looking forward to the evening, partly because the company was reviving a little-known opera of Handel which he wanted to hear.

The assignment made him nervous, though. Although Graham hoped to match the high standard his boss had set as an opera critic, he had less experience in reviewing opera. Besides, Graham couldn't compete with the knowledge of stagecraft his boss had acquired as a combined theater and music major. Graham wondered what he would say if the acting tried to recreate a Baroque style of movement, since he couldn't visualize what one should look like.

During the first act he moved from seat to seat throughout the opera house (with the general cooperation of the sometimes surprised ushers) to test the acoustics and sight lines. Although somewhat variable, they were still good on the whole, and he sat in his assigned seat for the remaining acts.

Soon after the curtain went up Graham began to relax, for the acting and staging presented no challenges to him. Like the rest of the production, they were in a mixture of styles with no pretense of authenticity. Although some performers sang with an appropriate Baroque sound and ornamented gracefully, others used a wide vibrato that would have been more at home in Verdi. The opera had also been badly cut and the order of numbers rearranged, which Graham could spot because he had studied the score carefully during the previous week.

After writing the review Graham felt exhilarated, for he knew he had finished a busy week with an article that sparkled. And tomorrow he and Martha were going on vacation!

Chapter Four

Music Criticism and Journalism

The relationship between music criticism and other aspects of journalism is intricate and often surprising, since what appears in print may be shaped by a host of concerns besides the critic's wishes. Sometimes an editor restricts what the critic can say (as happened to Graham in the last chapter), sometimes the publisher is stingy with space, and sometimes pressures from the outside world limit the critic's freedom. These are but a few of the reasons why the reality of music criticism often fails to match the ideal. The following pages explore these issues, along with others from the frequently troubled relationship between music criticism and journalism as a whole.

THE TYPES OF JOBS AND WHO FILLS THEM

If more music critics were full-timers, they might have greater power and be able to protect better what they write. Instead, a majority of music critics probably work only part time, and many also review dance or other performing arts.[1]

When they write for newspapers, these part-timers are picturesquely called "stringers." The nickname "stringer" began when they were paid by the number of lines they wrote. An editor would measure the length of each article with a piece of string, cut the string, and at the end of the month, total the length to determine their salaries.[2] Some of these often-underpaid critics review concerts on short notice and at inconvenient times without uttering a complaint, for fear that the person assigning reviews will not call on them again.

Although "stringer" and "first-string critic" sound somewhat similar, the terms refer to very different people. The first-string critic is the paper's chief one, whereas the stringer is only a lowly part-timer. Of course, a stringer may function as a second- or third-string critic on a small paper.

Occasionally a staff reporter—one trained to do any job—helps out as a music critic. Although some have decent music backgrounds, others are unqualified. One poorly trained critic, whom I knew casually, was fortunate enough to have a knowledgable wife or girlfriend who accompanied him to recitals and told him what to say. Why is such an ill-suited person chosen for the post? I can only guess at why my acquaintance was selected, but Shaw said in 1894 that editors are notoriously ignorant about what to look for when employing a critic.[3] (Some suggestions for finding a good one appear in the notes to this chapter.[4])

A system of accreditation for critics might be useful, but there is none available. An attempt to establish such a system failed because the participants couldn't agree upon a set of guidelines to use for evaluation, since the writing of music criticism is so very subjective.[5]

Newspapers in towns without enough music to justify a full-time critic have a problem when hiring. Using part-timers would seem to be a logical solution, but often those qualified musically for the job are too involved with the local music community to be objective. For this reason, some papers try to find somebody to cover all the arts rather than hire a part-timer for each.[6] This practice may be particularly common on papers whose circulations range from 60,000 to 100,000.[7] (To be successful, though, such a critic must begin with a strong background in music.) Larger papers usually have a different approach when they have an opening. Their editors are likely to seek someone with the needed specialization and then teach that person journalism.

PRESSURES ON CRITICS

Critics are subject to pressures from a variety of sources, including letters from the general public and from composers such as Ned Rorem and Benjamin Britten.[8] The *Montreal Gazette,* for example, printed a letter in 1979 that charged that a reviewer was incompetent and suggested that she should be replaced.[9]

Sometimes the critic deserves the blame, but many letters of complaint contain nothing objective upon which to base their charges. Publishing such letters may show the paper's interest in the opinions of readers, but if the critic can't reply, the public learns little or nothing and the critic is insulted. To avoid hurting the critic, one editor prints the critic's credentials immediately after such letters,[10] though doing this insults the letter writer by making that person's opinions seem worthless. If such letters are to be published, a better approach would be to have a critic, editor, or outsider respond tolerantly on the same page with possible reasons for the disagreement. The public might then learn from the interchange.

Sometimes elaborate letters of complaint appear in print. In 1981, 49 members of the Philadelphia Orchestra took on the critic of a weekly suburban newspaper with a circulation of about 24,000. In their letter the musicians tried to document their charges by quoting from the critic's reviews and commenting on their flaws, but the musicians' writing is confusing and some of their points are controversial.[11]

At times, too, that orchestra's members have gone after bigger game—a critic for the city's main newspaper, the *Philadelphia Inquirer*. In a 1993 article evaluating the work of music critics in the Philadelphia area, Davyd Booth, an orchestra member, says:

> On two occasions in the past 20 years, Philadelphia Orchestra musicians have sent a joint letter to the *Inquirer*, each signed by more than 90 members, complaining of mistakes and misrepresentations in [Daniel] Webster's articles—mistakes apparently caused not by malice or ill will, but by simple carelessness.[12]

Booth doesn't indicate what the musicians wanted the *Inquirer* to do about the problem nor whether the paper ever published either letter.

Despite these examples, it remains debatable whether performers or composers should make a fuss about a review they think unfair. Doing that could hurt a musician and might let the critic get the last word by replying to a printed letter. Still, Andrew Porter believes that one should challenge an inaccurate or incompetent critic and even complain to an editor if necessary. Porter thinks that requiring this kind of accountability will produce better criticism and critics.[13]

Unfortunately, competent critics can be attacked, too. When Virgil Thomson first wrote for the *New York Herald Tribune*, there were immediate demands for his "beheading," as he put it—most persistently from the Metropolitan Opera but also strongly from the New York Philharmonic. The orchestra soon changed its tactics, however. First, it tried to seduce him by offering him a membership on its board. When he declined, Arthur Judson, who was both manager of the New York Philharmonic and president of Columbia Concerts

Corporation, threatened to have Columbia withdraw all advertising
from the paper. How practical this would have been is debatable,
though, since it would have penalized Columbia's artists.

Several things saved Thomson, including letters of praise to the
paper from various intellectual and cultural leaders and an offer from
Ira Hirschmann, the advertising manager of Bloomingdale's, who was
a music lover and sponsor of a chamber music series. Hirschmann
said, "Mr. Thomson has not yet reviewed my concerts unfavorably,
though he may well do so. But whatever happens, I shall match, line
for line, any advertising you [the paper] lose on his account." To their
credit, the editors of the *Tribune* told Thomson nothing about this
incident until two years later.[14]

The very thought of interference by advertisers is upsetting. It's
hard, though, to tell the extent of the problem for music criticism since
editors may deflect much of the meddling, and most of what happens
may occur orally and leave no paper trail. Harold C. Schonberg said
that on a well-run newspaper the advertising and editorial sections are
separate. (When used as an adjective, "editorial" refers to the literary
contents of a paper as opposed to its business aspects.) Schonberg also
added that the advertising department of the *New York Times* never
told him what programs to review.[15] Still, conditions were not ideal on
the *New York Herald Tribune* when Thomson began working there,
and they may not be on other papers. When I asked critics in my
survey, "Have pressures ever been exerted upon you which threatened
your integrity as a critic?" one person replied, "Not as a critic. As an
editor, yes—from advertisers, mostly."

My question brought forth other interesting answers, including six
reports of unsuccessful attempts to get a critic fired. Four of the replies
now follow, exactly as they appeared except for the omissions needed
to protect privacy:

1. Indirect pressure to give favorable [review] to person
   considered interesting by editor.
2. "Please go easy on ———," says editor. I have never
   complied. I am still employed.
3. At my former job, in ———, my publisher ordered that I be
   kept from reviewing important opening night
   [performances] . . . following my negative review of ———
   which he attended. That, in large part, was the reason I
   moved here.

4. Sure. Everyone attempts to influence you—except the editors, who are impartial.

FIGHTS BETWEEN CRITICS

Although critics can be scathing when reviewing the work of a performer or composer, they seldom charge a fellow critic with incompetence or bias. Such tolerance may result not from a spirit of camaraderie but from prudence, cowardice, or fear that the resultant bloodletting could hurt the profession. Unfortunately, this cautious behavior makes it hard to weed out the unfit.

Nevertheless, fights between critics, or at least debates, have appeared in print. In the 1920s Olga Samaroff of the *New York Post* sparred with Samuel Chotzinoff of the *New York World.* In 1975 John Rockwell reported Paul Jacobs's complaint that a group of New York critics had been hoodwinked by Marie-Françoise Bucquet's performances of Schoenberg in her New York debut. Rockwell also suggested, however, that Jacobs, another pianist who performed Schoenberg, might have spread the word for selfish reasons.[16]

One critic, B. H. Haggin, confessed to having an "undisguised loathing" for most of the work of his colleagues. A 1968 article by him grumbled about nine of them (eight well known), though he grudgingly admitted that two have merit at times. Of the critics he named, only George Bernard Shaw and a novice writing for *Commentary*, the journal in which his tirade appeared, emerged unscathed.[17]

And so Michael Steinberg's implied criticism of Harold C. Schonberg, then chief critic of the *New York Times*, is not unique. In 1973 both men heard Claudio Abbado and the Cleveland Symphony play Mahler's Sixth—Schonberg in New York, and Steinberg two days later in Boston. Steinberg's review in the *Boston Globe* reported that Schonberg thought Abbado, like most of the younger generation of conductors, missed the work's tempo fluctuations and gave an "unrelaxed and literal" performance. Steinberg, however, heard "an interpretation in which the many tempo changes in the score were exactly observed and in which, wherever flexibility was built in—most in the second and third movements—the approach was elastic to the point almost of risk."[18] It's possible, though, that Abbado's conducting was freer and more at ease in Boston than in New York, which would explain the disagreement between the two critics.

CRITICS WITH SHARP TONGUES

Usually, however, any acid in a critic's tongue is directed toward a musician and not another critic. Some critics even thrived on being cutting, such as Claudia Cassidy who wrote for several papers in Chicago from 1925-65. Olga Samaroff says:

> The brilliantly censorious critic is the virtuoso of the profession, and no musical showman who yields to the temptation to play to the gallery can be more sure of applause than the music critic who can add wit to severity.[19]

Samaroff's correspondence taught her much about the public's attitudes. She says:

> I learned the melancholy fact that a great many people prefer and enjoy adverse criticism. In fact, to them the word criticism has just one meaning: censure. . . . From time immemorial there have been human beings who enjoyed witnessing torture and death. Perhaps, in a milder form, the critical "roasting" of a musician satisfies this urge. The severe critic is therefore giving the public what most of it wants.[20]

Today's public, though, seems less bloodthirsty than Samaroff's was in the 1920s, at least when it reads music criticism.

Samuel Lipman complained in 1977 that critics in major metropolitan areas sometimes tried to find "an approving and admiring audience . . . [by competing] with each other to see who can write more destructive and vicious attacks."[21] If such competition ever existed, however, it had probably died out by 1977, at least in the United States. (Lipman gives no evidence to support his charge.) By then only two or three major newspapers survived in most major cities, which left few reviewers to indulge in this cruel sport. Besides, the replies to my questionnaire suggest that editors would discourage it today.

LIBEL SUITS AGAINST CRITICS

Although one seldom hears of American music critics being sued for libel, it occasionally happens, as was reported by one respondent to my questionnaire. In other countries, though, the fear of such suits may greatly hamper a critic.[22] Ludwig Rellstab even went to prison in 1825 because of a pamphlet he wrote about Henriette Sontag, the coloratura soprano.[23] A century later, in 1925, Ernest Newman observed:

> I often think, with mingled sadness and amusement, of the case of Dr. Leopold Schmidt, the musical critic of the *Berliner Tagblatt*. A few years ago he wrote a very disparaging notice of a German work that had been extensively and expensively advertised. The publishers took phrases here and there from his article, and by cunningly joining them together converted it into one of warm commendation. Dr. Schmidt, in his righteous indignation at this piece of sharp practice, wrote another article in the *Tagblatt*, telling the publishers precisely what he thought of them. Thereupon *they* brought an action against *him* for defamation, and actually obtained substantial damages.[24]

CRITICS OR REVIEWERS

Besides worrying about what the world thinks of their writings, including how to say what they want without being sued, some critics fret over the social status of their jobs. One common ranking within the profession places the true "critics," usually magazine writers, above the mere "reviewers" who work for newspapers. As is to be expected, many writers for the daily papers irately reject this distinction. In truth, many excellent music critics work for newspapers and many poor ones for magazines. And how can one rank critics without first examining their writing? Consider Andrew Porter, a highly respected figure, who wrote for the *Financial Times* (London) for nineteen years before changing in 1974 to the *The New Yorker*. Did he suddenly become a critic after his long service as a reviewer? And did he change back into a reviewer when he left the *The New Yorker* in

1992 to work for the *Observer* (London)?[25] Applying such
classifications mechanically is ludicrous.

The division between high and low criticism plagues the literary
world, too. Eudora Welty, the novelist and short-story writer, cast
aspersions on her own work as a critic when interviewed by Scot
Haller in the *Saturday Review*:

> SR: Since you also write criticism, can you tell us how
> being a critic can be helpful to a writer?
>
> WELTY: I don't think I really am a critic. I like to
> respond to a work and to do so with a full heart, but I'm
> not a *learned* person and don't know the histories of
> things. I could not write a critical evaluation of anything. I
> just review the things I respond to. I'm a reviewer, if
> anything; I'm not a critic.[26]

If one wanted to make the literary and musical usages parallel, one
could call the writers for newspapers and magazines *reviewers* and
label the musicologists who write academic criticism *critics*. After all,
musicologists often study a subject in greater depth than those writing
for newspapers and magazines. That proposal, however, violates
standard usage, for the public thinks that the writers for newspapers
and journals are the music critics, *not* the musicologists.

Another reason why the literary model doesn't work for music
criticism comes from the differences between the arts. Music is a
performing art, unlike literature, and critics must consider both the
music and the performance. A curious division of labor along
chronological lines then occurs for performance. Academic criticism
generally prefers the past to the present and is more likely to analyze
the patterns of nineteenth-century concert going and performance than
to discuss what is happening today. That task is usually left to
newspaper and journal writers, the people whose work has *actualité,*
or some relationship to what is occurring now. In fact, the day-by-day
chronicle of today's concert life provided by music critics often serves
as the raw material for later study by musicologists.

The distinction between musicologists and music critics shouldn't
be made too rigidly, however. Some people have worn both hats at the
same time, particularly in England.[27]

One might ask whether those writing about music for the popular
magazines have advantages denied to their colleagues on newspapers?

In some ways the answer must be yes, for they often profit by a more relaxed format, and greater space. Consider one reason Porter gives for moving to the *The New Yorker:*

> In the pages of *The New Yorker* I was invited, encouraged, to attempt a kind of criticism for which the British press had ever less space—part descriptive chronicle, part essay in which a particular performance may be viewed as the latest addition to the long history of a work and, more personally, to a critic's experience of it.[28]

Another advantage possessed by magazine writers is a greater freedom of schedule which often allows them go to a second performance of a difficult new work or to hear a tape of it before setting their thoughts down on paper. Some newspaper reviewers blessed with ample space can combine the newspaper and magazine styles of criticism, however. First they write a review that is primarily descriptive and non-evaluative and then, after further study, give an evaluation in a Sunday essay. Nevertheless, an elaborate opera existing in different versions requires extensive prior study to decide whether the right one was chosen—doing this is one of Andrew Porter's specialties—and the process may be too time consuming for most newspaper writers. And even if they prepare carefully beforehand, the performance may reveal something demanding further study, which the newspaper deadline doesn't permit. Indeed, Porter often studies a subject in greater depth than his colleagues and comes closer to the literary conception of a critic.

Still, it would be wrong to say that magazine writers are the music *critics* because they analyze a subject more thoroughly than newspaper writers. After all, some newspaper writers still manage to produce first-rate music criticism while some magazine writers churn out fluff. Besides, all critics worth their salt should be able to say immediately whether a concert of standard repertory was played well. Some aspects of performance can be described clearly without a great deal of space or time for reflection.

Indeed, since the general public doesn't distinguish between "critics" and "reviewers," it makes more sense just to say that some music critics are better than others, or that some study a subject in greater depth than others. It's unnecessary and confusing to give the better one a separate title. Perhaps separating critics and reviewers is more feasible for some other arts, since we all speak and write the language of poets, playwrights, and novelists. Paintings, statues, and buildings are also considerate enough to remain still so we can see what they are about. Music, though, can't be stopped and analyzed this way except by someone fluent in musical notation and capable of grasping a complex score. Because it often takes great skill to evaluate even a seemingly simple concert, distinguishing between "critics" and "reviewers" is pretentious and unworkable for music. For this reason, the two terms are used interchangeably in this book. Music critics are either qualified or unqualified or good or bad, but they are *not* either critics or reviewers.

THE MYTH OF THE OMNISCIENT CRITIC

When critics write such an evaluation and disagree with a seemingly enthusiastic audience, how can they know they are right? The answer is that they can't, even if they or the public believe otherwise. This eternal problem of the validity of criticism, which surfaced in the preface and will occupy much of chapter five, demands our attention now to consider its ramifications for journalism.

In 1979, at the Carnegie Hall conference on music criticism, the consensus was that few critics now believe their judgments present objective and universal truths. When David Cairns of the *Sunday Times* (London) stated that the image of the critic as Olympian arbiter is declining, nobody disagreed, though anybody who felt otherwise may have decided it was not politic to dissent. The public stance of critics may give the opposite impression, however, since they often fight strongly for their viewpoints, as they must to function effectively. (At their best, though, critics support their conclusions with crisp, clear-cut reasons.) Not only does faint-hearted criticism make dull reading but, as Harold C. Schonberg said, "Modesty will get you nowhere in this profession."[29] Besides, an editor might consider a review which admits other points of view to be unacceptably wishy-washy.

Another possible source of the public's belief in the critic's infallibility was the largely English custom of publishing unsigned criticism, which suggests that God wrote the review and not man.[30] The practice persisted in the music reviews of the *Times* (London) until 1967 but is largely extinct now in most papers, though it crops up occasionally, sometimes when a by-line is omitted by mistake.

The various forms of anonymous music criticism, including criticism signed with a pen name and ghostwritten criticism, have had a long history. Anonymous criticism is found as far back as the music magazines of the Classic period according to Max Graf, who observes that "Anonymity assured complete independence."[31] This independence is the sole virtue of the practice, though an important one, since nobody can pressure a critic who is unknown. Still, the anonymity may not be complete. For instance, anonymous criticism persisted in India after the British departure in some English-language newspapers, yet the music community in Bombay (and perhaps elsewhere) generally knew who reviewed a concert of Western music.[32]

Unfortunately, anonymity sometimes exists to disguise a critic's bias. For instance, Carl Maria von Weber and his friends formed a secret society to foster the "good in art" and the careers of its members. These friends then wrote anonymous and pseudonymous reviews praising the music of other members of the society.[33]

Signing reviews with initials alone is still prevalent, though this, too, can hide the author's name. To find it, readers must look at the magazine's masthead, which may not be up to date. Both music magazines for which I wrote used initials, but during my brief stay at *Musical America* my name was never listed, and it took a while to appear at *Musical Courier*.

Another journalistic convention leading to the myth of the critic's infallibility is the use of the editorial "we." For instance, in 1925 Olin Downes said about a performance of the Schubert C Major Symphony, "We have heard the introduction of the symphony given a serenity of spirit which was not present last night."[34] The editorial "we" is still found today, though less frequently. It creates the illusion of a collective judgment dispensing its wisdom, even when a single individual signs the review. When a newspaper frowns upon its critics using "I," saying "we" is a convenient, if pretentious, substitute. Other and possibly better options include expressions like "this reviewer," "this listener," "to these ears it sounded," and "one," as in "One wanted more tone at the climax." Still, all are inferior to "I," in my opinion, because they are awkward and artificial. (Some newspapers and news services have style manuals indicating what they allow.)

Every "we" in criticism isn't an editorial one, however. Writers often use that word (or its alternate grammatical forms, "our," "ours," and "us,") when addressing a group to which they feel they belong, or when expressing thoughts which they think they share with their readers. For instance, the first paragraph of this section on the myth of the omniscient critic says: "This eternal problem of the validity of criticism . . . demands *our* attention now to consider its ramifications for journalism." Unfortunately, unless the context makes the meaning clear, readers may become confused about which usage of "we" is intended.

Omitting such phrases as "I think" or "in my opinion" also perpetuates the image of the omniscient critic. Although nothing becomes more tiresome than repeating these phrases, particularly when the thoughts are clearly the critic's, leaving out such words helps make the critic seem all-knowing and infallible to the naive.

DECLINE IN NUMBER OF REVIEWS

The decline in number of newspapers also helps create the impression that the critic knows all. Years ago, when there were more papers, opposing opinions were common, but with fewer critics in print today, disagreements are rarer and the individual critic is more likely to seem infallible. As long ago as 1934, Oscar Thompson lamented that consolidations of newspapers had reduced New York City to seven, excluding tabloids, regional, and foreign language papers.[35] Today, when only one paper in New York City, the *New York Times,* covers music extensively and many American cities are no better off, readers of reviews recall the past with nostalgia. Since many opinions are needed for criticism to flourish, everyone loses without them. One-newspaper towns are particularly bad for all, including the critics, who need competition to stay sharp. Some readers may also feel alienated from criticism when their response to a concert differs from a reviewer's and they can't find another opinion in print.

Newspapers sometimes commission surveys of readers' opinions and then respond to the results in an unfortunate manner. If the public seems disinterested in music criticism, some publishers automatically cut back on the space, without considering whether expanding the music coverage might attract a new group of readers.[36] Still, regional newspapers in areas surrounding the big cities may fill in some of the gap. Magazines that review concerts help, too, but magazines appear less often, are harder to locate, and generally have circulations which can't compete with that of a major newspaper.

London is a fortunate city today because about eight newspapers review classical music. Since distances are relatively small in the British Isles and newspapers circulate widely, music criticism is better in that region than in the rest of the English-speaking world.

PUBLIC RELATIONS AND REPORTING

Because reviews are the most prominent things that critics write, it's easy to forget that that they do other kinds of work, including publicizing future musical events. That task largely involves preparing lists or calendars of coming concerts and writing descriptions of some. Although these are everyday activities for critics, some analysts complain that such writing usually lacks real criticism.[37] (If true criticism appears, the objection vanishes.) In any case, publicity articles seem most appropriate for a program which needs an audience or for an evening of difficult or unusual music which the critic can help explain.

Unfortunately, attending to public relations can overwork a critic and leave little space for real criticism.[38] Indeed, in some papers today, listing and publicizing future events seem to have a higher priority than reviewing the music. Another drawback with writing publicity articles is that careless critics can lose their independence and become lackeys of the organizations about which they write. One reply to my questionnaire complained that "Boosters want to enlist me for public relations campaigns." Critics who publicize a concert glowingly beforehand also look silly if they later give it a bad review.

Serving as reporters is another time-consuming but essential duty of music critics, essential because their familiarity with the music world lets them do a better job than staff reporters. At times the duties of critic and reporter may even overlap, such as when covering a music contest. Besides telling the outcome, a critic could evaluate the playing and rank contestants, perhaps in an order different from that of the judges. Sometimes reporting produces an article that is part news story, part essay, and part concert review. When Nicholas Kenyon wrote in the *Observer* (London) about a symposium and festival on the Mozart piano concertos held at the University of Michigan, his report included a review of the concerts and an essay on approaches to performing Mozart's piano concertos.[39]

INFORMANTS, AND CONFLICTS OF INTEREST

Much reporting, however, is about less artistic matters. If the local orchestra or opera company is involved in a labor dispute, it's usually the music critic who writes about the negotiations. To do this well, a critic needs friends or informants placed throughout the management, orchestra, chorus, and soloists.

Informants can also tell how the new conductor gets along with the orchestra, or explain why the wind section sometimes sounds peculiar, or give clues about why the acting of an opera was so stilted. Good informants can reveal, too, how the baton technique of a conductor affects an orchestra's sound. Indeed, they can help train the eyes and ears of a critic.

Yet the use of informants can be dangerous, for their information may be inaccurate or biased, and critics can become overly dependent on their services and end up hearing little more than what an informant predicts. Even when the information seems accurate, it must be used with discretion. If an informant discloses that the conductor had rehearsed the soprano for an hour and a half on the day of the concert, that could explain why she sounded tired. Still, despite any sympathy the critic might feel for her, it would be dishonest not to tell readers what her voice sounded like, though the review might also mention the rehearsal schedule.

What happens if an informant—perhaps a violinist in the orchestra—and a critic become friendly, and the critic must then review the informant's recital? The situation is awkward at best and at worst leads to a biased review. Because of these problems, some newspapers discourage fraternization between critics and musicians and don't let composers or performers serve as critics. Harold C. Schonberg says this about writers for the *New York Times*:

> Naturally, we meet many musicians on a professional basis—for interviews, background material, feature pieces, gossip. As newspapermen, we have to know what is going on. We cultivate a network of sources and even of Deep Throats. But that is acquaintance, not friendship. . . . As a matter of policy, *Times* critics are not supposed to be close to musicians they may be in a position of reviewing. If they are close—and sometimes

that is unavoidable—the critic is supposed to disqualify himself.[40]

Here is an example of how Schonberg enforced this philosophy. When he became chief music critic for the *Times* about 1960, Schonberg objected to Eric Salzman's presence on the staff because his work as a composer presented a conflict of interest. The newspaper tried to compromise by offering Salzman an alternative position as a cultural news reporter, but he didn't want that and had to leave the paper, though with full severance pay.[41]

Maintaining the purity of critics is a controversial ideal, however. William Littler, representing the viewpoint opposed to Schonberg's, once asked tongue in cheek whether critics should be vestal virgins and avoid all contacts with musicians which might soil them.[42] His tone suggested this was impractical, particularly for critic-reporters who need information. (Few can tread the fine line between being an acquaintance and a friend as neatly as Schonberg.) Since critics would become sterile and inbred if denied intercourse with other musicians, isolating them seems to be an impossible and unhealthy goal.

One critic who didn't maintain his distance was Tom Johnson, a writer for the *New York Village Voice* and a composer and performer of experimental music, the very scene he covered as a critic. Such proximity makes it harder to evaluate works objectively but gives an understanding that is valuable for descriptive reviews.

Still, the actions of some critics add fuel to the debate. For instance, Virgil Thomson had an easy-going—or was it self-serving?—attitude toward these ethical questions. During the negotiations for his becoming the chief critic for the *New York Herald Tribune*, he was asked how he felt about taking the position. Here is one reason he gave for wanting it: "Also I thought perhaps my presence in a post so prominent might stimulate performance of my work."[43] Shaw's description of *Thorgrim*, an opera doomed by its stilted libretto, provides another classic example of the abuse that results from lax ethical standards. With wonderful irony he suggests that only fear of offending its librettist, music critic Joseph Bennett, could have persuaded the poor composer to set that piece of trash.[44]

When critics are unwise in their associations, the fault may not be completely theirs, however. Max Graf describes how people tried to become friendly with him from motives that were not the purest:

Musicians doffed their hats and whispered to me (when
no other critic was close by) that I was the only one who
understood. The worse they sang, the more tenderly opera
singers caressed my hand. . . . [Musicians] called critics
their friends and assured them of highest esteem. In reality
they wanted to be sure to be praised as much as
possible.[45]

Writers of program and liner notes face the same conflicts if they
must later review the people about whom they wrote. Harold C.
Schonberg says, "[No] *Times* critic [is] allowed to write for any
publication that would even remotely suggest a conflict of interest.
That, of course, includes writing program or liner notes."[46] Students
who write for school papers also face problems if they must review a
performance by faculty or friends, since saying something negative
might put them in an awkward position.

BRIBERY AND FREE TICKETS AND RECORDS

Submitting to bribery should be unthinkable for a critic, but
unfortunately some critics haven't seen it that way. The issue is an old
one, predating the premiere of *Carmen*, and was discussed by Balzac
during the reign of Louis-Phillipe (1830-48).[47] Here are some
instances of the problem: Among the guilty was the German poet
Heinrich Heine, who lived in Paris for many years and wrote music
criticism there (in German). Heine accepted and even solicited
bribes.[48] Other German critics were also corrupt, for in 1854 the
English critic Henry Chorley (1808-72) complained about their
willingness to accept payments.[49] Later, Gilbert Chase, Ernest
Newman, and Virgil Thomson reported attempts in the 1920s and
1930s to bribe critics on the Continent, particularly in Paris where the
practice may have been at its worst.[50]
In the United States the issue seems better, at least in its overt
form, though one critic said in reply to my questionnaire, "A small
record company sent me records several years old and hinted it would
be worth my while if I reviewed them. I did not." Edward Downes
believes that American critics reject outright bribery and return the
occasional gift a European artist ignorant of our tradition sends to
them.[51] The usual approach here is subtler: inviting critics to free
lunches or cocktail parties or paying all of their expenses while on tour

with an orchestra which they are reviewing. The aim is to make a critic feel obligated to repay this hospitality by writing something favorable. To avoid these temptations, many newspapers refuse such offers.[52]

The practice of giving free disks and tickets to the press for review poses similar ethical questions. Although some papers and journals probably reject such gifts,[53] many or most seem to accept them. The cost to the public may be high, however, since the number of reviews tends to be skewed in favor of the producers and artists supplying the free goods, regardless of the merits of the music. Yet, without free tickets and recordings, editors might restrict what their reviewers hear, particularly on small journals with limited budgets. And the public might suffer if newspapers and journals kept critics from hearing programs because the tickets were too expensive. A press seat for an opera abroad can cost over $300.

BAD HEADLINES, ALTERED AND CUT REVIEWS

Rare is the critic who has been spared the embarrassment of having copy appear in a distorted form. One common problem, a headline that doesn't fit the article's content, arises when the headline writer reads (or misreads) the article in a hurry. (Critics seldom write their own headlines, because they usually don't know the shape the article will take on the printed page.)

Having words altered in the review proper is generally more serious than a bad headline. One critic said in reply to my questionnaire, "I have had reviews which were unfavorable to the establishment cut extensively or not printed." And someone maliciously inserted lines she never wrote into Olga Samaroff's by-lined reviews.[54] The most frequent problem, however, is having a review cut for lack of space. Some critics are spared these indignities, particularly important ones such as Harold C. Schonberg, who said that his reviews were never touched.[55] In a situation of trust and courtesy, if a review must be changed, the editor first confers with the critic, particularly when the deadline permits.[56] But when an editor makes changes without consultation, the critic is often bitter.[57]

To some extent critics can protect themselves by knowing the available space before writing or by making friends on the paper who will consult with them if there is time when something must be cut.[58]

(Critics also need to know whom to ask for the extra lines that an unexpectedly brilliant program may deserve.)

When a review is cut, the critic may suffer most because of the way it was done, since those doing the cutting usually find it easier to lop off paragraphs crudely than take time to select the less important details. (Sometimes, though, nothing would work short of having the critic rewrite the review completely.) Frequently, the ending goes when a review is shortened, as happens with a news story. (In a news story the most essential paragraphs come near the beginning, the less essential later on, so the writing can easily be cut from the end.) Doing this to concert reviews can be disastrous, however, since few of them follow that structure. At a meeting of music critics, one woman said that she seldom tried to close a review with a strong ending, because the ending usually disappeared anyway.[59]

Other passages can be chopped, too. When the Curtis Institute of Music presented three little known, one-act comic operas, my review in the *Philadelphia Evening Bulletin* praised the venturesome quality of the repertory while noting that "only one of them proved to be a complete success."[60] Unfortunately for my review, a play starring Bette Davis suddenly closed that evening in Philadelphia, and the news preempted most of my space. The report on the best opera remained, but what I said about the two weaker ones disappeared except for their titles, composers, and a few miscellaneous facts. A largely negative review had been changed into a largely positive one by cutting out most unfavorable statements.

How can the reader tell that a review has been cut without authorization? Often there are no clues, but at other times an abrupt transition, some curious omissions (as in my review), or the failure of subject and verb to agree suggest that someone has tampered with the writing.[61] Of course, all changes in a review aren't bad. Copy editors routinely catch misspellings and other minor mistakes, and some critics look good only because of an editor's help.[62]

DEADLINES

Critics are most likely to talk nonsense when they have little time to write. An early deadline after a long concert is particularly problematical for those working for a morning paper, since the review cannot—the cynical might say should not—be written before the concert.

An early deadline had a profound effect on the life of Daniel Schorr, a commentator for National Public Radio. When still in his teens he wrote music criticism and contemplated a career in that field. After the *New York Times* published his interview with composer Ernest Bloch, Schorr met with its chief critic Olin Downes. Just before the meeting, however, Schorr read the morning paper and Downes' review of a recital by violinist Joseph Szigeti. One of its sentences said, "Szigeti's tone was impeccable but the profile of the tone lacked something." This remark puzzled Schorr and he asked Downes how the tone could be impeccable and still lack something. Downes replied, "Don't worry, my boy. It's the kind of bullshit you have to write when you're writing on deadline." These words discouraged Schorr and helped make him choose a different aspect of journalism for a career.[63]

Since many newspapers no longer print reviews the day after a recital, the later deadline lets morning-paper critics hear the end of a long program and gives them more time to write. It's unlikely that pure idealism brought about the change, however. The decline in number of newspapers probably helped, for if a city has only one major paper, no competitor can beat it to the punch. Readers prefer, though, to see reviews no later than the second day after the concert and not helter-skelter throughout the week. It's also aggravating when a review is buried in a hard-to-find place.

Sometimes, though, because a group of concerts or even a whole festival is covered in one write-up, some concerts are reviewed later than usual. Magazines commonly use this style and newspapers follow it occasionally. Both the *New York Times* and the *Boston Globe*, for example, have summarized in one article an entire weekend of Boston Symphony concerts at Tanglewood, the orchestra's summer home. This approach can work if the programs form a natural unit and the review appears soon after they're over.

CHOOSING WHAT TO REVIEW

When there are more concerts than space or reviewers, making the choice can be difficult. An omitted review can cause more bitterness than a bad one, particularly when a program was given primarily for the reviews. Newspapers sometimes follow certain guidelines when deciding what to review, though these principles can't be applied automatically because they're hard to rank in order of importance. If, for example, guideline (2) suggests reviewing one program and guideline (5) another, the critic or editor must make the final decision. Here are the guidelines:[64]

1. Choose what is news, whether it be a new composition, conductor, or production of an opera.
2. Select a new piece in preference to an older work.
3. Give precedence to the rare or unusual piece.
4. Give the space to a major orchestra or established chamber music group.
5. Review a concert in a major hall.
6. Describe a concert by a musician of international reputation.
7. Give coverage to a performer making a debut.

In recent years the last guideline has become less important in New York City and perhaps elsewhere. The *New York Times* now usually ignores the traditional debut recital by an unknown, since the paper feels that a debut recital is no longer a viable way to establish a career.[65] A first performance by an artist with a reputation from recordings, other engagements, or from winning a major contest may be reviewed, however.

8. Review only the first concert when a program is repeated several times. (If the cast changes for an opera, however, the *New York Times* often gives a second and shorter review devoted primarily to the new performers.)

During Virgil Thomson's first two years (1940-42) with the *New York Herald Tribune*, some of his choices fit none of these patterns. Besides reviewing some standard soloists, orchestras, and operas, he reviewed a night-club performer, incidental music for a production of *Twelfth Night*, books and magazines, church performances, a Broadway musical, student and youth orchestras, operas, and choruses, and lots more.[66] Indeed, Thomson's colorful columns suggest another principle:

9. Show the variety of music and ideas in today's music world.

Even with this example to follow, no critic today writes as varied a column as Thomson's to the best of my knowledge. Sometimes the critic is at fault for being unimaginative, but often an editor or publisher has stifled creativity. Newspapers with large staffs often cover much of Thomson's ground, but each critic is then usually assigned a specialty.

When choosing what to cover, record critics have an advantage over concert reviewers, since they aren't pressed to review more concerts on an evening than there are critics or space. Although their reasons for making choices tend to be less obvious than those for concert reviewers, making the right decisions is still important, since more disks are released each year than any paper or journal can describe.

The work of established performers remains of interest, but reviewing what is news is crucial, whether it be a new or unusual piece, a new star among performers, or a new technology. For instance, when the first CDs came out, they were widely reviewed, whereas the latest LP of *Symphonie Fantastique* might have been ignored, even if by a major orchestra and conductor. Record journals, though, sometimes follow three more criteria when choosing what to review:

10. Review a free recording instead of one the journal or paper must pay for.
11. Don't waste space reviewing recordings nobody should buy. (Since record reviews serve as marketing guides, editors and critics often screen recordings beforehand to select those most likely to be worth recommending.[67]
12. Review a recording by an artist who will soon be appearing in town. (Such a review serves as advance publicity for the concert.)

ALLOCATING SPACE AND ASSIGNING CRITICS

When space is limited, dividing up what is available becomes a major decision. Granting only a little space to a varied contemporary program with many short pieces makes no sense, for a critic can't do justice to the concert under the circumstances. Lack of space also breeds lack of grace, since the need to convey the essential facts may leave no room for the extra words that could make the writing more appealing.

Occasionally, a news service article, perhaps a biography of some popular diva with no relationship to the community, appears on the music page without the music editor's knowledge or approval. Better use could have been made of the space if the music editor had been given a chance.[68]

When in charge of critics for the *Financial Times* (London), Andrew Porter tried to send his reviewers to what interested them in order to avoid bored, routine reporting. Unfortunately, doing this risked ignoring an important program that nobody wanted to hear, for example, "[Rubinstein] playing the Brahms Second Concerto for the umpteenth time." Porter adds, "And sometimes the editor was cross. But as the team grew, it usually included someone who would leap at the chance of hearing Rubinstein."[69] This approach may work best on papers with large staffs, as Porter suggests.

James Wierzbicki of the *St. Louis Post-Dispatch* has an interesting approach to assigning critics. If an ensemble gives a series of concerts, he sends a different critic to each, using stringers if necessary, in order to present a variety of viewpoints.[70]

When reviewing televised concerts and operas, some newspapers unfortunately assign a television critic rather than a music critic. Although an occasional television critic can write intelligently about music, even the best are sometimes out of their depth. At such moments, the need to have a music critic on the job becomes obvious.[71]

THE CULT OF PERSONALITY

Unfortunately, music criticism, like other aspects of journalism, indulges the public's insatiable craving for news about personalities. Managers, publicists, and others pander to this desire by trying to create stars out of lesser individuals and manufacturing "events" out of minor occurrences.

An example would be the excessive publicity given in 1973 to the sudden reappearance of pianist Erwin Nyiregyházi. He was a well-known performer as a child prodigy and young man, but he disappeared from public view when in his twenties. After neglecting the piano for years, Nyiregyházi resurfaced when about seventy, with a solo recital and some creative recordings of Liszt. His story is colorful, and what he achieved with little practice adds to our knowledge of how pianists learn. Nevertheless, the success of his comeback was exaggerated, and the publicity by music critics and others was overdone.[72]

Or consider the egregious waste of space when the *New York Times* in a 1990 Sunday edition devoted more than a full page (including pictures) to the 88-year-old Rudolph Bing. Yet his career had ended eighteen years earlier when he retired as general manager of the Metropolitan Opera! It's true that Bing's recent marital troubles had kept him in the news, but he was now in a nursing home, apparently suffering from Alzheimer's.[73]

Some critics hate the demand for news about stars. Thomas Willis said that he quit the *Chicago Tribune* because he was ordered to write articles devoted to the cult of personality, such as why Karajian, for example, is or is not the world's greatest conductor.[74]

Such situations and others like them are stressful for critics, a point confirmed by many replies to my questionnaire. Negative reviews (especially of local artists) caused the most trouble, since the public often responded by putting pressure on a critic. On a few occasions someone even organized a campaign against a critic.

Fortunately, only a little more than 10% of those surveyed had to review music of a type distasteful to them. About 43% observed, though, that important areas of music, often contemporary, did not receive adequate attention in their papers, journals, or radio or TV stations. This failing could trouble a conscientious critic.

In short, much that they wrote was disturbing and reflected less than ideal conditions. Nevertheless, many critics fought with admirable courage for what they thought right. The words of these people were reassuring, as were the remarks of those who found their jobs satisfying.

SOME OMINOUS SIGNS

Unfortunately, since those replies were written in 1980, the pressures on music critics have increased, largely because classical music in the United States has lost much of its public in recent years, particularly among the young.[75] As a result, many newspaper editors, ever sensitive (or oversensitive) to the wishes of their readers, give less space to classical music and more to pop and rock. Instead of fighting the trend, as they should, these editors promote it.

In addition, editors frequently mirror the increasingly superficial tastes of the public by favoring the profile and feature story over the supposedly more difficult and esoteric review. If this course persists, the results could be disastrous for music criticism. Scott Cantrell of the *Kansas City Star* said in 1994, "The review is the one forum [about music] where issues of quality and performance are at least raised in public. . . . If reviews disappear, an essential part of the artistic dialectic will be lost."[76] Some papers also favor the glamorous event and send a critic to New York for a routine revival at the Met, although a concert at home might be more deserving of attention.

Another concern, still in the embryonic stage, is that some newspapers may be going on-line, so they can provide readers by computer with a newspaper that is updated throughout the day like television news. Although it's too early to predict the effects this might have on music criticism, one worry is that critics who work for on-line newspapers might have to write for an immediate deadline.[77]

Even the appearance of American reviews is changing. Often one sees other aspects of the story placed above, below, or alongside the main article, surrounded by black lines forming two-dimensional boxes. The contents of the boxes may be logical, since a review of an opera might list the cast in one box, describe the opera's history in another, and give a biography of the composer in a third. The boxes provide many points of entry into a review and presumably make it easier to interest the reader.[78] Unfortunately, they can also fritter away so much space that little is left for other criticism.

Another headache for some music critics is not being allowed to review a concert unless the program is repeated.[79] Equally aggravating is being forced to compete for space and a good position on the page with critics of the other arts, including film. Sadly, the article with the best photos, *not* content, often wins.[80]

Many of these changes reflect a shift in emphasis in newspaper coverage. Although many newspapers still try to appeal to a variety of readers, the belief that every story must reach a broad segment of the readership is becoming stronger in the industry. As a result, a music critic can still write about a celebrity, but in some communities an article about an unknown local musician is less likely to be allowed, because fewer people will be interested in it.[81] Now, more than ever, the vitality and quality of the music criticism in American papers seems pale in comparison to what is found in London.

The fear of censorship may also sap energy from American criticism. The following example may be only an aberration, but it must have cast a chill upon all who wrote for the *New York Times*. On August 25, 1992, the *Times* printed a lengthy review by Allan Kozinn of a festival at Bard College called "The World of Richard Strauss, Murky and Not So Honorable." The festival included eleven concerts (with a lecture before each), some panel discussions, and an exhibition. Here is part of what Kozinn says:

> An issue that cropped up frequently both weekends was Strauss's connection with the Nazis, itself a complex matter. As German music's elder statesman, he accepted an offical cultural post. But he and the Nazis gradually parted ways. Strauss was not a party ideologue (as were Hans Pfitzner and other composers); he had a Jewish daughter-in-law, and he belatedly recognized the regime for what it was.
>
> He is fleetingly present, though, in one of the festival's central elements, an exhibition that looks at the cultural suppression in which Strauss's political overlords engaged. In 1938 as part of a grand hootenanny of German music staged in Düsseldorf, the Nazis put together a "Degenerate Music" exhibition. Last year two musicologists, Albrecht Dümling and Peter Girth, recreated the exhibition for the Los Angeles Philharmonic, and Bard has brought it East.

In it, one sees pictures of Strauss and Goebbels beaming at each other, and Strauss conducting beneath a swastika banner. More broadly, the exhibition's posters vilify composers whose music, in the Nazis's view, did not represent pure German values and would corrupt the morals of children. Music lovers are exhorted to reject these dangerous currents and protest against them.

A visitor taking in the exhibition just two days after the Republican National Convention could not help but notice a similarity between this rhetoric and that of the American right wing. Such a comparison was clearly intended: An adjacent exhibition presented 15 prints by Robert Mapplethorpe, the photographer whose work was a focus of the conservative attack on the National Endowment for the Arts. And at the concert on Saturday evening Mr. Botstein pointedly described Pfitzner's belief that all modernism represented degeneracy and moral decline as proceeding from "a kind of Dan Quayle logic."[82]

The day after this review appeared, an "Editors' Note" was seen on page two of the *Times,* just below the index to the paper. After a brief introductory paragraph describing how the festival recreated the Nazi attacks on "degenerate" modern music, came the following statement:

The review said there was a similarity between such propaganda and some views expressed at the Republican National Convention this month. Such an offensive comparison was out of place in a music review.[83]

But it is the *Times* that is out of line, not Kozinn. A music review should present a personal opinion and need not be written in the seemingly objective style of a news story. Kozinn's remarks appeared under his own name and clearly represented his viewpoint and not the official one of the *Times.* Regardless of the merits of his comparison, chastising Kozinn this way threatens the freedom of expression of all critics. The arts do not exist in a vacuum, and a newspaper should encourage its writers to discuss any political issues they reflect without fear of censorship. Besides, if an issue is important and a critic has taken a controversial stand, some reader is certain to write and complain, thus giving the paper a chance to print a letter presenting another point of view.

What will come of these nasty trends is hard to say. Some of these concerns, however, have important ramifications which need further study on our part. The epilogue will consider them again during its discussion of the responsibility of the public in these troubled times.

Chapter Five

The Principles Behind Value Judgments

Because they have never been above reproach, critics inevitably became the butt of jokes. For example, in *Waiting for Godot*, during the scene in which Estragon and Vladimir toss insults at each other, Estragon's final and crushing gibe is "Crritic!"[1] Besides the amusement of seeing Beckett thumb his nose at reviewers, the remark has a serious meaning, the suggestion that critics are no better than base animals.

Such a low status may have arisen because some critics have bizarre opinions and because it often seems impossible to resolve critical disputes. If critics can't agree and there is no methodology for getting them to agree, what good are they and their statements? Yet differences of opinion are central to the critical process, for if there were none, there would be no criticism. We must look further and try to find the causes of these disagreements if we are to prove that critical judgments are more than arbitrary expressions of opinion.

THE POSSIBILITY OF OBJECTIVE CRITICISM

It's always difficult when undertaking such a search to decide where and how to begin. Perhaps, though, we could start by asking whether some form of objective criticism is even possible. This approach requires us to consider what "objective" can mean in this context. James S. Ackerman gives one common usage. He holds that an objective opinion is one which matches the generally accepted views of others or could receive confirmation under appropriate conditions. Those opinions we recognize as highly personal we call subjective.[2] This viewpoint makes much sense and is in common use, but problems remain. If there is no generally accepted consensus about a work, as might happen after a first performance, under what conditions could one try to confirm the opinion?

Unfortunately, there is no easy answer to that question. In view of this difficulty we might seek another definition of "objective" to help decide whether objective criticism is even possible. Here are two definitions of that term I propose for consideration now:

1. Impersonal and uncolored by the feelings and prejudices of the critic.
2. Containing clear-cut descriptions of the object in question.

Can a critic write criticism that is objective according to these definitions? In regard to the first one, one must answer not completely. Trying to write criticism without feelings would be unnatural and dishonest, because music and the other arts affect the feelings of those who care about them. Besides, eliminating prejudices is an ideal but unachievable goal even though prejudices are so unwelcome. It's impossible to exclude all of them (and our feelings, too), for they are buried in the subconscious and can be perceived only with difficulty, if at all.

Since prejudices hide so well, it would be difficult to implement John M. Robertson's suggestion that critics should tell readers their biases.[3] His idea also has two other problems. Even if critics could know all of their prejudices, which they can't, making such a confession might cause them to become smug, complacent, and neglectful of the constant need to try to overcome them. Besides, it's difficult to differentiate between a prejudice and a well-reasoned viewpoint which runs counter to fashion. What seems biased today might in a hundred years be considered a praiseworthy judgment ahead of its time.

Is objective criticism by the second definition, "Containing clear-cut descriptions of the object in question," more practical? The answer must be sometimes, but not completely. If simple music is heard by listeners with modest training, they can often tell whether a work begins loudly or softly, is in major or minor, or is slow or fast. Many can also name the instruments that play. These descriptions are objective. Listeners with talent and extensive training can go further and answer harder questions about more complex music. Even so, disagreements will arise, regardless of the level at which people listen. Sometimes this happens because listeners concentrate on different things. One person might focus on the melody, another on the harmony, another on an apparent stylistic clash between sections, and so on. Although experienced listeners can follow many things at once, this ability has its limits.

All differences of opinion aren't bad, though. Several descriptions of a complex work, each giving a variant viewpoint, may paint a richer and truer picture than a single, unified one. When sharply contrasting evaluations appear, however, the public, ignorant of the cause, may become bewildered.

How can people agree on the worth of a work if they don't perceive the same thing? Their perceptions may not be that far apart, though. Trained listeners can often describe works with reasonable, though not foolproof, assurance that they are talking about the same thing. If listeners compare notes and hear the music again, as happens sometimes when friends listen to a recording together, many disagreements can be resolved.

Some philosophers and critics don't accept this argument, however, and hold that objective criticism isn't possible. Their beliefs have spawned another type of criticism, impressionist criticism.

IMPRESSIONIST CRITICISM

According to Monroe C. Beardsley, impressionist critics hold that we can only talk about our impressions of music and not about the music itself—an extreme position if carried through consistently.[4] Beardsley holds that critics may function as impressionists on some occasions but not others. A reviewer who often speaks objectively could hedge upon hearing a first performance of a complex work and say it *seems* like such and such, without being committed to saying it *is* such and such. This caution can be a wise form of self-protection.

Shaw says critics are impressionists if they give only first impressions of a work without serious study, in contrast to other critics who analyze a work carefully before committing a word to print.[5] His usage fits into Beardsley's broad category.

Impressionist criticism is often associated with these words of Anatole France:

> The good critic is he who relates the adventures of his soul among masterpieces. Objective criticism has no more existence than has objective art, and all those who deceive themselves into the belief that they put anything but their own personalities into their work are dupes of the most fallacious illusions. The truth is that we can never get outside ourselves. That is one of our greatest misfortunes.[6]

I agree that criticism is only the opinion of an individual. Nevertheless, as the previous section has shown and later parts of this

chapter will affirm, there are alternatives to Anatole France's position
and the severe limitations it imposes on criticism.

The following example by Paul Rosenfeld illustrates what happens
when impressionist criticism is carried to the extreme:

> ERNEST BLOCH's sonata for violin and piano calls
> to mind certain pages of "La Tentation de Saint Antoine."
> It calls to mind the adamantine page where the devil slings
> the saint upon his horns, and carries him out into the
> empyrean amid the planets, and makes him to perceive the
> infinitude of matter; thought encased in matter; and matter
> higher than sight however high one lifts one's eyes. It calls
> to mind also the final scene, where the monstrous
> animality of the earth becomes visible to the delirious
> dreamer, and he imagines himself viewing the origin of
> life. For in Bloch's music, too, we come to perceive with
> impersonal eye, the titanic, virulent and incommensurable
> forces upon whose breast man lies tiny and impotent. We
> are as though placed on a platform somewhere without the
> universe, and nevertheless permitted to see ourselves in
> the grasp of the natural powers, spurned about as a
> football. In the roaring of the piano and the impersonal
> singing of the violin, we feel nature before man, nature
> which is grandly impervious to man and his woe, nature
> which tramples ruthlessly upon him, and drowns his
> wailing in her unending storm.[7]

The writing is so bizarre and far removed from today's conception
of criticism that it may provoke laughter in some readers. Though
Rosenfeld's pictures are impressively vivid, they have little to do with
poor Ernest Bloch's violin and piano sonata. The highly florid
imagery and the emphasis on the impressions of the listener (critic) at
the expense of objective description are typical of this overdone form
of critical impressionism. The absence of simple description suggests
that Rosenfeld forgot what the music was like after it stimulated his
flights of fancy.

This style of criticism was once popular, but today's readers
demand criticism that is more objective, less personal, and less self-
centered. Even Rosenfeld, who was active from 1916 through the
1930s in New York City, was out of date toward the end of his career
when the public taste had turned away from such exaggerated prose.[8]
Yet such writing still turns up occasionally, though usually in a milder

fashion, perhaps in a paragraph or two embedded in a more objective setting.

THE INSTRUMENTALIST THEORY AND THE AESTHETIC EXPERIENCE

We must now turn to a question that was postponed from chapter one: What does it mean to say that a piece is good or, in the terminology of some aestheticians, that it has aesthetic value? One major hypothesis, Monroe C. Beardsley's Instrumentalist Theory, provides an answer that is impressive both for its plausibility and for the way it surpasses any other theory in matching what critics actually do today.[9] The Instrumentalist Theory holds that the value of aesthetic objects (a term broader than "works of art" since it includes nature) is their capacity to produce an aesthetic experience. (It is assumed that such an experience has value to human beings.) A more precise way to say it would be, " 'X has aesthetic value' means 'X has the capacity to produce an aesthetic experience of a fairly great magnitude such an experience having value.' "[10] (Having aesthetic value and being a good aesthetic object are thus equivalent.)

In other words, what makes an aesthetic object good is its ability to produce such an experience. Beethoven's *Eroica* Symphony is great (an extreme form of good) because of the kind of response it can produce within us. It is also greater than Beethoven's First Symphony because it will produce an experience of greater magnitude than the First.

The nature of the aesthetic experience, however, has been much debated. Philosopher George Dickie even denies its existence,[11] but the concept probably survives his attack.[12] The aesthetic experience, of course, is broader than the musical, since it can arise from the other arts and even, according to John Dewey (I think rightly), from non-artistic events such as a meeting between two individuals.[13]

Unfortunately, these topics are complicated, although intriguing. Since this is primarily a book on music criticism, it appears best to simplify matters and confine the discussion to the issues presented by music alone.

Most music lovers can recall some intense and memorable musical experiences, moments when we forget ourselves and outside distractions and become completely engrossed in the music. I will recount some such moments of mine. At times it was largely a response to tone color, for example, to Ravel's shimmering sounds in portions of the orchestral version of the *Mother Goose Suite* or to the beauty of Eleanor Steber's voice floating through Carnegie Hall in Berlioz's *Nuits d'été* with the New York Philharmonic. Or it could be a reaction to a dramatic moment, such as my surprise at an entrance of the brass in the finale of Brahms' Third Symphony. Or it could be a complex experience made up of many smaller ones, as happens when I am moved by Beethoven's Ninth.

Usually, when discussing a work that produces such an experience, we don't go into detail about our experience but simply say that the piece is good or great. Those words are both convenient and valid, since being good means that it has the potential to produce such an experience, something a bad work cannot do. Similarly, when comparing works we merely assert that one is better or greater than another. That is how these terms are used throughout this book.

The emphasis on experience suggests that critics get their knowledge of a work, including its value, empirically. Few would hold, assuming they think through the issues, that intuition plays a part. If it did, their judgments could be correct and objective since intuition in the form used here bypasses sense experience and reaches conclusions independently of it. Yet, as we have seen, it is doubtful that any critic could have the infallibility that comes from this form of intuition.

One factor, though, suggests a role for intuition in evaluation. Often, after hearing just a few notes of a piece, a good listener can name the composer and work, tell whether the performer has talent, and sometimes even name the performer if the person is well known. Still, what seems like an intuitive process is probably just one in which the mind processes the information so quickly that the listener can't perceive the steps involved.

THE LOGIC BEHIND AESTHETIC JUDGMENTS

When giving reasons for their opinions, most critics do so in incomplete form. If they say a piece is good because it has rhythmic vitality, they omit the following crucial premise of the syllogism: "Works with rhythmic vitality *tend* to be good."[14] Repeating this sentence would soon become tedious, but omitting it leaves an essential step of the logic unexpressed.

To claim more boldly that "works with rhythmic vitality are *always* good," would be wrong, for the structure might be poor or the harmonies crude, which could ruin the effect. Unfortunately, throughout the history of music, composers and theorists have issued arbitrary and inflexible rules for achieving musical beauty which can't be literally true. When they claim that doing such and such produces a great piece, they forget that this happens only if the other elements fit in. Often, though, they don't.

As a result, all value judgments are tentative and not absolute, since one of their basic premises must be only an inclination and not a definite rule. To be precise—which we seldom are when expressing a standard for a value judgment—we should say, for example, that a piece with clear-cut structure *tends* to be good but not that it *is* good.

Value judgments in art share with scientific hypotheses the possibility of being mistaken. The principles of scientific method and of inductive thinking also apply to the critical process in art. If either a premise or a step in the logic is wrong, so is the conclusion. The initial response, the "Aha!" after a glittering performance, the tingle down the spine at an exquisite moment, come immediately. Logic and thought then translate these feelings into a value judgment.[15] The process is particularly complex for some judgments, like ranking a symphony among the works of its composer and period.

Those who believe that the pronouncements of chemistry, astronomy, or medicine are more accurate than critical judgments about music and the other arts, should reflect upon the history of those sciences. Their record is far from perfect.

STYLE

Many of the standards upon which critics base their judgments tend to be valid only for particular styles. To understand why, it's necessary to study the nature of a style and to see how it functions.

Basically, a style is a repetition of patterns, the use of certain traits again and again.[16] There are many kinds of styles. For instance, musicians talk about the style of a single work, artist, period, country, or culture and of genres like nineteenth-century French opera or English folk song. In each case, a pattern is repeated either throughout a piece or over many pieces. Here are three examples of mine to illustrate this.

The style of a single work: Debussy's *La plus que lente* (1910) for piano is in the style of a Boston waltz, one in which beats, or even measures, are sometimes suppressed in the accompaniment. The character is reminiscent of salon music, but the subtlety of the writing, the rhythmic sophistication, and the occasionally tart harmonies keep the sweetness of the melody from becoming cloying.

The style of a composer: Domenico Scarlatti's output consists of over five hundred short keyboard works called *exercisi* or *sonatas*, some intended to be played together in groups of two or three. Each sonata divides into two parts each of which is repeated, but the formal relations within a part vary from sonata to sonata. Often they develop a figuration in etude-like fashion requiring considerable virtuosity. Patterns with trills, repeated notes, rapid passagework, leaps, crossed hands, and octaves abound. Other passages sometimes imitate the sound of a person slapping a guitar.

The style of a country's folk tunes: Hungarian folk melodies tend to begin on a strong downbeat, since the language has no articles and sentences don't start with an unaccented "A" or "The." Often the structure transposes phrases regularly up or down an interval of a fifth. Frequently, the melodies are pentatonic and contain strongly accented rhythms in figurations of long-short or short-long rhythms. The meters are often duple, triple, or quadruple, but more complex asymmetric patterns are also found.

This emphasis on style doesn't mean that every piece or composer can be neatly pigeonholed into a style. Instead, a composer may be experimenting, or the composer's style may be changing, or the composer may resist acquiring a style.[17] Nevertheless, critic John Rockwell believes that a composer needs a style if only for purposes of marketing, since a style is the imprint which marks a composer's work. If each piece seems to be in a sharply different style, the composer lacks identity.[18]

Some contemporary pieces, though, lack a style or, to be more precise, are in a potpourri of styles which follow each other without fusing. Such a hodgepodge is usually a liability, but an energetic or humorous piece may make us overlook the stylistic mishmash. And in a program of theatre or dance, the changing musical styles may even seem appropriate if they match what happens on stage.

Another meaning of style is that of being fashionable (stylish). The latest style (fashion) is what everybody, or seemingly everybody, wears or does, whether it be in music, clothing, food, or dance. As I write this, my students wear blue jeans in winter, shorts in summer; everyone eats croissants—rolls once found only in French restaurants—and exercise of one sort or another seems popular for every age.

Some musical styles are fashionable, that is, commonly found, while others are not. Either they never caught on, or they became unpopular—out of style—the very fate that befell Bach's musical idiom at the end of his life.

The many styles of music present problems to listeners, for each style is like a language which has to be learned for comprehension. Look at only part of what can be heard any day in our culture: eighteenth- and nineteenth-century European art music; serial, experimental, jazz, rock, country and western, soul, and popular music. How many people can comprehend and enjoy them all?

Music is not a universal language despite the romantic legend to the contrary. Although it was once claimed that all cultured Frenchmen, Englishmen, and Germans, for example, liked Bach—substitute the name of another composer if you prefer—the people who were tone-deaf or couldn't tolerate him were conveniently overlooked. What was also overlooked was the educational process involved in learning to understand music.

Indeed, as Leonard B. Meyer eloquently argues, the appreciation of all musical styles is learned,[19] and nobody is born with an innate comprehension of a style. If two listeners hear the same piece for the first time, the one more familiar with the style probably enjoys it more, unless that person has become bored with the style.

SOME COMPLICATING FACTORS

Another issue makes the process of evaluation more difficult. Most listeners, including educated ones, don't want to be fed only the greatest pieces and styles but prefer to hear music of many types and moods, including the warm, humorous, sad, grotesque, ugly, playful, and erotic. The desire for variety is almost universal, which is something the planners of concert programs generally keep in mind.

To meet the demand for variety, even the greatest composers wrote modest pieces as well as big ones, modest and less important because of the scope of their designs, not their workmanship. Brahms, for example, wrote both waltzes and symphonies. Folk music—the genuine product of a community's creativity—provided another alternative for past listeners. (Its importance had faded in our society even before it was replaced in the 1960s by the pseudo-folk music of Bob Dylan and others.)

The music of Broadway shows, particularly in the pre-rock days, provided some of the needed variety for those whose normal diet was classical music. A Cole Porter tune may lack the depth of feeling of a great German Lied, but if it had that quality, it might lose the delicious wit and sophistication which are its charm.

Nevertheless, some who appreciate the depth and subtlety of late Beethoven quartets dislike all popular music. A form of cultural snobbery may restrain them, the belief that only the "best" kinds of music are worthy of attention, or else they refuse to accept popular music because its fine qualities are mated with traits less appealing to them.

Incidentally, liking a style or piece doesn't require thinking it good. For instance, the sensuality of rock tunes attracts many who know how primitive they are, and a personal association can also affect one's response. I'm particularly fond of the tune, "Where or When," not only because it's a good one but because—trite as it may seem—I heard the song at my high school prom and hearing it again evokes warm memories. Some people like hymns because their melodies remind them of church, while others hate them for the same reason. Old-fashioned sentimental tunes may evoke nostalgia and memories of a somewhat distant and (presumably) more secure age.

The capricious behavior of our feelings can make us like an inferior piece without our realizing what is happening. Much of the confusion regarding value judgments comes about because of the odd and seemingly illogical ways that feelings affect our judgments.

TASTE

Unfortunately, many listeners fail to realize the point made above, that one can like a piece without thinking it good. The most naive of them even believe that what they like is automatically good and what they dislike is bad. For them, nothing could be wrong with their taste. Before we explore what that statement can mean, it pays to consider what "taste" can mean in this context. Here are four major ways that the word is used:

1. The first usage lists an individual's preferences, what that person likes to do, in a value-neutral way which conveys nothing positive or negative about them. For instance, I might say that John goes fishing and hiking, wears tweed jackets, and watches Charlie Chaplin movies. My remarks divulge nothing about what I think of his tastes. Even if I make John more colorful and controversial and say he is a sharp dresser, drinks a lot, sleeps with many women, and drives fast sport cars, the words don't convey my approval or disapproval. Either the context or your knowledge of my values might tell you, or a facial expression or tonal inflection could give me away, but the words contain no value judgments. Similarly, if I say that Jane likes hard rock and Mary likes classical music, the words remain value neutral.

2. A second meaning, like the first but with a plural or collective subject, refers to what a group of people likes rather than to just the wishes of an individual. For instance, the work of Maria Callas, Beverly Sills, Joan Sutherland, and Montserrat Caballé has increased the American taste for coloratura singing in Italian opera. This example helps contrast "taste" and "style." As used here, "taste" refers to the thoughts, feelings, and, in particular, likings of a group of people. The object of their likings is a kind of music, a musical style or sub-style, coloratura singing in Italian opera.

3. When I say "He has good taste," or just "He has taste," the words imply that I value his choices positively. "He has poor taste," "He has no taste," and "He lacks taste," all imply the reverse.

4. A fourth meaning was apparently first formulated by eighteenth-century English and German philosophers interested in the way human nature responds to the outside world. To them, in Kant's wording, taste is "the faculty of judging the beautiful,"[20] or, as Beardsley puts it, "A special faculty by which we appreciate or 'relish'

beautiful objects."[21] The *American College Dictionary* says a "faculty" is, among other things, "an inherent capability of the body: the faculties of sight and hearing." This meaning of taste is rarely used today, since we think less of dividing the mind into faculties.

Kant made an important point when he said there is no rule by which anybody can be forced to recognize something as beautiful.[22] Regardless of the supposed virtues of a work, if we don't think it beautiful, we can't be persuaded.

When discussing the accompaniments to two dances, *Playera* and *Evocación*, Deborah Jowitt, the dance critic, shows the impact of taste on reviewing:

> I like these [dances] even though I'm not a fan of solo piano Albéniz, Granados, and de Falla. I'm reminded of salon art and wish someone would use Scarlatti or Soler, or *something* besides these sweet old chestnuts.[23]

At their best, these works of Albéniz, Granados, and de Falla have a subtle structure, sharp dramatic profile, and imaginative piano writing, traits which help account for the music's popularity with audiences and pianists. Unfortunately for Jowitt, these fine qualities are combined with others—perhaps a hint of the superficial, commercial, or popular—which spoil her pleasure in the music.

Alan Rich provides a striking example of how a professional critic's taste or preference becomes a standard for judgment:

> Suppose I am going to *La Traviata.* . . . I have had plenty of time . . . to form my own set of ideas about the opera, the kind of voices I would ideally like to hear in the roles, the tempos at which it ought to move, how it should look onstage. This is the equipment I take with me to the opera house that night. . . . My colleague across the aisle arrives with a similar set of equipment—similar in scope, that is, but conditioned by *his* personality. We sit there, a few feet apart, listening to a Violetta with a perfectly awesome technique; she sticks an E-flat into the end of "Sempre libera" which goes off like a rocket. She may not know beans about what the opera is about; her exchanges with Germont in the second scene may seem so many vocalises. But boy! she can get the tone out, and the crowd goes wild. In next morning's papers my colleague erupts in ecstasy, I in fury. There's something I want from *La*

Traviata that has to do with drama and sentiment and
reaction to the text; my colleague is mad for vocal
prowess. I am not immune to great singing, nor is he to
dramatic values, but each has made his own decision as to
which is the element more highly to be prized. Our
reviews are opposed, and the strange and wonderful thing
is that neither of us is "right" or "wrong."[24]

It's hard to be so tolerant of a colleague who takes the dramatic
values of an opera lightly, but the fellow critic may be fictional or Rich
may have exaggerated the positions to make a point. In any case, the
passage shows how a significant difference in taste—wanting good
vocal sound versus wanting dramatic plausibility—results in two very
different verdicts.

Still, two reviews with such different conclusions can disturb
readers and make them wonder whether such judgments are objective
or just the expression of a writer's taste. And if judgments are based
on standards, why were two different and incompatible sets used? Is
there any way to decide which standards are the right ones? Because
these questions are difficult, perplexing, and frustrating, many
conclude that objectivity in criticism is impossible and that relativism
is the only plausible alternative.

RELATIVISM

Although there are many kinds of relativism, the following two
definitions show some common usages regarding value. Antony Flew
says, "To be a relativist about value is to maintain that there are no
universal standards of good and bad, right and wrong."[25] The
Encyclopaedia Brittanica defines ethical relativism as "the view that
what is right or wrong and good or bad is not absolute but variable and
relative, depending on the person, circumstances, or social situation."[26]

People have long known of the problems leading to relativism, as
Aristotle's comment shows: "Fire burns both in Hellas and in Persia;
but men's ideas of right and wrong vary from place to place."[27] Here
is a contemporary example that should set the stage for our discussion.

Two musicians, one a native of Ghana and the other an American
unfamiliar with African music, are listening to a recording from the
Ashanti people of Ghana. The African admires the work's rhythmic

vitality, its many polyrhythms and syncopations, the enthusiasm of the overlapping call and response between the leader and the chorus, and the variety of timbres of the drums. He notes that though the piece was improvised, the ensemble holds together well when the leader starts the transition to a new section. The American complains, however, that the harmony and counterpoint are rudimentary; the tone color of the voices, coarse; and the form, repetitive and elementary, since it often repeats the same material again and again, though with modifications.

It's tempting to explain their disagreement relativistically, perhaps by saying that each person has different criteria for what is a good work. The Ghanaian's are derived from the African tradition, the American's from the Western, and neither one is absolutely right. This viewpoint would be a form of cultural relativism, the philosophy which claims that all aspects of the culture must be judged by its own standards. According to this belief, only the Ghanaian standards apply to this music.

Much of the spread of cultural relativism in this century came about because anthropologists studying so-called "primitive" societies discovered that their social mores and principles of conduct differed radically from each other. Within a particular culture, however, there are objective standards of conduct, although these may differ from those of its neighbors. It's not true, even in a primitive society, that anything goes.

Nor does such freedom exist when judging music by the principles of cultural relativism. Music is judged according to (in relation to, relative to) standards, but the standards are not universal and vary with the culture. In addition, some forms of cultural relativism claim that only people of the culture can know these standards and apply them properly.

A problem appears, though, if we consider how the quality of German art declined under the Nazis, as the first chapter described. Even though the Nazis severely restricted what could be painted, a consistent cultural relativism would claim that only the standards of the Nazis apply to this art and that the works must be considered good. This conclusion, though, is probably unacceptable to most people.

Historical relativism, another popular kind, holds that only those living in a particular period could know the standards and be qualified to judge its art. The difficulty remains, though, of trying to judge the maverick artist who doesn't fit in, say, a William Blake who painted in

his own mystical style regardless of what everybody else was doing. A
sub-culture would be needed to evaluate him since his work doesn't fit
into the main one. It thus becomes difficult to maintain any objective
standards at all even for a particular period, since smaller and even
smaller groups might be needed to find qualified judges for unusual
artists.[28]

In short, attempts to maintain some objective standards by allowing
only a partial relativism, like those of cultural and historical
relativism, soon break down. Either the attempt leads to patent
absurdity, as with Nazi art, or other problems appear. For instance, in
order to find somebody to evaluate a work, one must first decide on the
group to which it belongs. Yet how could one do this with a work of
unknown date, authorship, and place of origin?

An extreme relativism which grants each opinion the same worth
as the next, regardless of the education, training, and talent of its
maker, would breed artistic chaos. Value judgments would be reduced
to mere statements of personal feeling without other validity. To avoid
this disturbing situation, we must seek an explanation for artistic
disagreements other than relativism. Let us begin by reconsidering our
example of Ghanaian music.

Although the American showed no comprehension of the music he
heard, could he learn to acquire it? Many of his countrymen have
become sensitive to the style of African music and have learned to
appreciate it and even perform it. They have learned that the tone
color of the voices, coarse though it may seem initially, fits in with
other stylistic traits of that music. Trained Western voices would be
out of place. Even the problems with the form can be explained away
by showing that the constant changes in the solo text add interest to
the music. The success of Steve Reich's *Drumming*, an American work
based on Ghanaian music, whose popularity extends beyond the circle
of regular listeners to African music, indicates that Americans are
capable of comprehending and appreciating that country's music.

A cultural or historical relativism implies that only a person born
into a certain culture or period can comprehend it. Education,
however, can teach one to comprehend a foreign culture or period of
the past. Today's pianists, for instance, are expected to perform works
from five periods, the Baroque (though some leave this to
harpsichordists), the Classic, the Romantic, the Impressionist, and the
Contemporary, with the assurance of a master who is thoroughly at
home in each style.

The concept of bi-musicality, developed by ethnomusicologists, assumes that with talent, hard work, and proper instruction, one can learn to perform and teach the music of another culture with the fluency of a native, just as one can learn a foreign language.[29] Ethnomusicologists, with the help of anthropologists, are also codifying the grammar and aesthetics of the music of other cultures.

One argument for relativism is that tastes are inflexible and once set can't be changed. A well-known saying goes, "I don't know anything about art, but I know what I like." Those who say it pride themselves on their ignorance, but they really should be ashamed. Evidence shows that tastes can change. Indeed, developing and broadening an individual's tastes is a large part of what education in the arts is about.

We must not forget the importance of the aesthetic experience in appreciating art. It may take time and effort to comprehend the style, content, or structure of a piece, and not everyone will succeed. Still, if a work can give an experience of depth and intensity after this, then it has value. Many arguments for relativism evaporate when it is realized that saying a piece is good means that it has the potential for giving such an experience.

This knowledge helps explain the error of genre criticism, the belief that works can be compared only with similar works—string quartets with string quartets (or possibly other chamber music), oratorios with oratorios, and so on. Genre critics hold that comparing small pieces with large, or waltzes with symphonies, is wrong.[30] As a result, genre criticism is a form of relativism, since it implies that universal standards don't apply to all works.

In practice we usually make comparisons the way genre critics suggest. Comparing a brief prelude to a symphony seems grotesque (unless the symphony is a dud) because the symphony's greater length and stature make it likely to win. Still, in principle we could compare the aesthetic experiences created by two such works, though we seldom do because the conclusion is usually obvious.

A form of historical relativism prevalent among musicologists claims that the music of all periods (at least of Western art music) is equally great. This belief assumes that works should only be judged against others of the same era, which makes it relativistic. Such a philosophy may have arisen to meet the subconscious needs of those studying a period to justify their efforts by asserting that its music is as good as any performed today.

APPLYING STANDARDS

When listening to new music, the critic's immediate gut reaction may determine whether the review is favorable or unfavorable. Since most readers want more than a gut reaction, however, a critic usually supplies some objective reasons, reasons which come to mind either while listening or afterwards.

The language of a review usually suggests rather than states the standards being used. For instance, a review might say that the piece was poor because the melodies all sounded alike, the middle part went on for too long, and the music was so continuously bombastic that the apparent climax could make no effect. The standards behind these observations might be formulated as follows: New themes should contrast with the old; a section must end before it becomes boring; a climax should stand out from its surroundings.

The standards used to judge performance are often more obvious and easier to apply than those for composition. Most people can tell that the soprano is poor if she sings out of tune or is barely audible over the orchestra even in soft passages. Other situations are more difficult, though. To evaluate, say, the many pianists who graduate from the major conservatories with good technique, memory, and a basic conception of musical styles, is challenging. Separating the truly talented from the merely well trained requires subtler standards which are harder to learn and apply.

At times, though, when there is no agreement about which standards to apply, sharply differing verdicts from critics may result. Even the most practical substitute for relativism, a criticism based on standards, can't guarantee critical agreement.

Since standards apply only to particular styles, when a style changes, the old standard may become obsolete, which is something that conservative critics seldom realize. For instance, any critic of 1910 who attacked a mature composition of Debussy because it used parallel fifths and octaves was out of date, since those traits fit his later music even though wrong for most nineteenth-century pieces.

Some readers may raise an eyebrow over this last paragraph, however. If standards apply only to a particular style, isn't this a form of relativism, stylistic relativism? Monroe C. Beardsley finds a way out of the problem, however. He explains that the specific standards all belong to one of the three large standards (canons) which give a work value: unity, intensity, and complexity.[31] Since the canons apply to all styles, relativism is avoided, though the problem of choosing the right standard remains.

Unity (whose opposite is disunity) is probably the easiest of the three canons to understand. Unity—the way something holds together—is a virtue in a work; disunity, a weakness. An aspect of music which helps give a piece unity is form. Consider how the following statements refer to a work's unity or lack of it. (All of the examples illustrating unity, intensity, and complexity are mine.)

- The last movement had so many themes that it fell into fragments. [Disunity]
- The return of the opening theme tied the work together. [Unity]
- The music alternates in style between passages which sound like Bach, Prokofiev, Puccini, and boogie-woogie. [Disunity]
- The start of the development, with its abrupt change of key and disturbingly chromatic harmonies, seems too agitated for an otherwise tranquil movement. [Disunity]

The next canon to be considered, that of intensity, assumes that music can have qualities we associate with humans. Indeed, "intensity" is a short way of saying "intensity of human feeling." For instance, we often say that music is sprightly, somber, vivacious, pensive, questioning, anxious, or majestic. Having a strong character (or mood) adds value to a work, lacking one subtracts from it, and a piece lacking any intensity at all is boring. The following examples consider intensity, first alone and then in combination with unity.

- The thematic material was routine and uninteresting. [Lack of intensity]
- The mood alternated convincingly between whimsy and pathos. [Intensity]
- The cheerfulness of the piece was diminished by the thick and muddy orchestration. [Defect weakens intensity]
- The even and constantly flowing figuration of the first movement of the "Moonlight" Sonata creates an ethereal, romantically tranquil mood. [Unity and intensity]

- The variations built up effectively by increasing the number of notes while keeping the pulse steady. [Unity and intensity]
- Although the long cadenza for harpsichord in the first movement of Bach's Brandenburg Concerto No. 5 is exciting when played well, in one respect it's a mistake. The work is a concerto grosso for three otherwise equal soloists—violin, flute, and harpsichord—and giving such a lengthy solo to one instrument upsets the formal balance. [Intensity achieved at the expense of unity]

The last canon, complexity, assumes that a more complex piece is better than a simpler work, all things being equal. A more complex piece tends to have greater magnitude, which makes complexity a rough indicator of a work's magnitude.[32]

The opposite of complexity is simplicity, not unity. Although we often think of simplicity as a virtue, simplicity alone can be cold and barren. When simplicity is appealing, it unifies a work or helps create an attractive quality, which adds intensity to the music.

Here are some examples illustrating complexity:

- Any movement by Beethoven like this one, with its many themes developed at great length, is certain to be an important one. [Complexity]
- Mozart's rondos for piano, despite their charm and occasional emotional depth, are only minor works when compared to his more elaborate sonatas. [A judgment based on a comparison of complexities]
- In the first movement of Brahms' Fourth Symphony, a large number of themes and motives, some radiantly beautiful, follow one another in the second subject. Despite the abundance of material, Brahms keeps the movement under control and a balanced structure emerges. [Complexity, intensity, and unity]
- Mussorgsky's *Pictures at an Exhibition* is best known in the arrangement for orchestra by Ravel. Although many prefer that version's richness of color to the original for piano, the original has its proponents, including some who think that it wears better. Ravel's orchestration restricts the way a conductor and orchestra can change the color of the music. A trumpet will still sound like a trumpet. An imaginative

pianist with subtle pedaling, however, can suggest an infinitely greater range of colors. [A tricky example which compares two versions of a work in terms of the complexity of the shadings listeners perceive after repeated hearings. The version with the more complex shadings at that time is probably more intense.]

Complexity is the most problematic of the three canons. When an increase in complexity produces an increase in magnitude, the result is fine, but that doesn't always happen. When a complex piece is too difficult to understand, listeners can't follow it and so miss any changes in mood and tension that might add interest. Such music becomes tiresome to them and lacking in magnitude and intensity. When that occurs, the complexity becomes self-defeating and the music seems more pretentious than grand.

Indeed, when a work or style is very hard to understand, it may survive only as the province of a clique or cult, if it survives at all. Even Bartok became aware of the problem, for he deliberately wrote some late works, such as the Concerto for Orchestra and the Third Piano Concerto, in a more approachable style.

The use of standards is embedded in our everyday language, for we sometimes speak of one person having higher standards than another. We could say, for example, that an acquaintance with little musical background loved the soprano's performance in the opera, but the critic, who had higher standards, did not. There is no way to avoid using standards, for many are generalizations learned from experience, often subconsciously and involuntarily, and we sometimes use them without recognizing or understanding what we are doing. A sensitive amateur may spot why one performance is good and another is bad and yet be unable to say why this is so.

Although standards are helpful, they shouldn't be applied mechanically, a point Wagner knew well. In *Die Meistersinger*, Beckmesser (a caricature of Eduard Hanslick, the Viennese critic) grades works by the number of times they violate the rules. Unfortunately, when the rules don't fit the music, Beckmesser misses the beauty of a piece.

Sometimes an entire work becomes the ideal against which others are judged. At a 1979 discussion on music criticism, Leonard B. Meyer remarked that Beethoven's Op. 131 String Quartet is the standard against which we measure other pieces.[33] Unfortunately, when asked how Op. 131 achieved this position, Meyer did not reply. His silence was troublesome, for it begs the question to say that a piece is the criterion of excellence without telling how it reached that exalted station.

Even if we could agree that Op. 131 is such a standard, this does not mean that everyone will appreciate it or that it will appeal to as many people as the latest popular tune. Greatness does not have to be certified by numbers, for some profound works have a more limited appeal.

In addition, even a seemingly objective piece of criticism may contain too much that is subjective to guarantee that it will stand the test of time. A broader consensus is needed, and even then errors may occur, as the constant reevaluation of the reputations of individual works and composers reveals. Look at the reverence accorded to Mendelssohn in much of the nineteenth century, his sharp decline in status later, and his current rank somewhere in the middle.

NORMS AND DEVIANTS

One philosophy which explains much about what makes music good is Leonard B. Meyer's concept of norms and deviants and their role in music. Meyer says:

> The customary or expected progression of sounds can be considered as a norm, which from a stylistic point of view it is; an alteration in the expected progression can be considered as a deviation. Hence deviations can be regarded as emotional or affective stimuli.[34]

These remarks have important implications for evaluating both music and performance. Assuming that the basic syntax of a passage makes sense, the progression that is out of the ordinary, the imaginative surprise, is what we respond to. A piece in which everything is predictable seems academic and routine, since we prefer in our music the unexpected, the fresh, the seemingly spontaneous, the imaginative. To create these qualities, passages must deviate from the norms of the style but without becoming so extreme that they seem jarring and out of place.

ORIGINALITY

Since we crave the new, the fresh, and the different, we praise both works and composers for originality. Originality is a quality that can be found in the style, form, or content, or indeed in any aspect of a piece of music or total body of works of a composer. One might wonder, though, both why originality is so important to us, and whether it contributes to a work's aesthetic value or to its other values, including historic, monetary, or moral?

Fortunately, the very last part of this question is easily answered. Although original works, like *Carmen*, have often been attacked on moral grounds, originality adds nothing to their moral value, though it may increase their monetary value. Bizet's widow became wealthy from the royalties to *Carmen*,[35] but it's uncertain how much was due to the opera's originality. Unfortunately many original and great works brought little or no financial reward to their composers.

Perhaps the chief value of originality is historic, for we remember innovative works and their composers. Nevertheless, innovation alone isn't enough to guarantee a work's survival, for an innovative work of slight musical value may be forgotten, while a later and better work is remembered instead for the innovation.

Beethoven's Fifth, Sixth, and Ninth symphonies are all important for their stylistic innovations. The Fifth connects two of its movements and brings back a theme from an earlier movement in a later one; the Sixth is the first program symphony; and the Ninth is the first work to introduce a chorus, vocal soloists, and sung text into a symphony. Even so, their musical value is what makes them survive, not their innovations.

The question still remains, however, about whether originality contributes to a work's aesthetic value. Although many people believe this is true, is it really so? A consideration of the recent history of this concept may help provide the answer.

The emphasis on originality arose with the nineteenth-century belief that each composer should have his or her own style.[36] (In earlier periods this wasn't required, and Bach could write the same kind of music as everyone else, only better.) The extraordinary proliferation of styles in the twentieth century seemed to confirm the importance of originality and led some critics to expect each composer to write in an original or "signature" style. Although Stravinsky's music was always distinctive, he treated each piece as if it was a new problem to be solved, with the result that each work became a new style or sub-style. (Yet, paradoxically, each piece also displays the stamp of his overall style.)

When critics took Stravinsky's approach as the model for all composers, the results were sometimes unfortunate. Consider, for example, the lukewarm receptions given to the late operas of Richard Strauss at their premieres because they broke no new ground. Only in recent years have these works been recognized as the masterpieces that they are.

The twentieth-century public displays a curious variety of attitudes toward innovation. Often it seems to want innovation, but not too much. Reviving a forgotten work can satisfy its craving for novelty, as shown by the tremendous appeal since World War II of little-known Baroque music, works which were new to their audience. The attraction of minimalist compositions may be similar, since the style of these works, though new, often shows roots with the past. The popularity of both Baroque and minimalistic works may be a reaction to the highly complex music frequently prominent in this century.

Earlier in this century, critics differed sharply in their attitudes toward composers who wrote in the latest school of composition. Some critics praised works in an innovative or "progressive style,"[37] even though the style was not original. (Consider the support some of the press gave to atonal and serial music and their composers.) Other critics, though, condemned anyone who worked in an established style, albeit a new one, because they thought a composer should invent a new style.[38] A third group managed to avoid alignment with either extreme.

An examination of the music of Charles Ives brings some of these issues into focus. Ives' works were long praised both for their beauty and their innovations, innovations arrived at seemingly without influence from other contemporary composers. It's disturbing, therefore, to learn that he may have faked the dates of composition for some works and quietly modernized others to make them appear more innovative.[39] Still, do these actions reduce the aesthetic value of his music and make it less beautiful? Probably not for most listeners. *The Unanswered Question*, for example, remains as evocative and poetic as ever, though perhaps less original than once believed.

Uniqueness is originality that is one of a kind. Although many original works lost their freshness by being imitated or copied, there are no copies of *Pelleas and Melisande*, of *Petrouchka*, or of *The Unanswered Question*, at least none that survive to influence our judgment. These works are the more precious because of their uniqueness. If some masterpiece had to disappear from existence, say, one of these three pieces or one of the more than 100 Haydn symphonies, many would give up even a favorite Haydn symphony. Aesthetically these three works may be no greater than the Haydn, but their uniqueness increases our capacity to enjoy them.

Originality, or the lack of it, helps determine the place in history of a composer or work. Originality can also give pleasure to a listener who enjoys novelty and freshness in music. The freshness can fade, though, from frequent hearings or listening to imitations, particularly if the imitation is better than the original. (In such cases, the original may have started a new style.) Originality by itself is more important for determining historic value than aesthetic value.[40] Although the *Rite of Spring* would still be a masterpiece even if preceded by many similar works, its significance comes from both its originality and its musical value.

The complexity of these issues and the vast range of topics they cover make the subject of value judgments a difficult, frustrating, and fascinating one. Crucial concerns, such as whether two listeners can hear the same things in a piece, the need of listeners for variety, the impact of taste on reviewing, and the problems in applying standards, to name just a handful, make it impossible for criticism to achieve the certainty that some desire. Still, seeking that kind of certainty is unrealistic, for it is no more available from the arts than from any other form of knowledge. Because people are used to wanting the best, it bothers them when they can't even agree on how to decide what is best. Perhaps, though, they should welcome the way the arts enrich our lives and accept the uncertainties that accompany them. Indeed, that touch of doubt adds to the richness and mystery of the arts.[41]

Part II: The Criticism

Chapter Six

The Concert and Opera Review

Music lovers often turn first to the concert and opera reviews on the music page when they pick up the morning paper. A review helps them relive the excitement of last night's concert or else take part vicariously in the pleasures of another program. Concert and opera reviews are central to their experience of music criticism and are what interests readers most. This chapter, the first of three on this topic, tries to satisfy their curiosity.

Many reviews are quoted below, some complete and some not, some of old music and others of new, most of them appealing to read, but at least one that may be distasteful. Together they show the variety of challenges facing critics and the ways those individuals overcome them, whether the program be of piano or orchestra, chorus or opera. Equally important are the analyses of the reviews. These discuss the strengths and weaknesses of each example, and also consider what belongs in a review and the different ways to structure the writing.

But no analysis can give a formula for writing a review, because no such formula can exist. Criticism must appeal to the imagination, which writing by rules fails to do. Besides, even if two critics like the same program and deliver favorable reports, they might respond to different aspects of the music and produce very different reviews.

The opening of a review, called "the lead," usually contains a creative description, perhaps a generalization about the program, which attracts readers and makes them want to continue. Although the who, what, where, and when of the story may be omitted from the lead, this news usually comes soon to help orient readers. Leads can be brief or lengthy, and most often are a paragraph in length, but not

always. Sometimes, it's hard to say where they end because their
thoughts flow into the body of the review without a sharp boundary
between parts.

Instead of beginning with some leads taken out of context, let us
start with an entire review to show how a lead functions in relation to
what follows. The first example, by Allen Hughes, called "Miss Darré
Brings Vivacity and Power To Liszt Program," appeared in the *New
York Times* on November 2, 1967.

> Marlene Dietrich is not the only chic sexagenarian who
> can put on a one-woman show and win cheers from a
> sophisticated audience. Jeanne-Marie Darré did just that
> Wednesday night at Carnegie Hall where she played a
> recital of Liszt piano pieces that glittered from start to
> finish.
>
> Miss Darré, a slim French-woman with extraordinary
> white hair, is not unknown here, of course, but her
> accomplishment on this occasion was no less remarkable
> for being not entirely unexpected. She is 62 years old, but
> when she walked out on stage in an off-the-shoulder ice-
> blue dress, you could hardly believe it, and by the time she
> had gotten well into the six Paganini Etudes, you were
> astounded at her vivacity and power.
>
> It was not simply Miss Darré's playing Liszt all
> evening that was unusual, though the physical challenge
> alone would keep most pianists from doing it. Nor was it
> the force and speed of much of her playing that provoked
> the most admiration. It was her ability to turn a tour de
> force into a valid and valuable artistic experience that
> made the recital so laudable.
>
> She opened the program with the Variations on a
> Theme of Bach (a basso continuo from the cantata
> "Weinen, Klagen, Sorgen, Zagen") and then, following the
> Paganini Etudes, played "La Leggierezza," "Un Sospiro,"
> "Feux Follets," "Harmonies du Soir," the Transcendental
> Etude No. 10 and the Twelfth Rhapsody.
>
> These pieces contain incredible numbers of notes in
> runs, octaves, arpeggios, trills and glissandos in countless
> combinations. As she made her way through them,
> however, Miss Darré separated the wheat from the chaff,
> as it were, and focussed the listener's attention upon the
> unifying and important elements of these vastly
> ornamented musical structures.

> Her most exquisite playing was probably in some of the
> Paganini Etudes, where delicate, lacy traceries in the
> upper treble were truly phenomenal. The entire recital was
> a triumph of virtuosity, concentration and taste.
>

The comparison of the elegant Mme. Darré with her contemporary, Marlene Dietrich, who was then appearing in New York, makes a colorful beginning, but Hughes wisely abandons its theme quickly to emphasize the musical values of Darré's playing. After the lead, following a common pattern for reviews, he organizes his thoughts into a series of generalizations about the works without concentrating on a single piece.

The writing emphasizes the performance rather than the music, the usual procedure when standard repertoire is played, since the performance is news, not the music. In such cases, observations about the music often elucidate the character of the playing. That happens in the fifth paragraph where the description of Liszt's style serves as a basis for describing Darré's strengths when performing his music. Although that description uses technical terms, they are elementary ones, and the overall point remains clear even for a reader who misses the meaning of one or two.

Saying "you were astonished by at her vivacity and power" at the end of the second paragraph may seem overly colloquial, because "one" as in "one was astonished . . ." is usually preferable in formal writing. Writing "you" could be a slip, or a conscious attempt by Hughes to avoid the more likely but ambiguous "one," in order to emphasize that others were also astounded and not he alone. (Reviewers often substitute "one" for "I" when their papers don't permit the first-person singular pronoun.)

Hughes skillfully makes the transitions from the initial description of Darré's appearance, to her power and energy, and then to her musical depth. Until the fourth paragraph, he doesn't risk losing the reader's interest by mentioning the works played. This information is needed to keep the review from seeming vague, but listing so many in a row may seem dry. Naming the works here does little damage, however, for readers who skip the paragraph will not abandon the review, since their interest has already been aroused.

Although continuously enthusiastic, the review never becomes boring. By making different points in each paragraph, Hughes avoids being repetitious, not an easy thing to do when dispensing only praise. Fortunately, he could say everything needed in a review of only modest length, largely because the works were all by Liszt, a composer with a unified style.

The brief concluding sentence, "The entire recital was a triumph of virtuosity, concentration and taste," summarizes the program and makes an effective close. Although a summary is perhaps the most traditional type of ending for expository writing, it works best in a review if the idea is restated in a fresh way. Otherwise, the repetition of thought becomes tiresome.

Reviews can have at least four other types of endings: (1) the striking phrase which stands out enough to make a good conclusion; (2) no ending at all, that is, just stopping when finished; (3) a series of left-over facts which don't fit in elsewhere; and (4) a new idea which will interest readers.

Often, an ending doesn't fit neatly into one niche. For instance, the conclusion to the Darré review is both a summary and a striking phrase. Allan Kozinn's ending to a largely positive review of pianist Mark Anderson also overlaps categories. Kozinn says, "And if his Brahms was sometimes overwrought, it did boast a gorgeously reflective Andante espressivo and a Scherzo that truly danced."[1] This colorful last sentence almost serves as a metaphorical summary, but on another level this review ends without a formal conclusion. When space is at a premium, such an ending is useful, but if the last sentence lacks punch, the conclusion may seem flat or too abrupt.

Endings that are routine compilations of leftover facts are also usually weak. Unfortunately, reviews of elaborate productions like operas often have them, because the structure couldn't include elsewhere the many points to be made, and the reviewer ran out of space or the energy to devise something better. Equally drab are conclusions telling when a concert will be repeated or the next program in a series takes place. Still, placing that information where it's easy to find is convenient for readers.

Will Crutchfield's ending to a 1989 review of Mozart's *The Marriage of Figaro* introduces two new ideas, though the second is the true conclusion:

> The English translation by Peter Westergaard was
> occasionally awkward but more often pointed, literate and
> witty. Every twist of the plot could be followed clearly,
> and the audience was often in stitches (especially at old

> Antonio's complaints.) At a performance like this, where
> the communication between stage and audience is direct
> and unmediated, one realizes that the advocates of
> supertitles haven't a leg to stand on, at least where
> comedy is concerned.[2]

Crutchfield's attack on what was then a fairly recent innovation, supertitles, adds an appealing bit of spice to the ending.

Unfortunately, many new ideas that close reviews are dull. For instance, by convention or bad habit, the evaluation of the accompanist for a solo recital is often left for last, though few writers can give such an ending color. The placement is often illogical, too, because the accompaniment is an integral part of the music making, and word about it usually belongs earlier. Nevertheless, Walter Legge found a way to make such a cliché sparkle in this review of an all-Wolf song recital by Ria Ginster:

> In Gerald Moore she [Ginster] had a perfect
> collaborator; both imaginatively and technically he stands
> alone among Wolf players. With the mastery and insight
> he displayed tonight he might well give a Wolf recital and
> announce it as "Gerald Moore, pianist: Hugo Wolf
> recital," and then, in the small type usually reserved for
> accompanists, "At the voice_____."[3]

Like the Darré review, the next example, "Schiff's Central European Assortment," by John Rockwell, comes from the *New York Times* (October 22, 1989), is professionally written, and finds no fault with a pianist. In other ways, though, the two reviews are very different.

> Sometimes the art of program-making rightly usurps
> the normal pleasures that attend concertgoing. Sometimes
> the very intelligence with which an artist has juxtaposed
> scores on a program seems so arresting that it takes
> natural precedence over the individual pieces or their
> performance, however excellent they may be.
> Such was the case Thursday night at Carnegie Hall
> when the Hungarian pianist Andras Schiff presented a

recital that was fascinating both conceptually and in its imposition of a disturbing, even intimidating atmosphere.

On paper, the Central European assortment seemed unexceptional: music by Haydn, Janácek, Bartók and Schubert. Yet every piece—and Mr. Schiff's way of playing these pieces, to be sure—conveyed a counter-image of cheerful Viennese, Czechoslovak or Hungarian folkish jollity and charm.

This came about partly because nearly all the music was minor-key or modal, with unsettling subversions of formal expectations and an overtly gloomy mood. Haydn's Variations in F Minor (H. XVII:6) consist of brooding, grave explorations of the curiously unsettling theme, in which ornamentation is used to trouble, not delight.

The subtitles of the surviving movements of Janácek's Sonata ("Oct. 1, 1905"), "Presentiment" and "Death," speak for themselves in this glum and defiant memorial to a murdered nationalist.

Bartók's "Dance Suite," which might have been expected to lighten the mood, did no such thing, at least in Mr. Schiff's idiomatic but fascinatingly driven rendition. A compendium of varied folk inspirations, the music emerged on Thursday as almost demonic in its insistent intensity.

Finally there was Schubert's Sonata in C Minor (D. 958), which is as far removed from child-of-nature Schubert stereotypes as the opening Variations stand from "Papa" Haydn cliches. This Beethovenian score, composed shortly before Schubert's death, pays outward obeisance to every formal property of the sonata, yet undercuts the emotional associations of those properties at every turn. The music casts a nearly unrelieved mood of lowering gloom, with themes disrupted curtly and expectations of emotional relief (as in the Menuetto) cruelly denied.

All this meant a not exactly upbeat evening, but the power and rigorous coherence of Mr. Schiff's overall statement easily compensated. As an interpreter, from phrase to phrase and piece to piece, the pianist seemed dispassionate, for all his subtle underscoring of his program's implications, as if he preferred to step back and let the music speak for itself. That it did so, strongly and grimly, spoke well not just for his program making, but for his pianism as well.[4]

The structure of this provocative review contrasts sharply with the one about Darré. Not only does the theme of the lead persist throughout, but the works are described in order of performance, one paragraph to each piece. Even the distribution of lines between performance and music differs from the first review. Rockwell concentrates on the music until the last paragraph which suggests that the music and performance are perfectly matched. Only now does the reader get the first clear-cut indication that the playing was fine, though there are hints earlier.

Although critics most often emphasize the performance rather than the music for a program of works from the standard repertory and use descriptions of the music chiefly to clarify a point regarding the performance, there are many exceptions like this one. In any case, concentrating on the music works here, largely because Schiff is an established pianist about whom readers can assume all went well. Those unfamiliar with his name, however, might have appreciated some word about his background early in the review.

It might seem that Rockwell has written what I call an essay-review. An essay-review is a cross between the two forms which surveys an entire program at least briefly and then reflects and expands upon one aspect of it. This example probably isn't a true essay-review, however, because it focuses solely on a single concert without comparing it to others—something essay-reviews tend to do—though some aspects of the program receive only minimal attention, as in an essay-review.

For instance, the Janácek sonata gets short shrift despite the many lines otherwise devoted to the music. This seems odd, because the Janácek is the work farthest removed from the standard repertory and would normally receive the most space. Even a brief description of its style, character, and quality would have been appreciated.

These omissions suggest that reviews which follow the theme of a lead so closely—even the ending imaginatively restates the theme—often omit information which doesn't fit. As a result, when they "hold up a mirror" to the music or the performance, to use Oscar Thompson's phrase,[5] the image may be a bit dim. A review with loose ends and a ragged structure might better picture what took place than one so tightly knit.

It's also unclear whom Rockwell is addressing. He must know that Haydn wrote music in darker moods, that Bartók's folk dances are often hardly "folkish jollity and charm," and that late Schubert can be gloomy. Rockwell is demolishing stereotypes, but are they ones widely held by his readers? It's hard to say.

Nevertheless, he deserves credit for writing a vivid, imaginative, and well structured article whose discussion of programming is refreshingly out of the ordinary. He has also shown another way to make a review interesting when it contains only praise for the performer.

———————

Less-than-perfect leads can also be instructive, as the next two examples reveal. The first, by William Mann, is entitled, "An enchanting curtain raiser: *Die Zauberflöte*: Glyndebourne," and is followed here by its second paragraph. The review appeared in the *Times* (London) on June 1, 1973.

> Glyndebourne Festival Opera has opened again for the summer. The London Philharmonic Orchestra is in the pit for its tenth successive season and its principal conductor Bernard Haitink was in charge of Wednesday's opening performance, Mozart's *Zauberflöte,* still with the enchanting toytown settings by Emanuele Luzzati, but with a production newly rethought by John Cox and Adrian Slack.
>
> The weather has not been kind to the Glyndebourne garden and as yet Londoners will mostly be enjoying the fresh air, grass, trees, and a few flowers, especially when the sun volunteers cooperation as it did during the afternoon for some minutes—better than at the dress rehearsal of Einem's *The Visit* on Tuesday which proved inclement for picnics.

Although the rest of the review is better, the opening lacks direction. The lead wades through routine matters before even mentioning the opera; then a discussion of the weather (of all things!) sidetracks the next paragraph. These observations may be directed toward a more limited audience, however, one which (supposedly) waits breathlessly for every word about Glyndebourne. This kind of writing may have its place, but such an opening to a review doesn't cross the ocean very well.

The next ailing lead, from one of my own reviews, appeared in the *Philadelphia Evening Bulletin* on Monday, February 18, 1974, with the title, "Art Songs Reveal Beauty of Pilar Lorengar's Voice."

> PILAR LORENGAR, the Spanish soprano, who has appeared with many major opera companies both here and abroad, provided Philadelphia with a wonderful concert yesterday afternoon at the Walnut Street Theater.

Although unimaginative, this passage makes a good introduction to what follows. Even so, the word "wonderful" is troubling because evaluative adjectives like "wonderful" are too easy to use and readily become trite. When lazy, people say something is beautiful, splendid, or gorgeous, without analyzing why or searching for a more creative or specific way to make the point. Since they accomplish so much when space is limited, such adjectives may still be appropriate for a review if used with discretion. Other kinds of adjectives, of course, are indispensable for giving precise descriptions.

Michael Dervan wrote this description of a chamber orchestra concert for the *Irish Times* (Dublin) of November 9, 1989.

Ferenc Liszt
Chamber Orchestra
at RHK
By Michael Dervan

Don Quixote Suite..Telemann
Concerto Grosso in B-flat, Op. 6, No. 7..Handel
Double Violin Concerto ....Bach
Sonata for Strings, No. 3 in C...Rossini
Serenade for Strings..Tchaikovsky

It's an odd feature of Irish musical life that the visiting chamber orchestras which appear most regularly in Dublin are not those nearest to hand, but two groups from Eastern Europe, the Polish Chamber Orchestra and the Ferenc Liszt Chamber Orchestra from Budapest.

Both of these orchestras perform to the highest standards and yet effortlessly maintain an individuality of character. The Poles drive the music harder and explore extremes of dynamics and colour with greater thoroughness than the Hungarians. The Hungarians' manner, as heard in the their concert at the Royal Hospital, Kilmainham, last night, is milder, more conversational in tone and not as hectoring in its effect as that of the Poles.

The style is less apt for baroque music than it is for music of later periods. In the works by Handel and Bach, the playing was more robust than pointed, and it was interesting to compare the Ferenc Liszt orchestra's Handel with the altogether defter rhythmic spring and lighter textures of the Irish Chamber Orchestra, who played the same concerto grosso under Nicholas Kraemer early last month. The Hungarians offered playing of considerably greater finesse, but the ICO were noticeably better attuned to the spirit of the music.

The Ferenc Liszt's finest offering was their performance of the third of the young Rossini's sonatas for strings. This is a piece which manages to be gauche in its construction (its composer, after all, was aged only 12) and yet witty enough to be thoroughly engaging. The Hungarians made it sound quite delectable, and they also responded vividly to the picture-painting of the opening "Don Quixote" Suite by Telemann.

The polished playing of the closing Tchaikovsky Serenade didn't quite allay an underlying feeling of blandness and, as with many a conductorless ensemble, it was easy to imagine that the presence of a conductor would have produced a performance more convincing in its musical purposefulness.

The heading and list of works simplify the writing by reducing the number of details needing mention later. Another interesting feature is Dervan's comparison of orchestras (first two, then three), which differs from the usual discussion of only the group being reviewed. The comparisons work here, at least initially, because they clarify the character of the orchestra being reviewed and paint a colorful picture of Dublin's musical life. Unfortunately, when the review mentions a third orchestra, some readers may become confused.

The witty language adds charm. But the description of the playing of Handel and Bach as "more robust than pointed," remains unclear, despite the hints to the meaning which follow.

The review describes the pieces chronologically, except for the Telemann, which is introduced later, perhaps because its performance differed in character from the Handel and Bach. The two main structures for reviews described earlier lend themselves to innumerable variations and modifications.

The ease with which the Telemann is mentioned is exemplary. Often, a skilled critic can casually insert an idea which another writer would omit for lack of space or a place to put it. There are limits to what can be done, however, and a review that expands on one idea may do so at the price of omitting another. Dervan's leisurely comparisons between orchestras apparently consumed the lines owed to the soloists in the Handel and Bach concerti. (Or did somebody cut the review?)

Instead of a formal ending, the last paragraph just discusses the final piece. This approach works here, because the suggestion that the Tchaikovsky might have been less bland if a conductor were used is sufficiently provocative to make an effective close.

The review that follows is unlikely to be anyone's favorite, but there is much to be learned from it. It appeared in the *New York Times* on March 1, 1982 with the title, "Recital: ———— Piano Debut," and is by Bernard Holland. (The name of the performer has been omitted.)

> Young, hard-working musical artists need room to perceive gradually their shortcomings and grow. We owe them our forbearance. ———— ————'s piano recital at Carnegie Recital Hall on Saturday night, however, stretched tolerance and good will to its breaking point.
>
> It was easy to forgive Mr. ————'s occasional memory lapses. And at times, one could also overlook his unrefined, unpleasant piano tone. But it was more difficult to deal with the utter chaos of his phrasing. Rubato, the elastic give-and-take within a melodic phrase, has an organic purpose—to explain and illustrate the gravitational pull of changing harmonies. Mr. ————'s gratuitous ritards and senseless, disruptive silences, on the other hand, dismembered the music before him. It was very painful to hear this lurching sense of phrase chop into hamburger Schubert's A flat Impromptu from Opus 90, the

Beethoven E major Sonata (Op. 109) and three familiar Chopin pieces.

There were a few engagingly lyric moments in Chopin's C sharp minor Fantasie-Impromptu and in Book Two of the Brahms' "Paganini" Variations. But Mr. ———'s parched piano sound managed only to strangle Liszt's "La Leggierezza" and Ravel's "Jeux d'Eau." His assault on the Ginastera Sonata at the end of the program was an act of thoughtless brutality.[6]

Critics generally use a double standard and treat young performers and composers more gently. This practice is fine provided it's not overdone, for when that happens it becomes dishonest and misleads both musicians and public. It's unfair, though, for this review to say that the pianist played so badly that the usual tolerance and forbearance—in other words, the double standard—can't be followed. A way to aid a new artist then becomes a tool for hitting him harder. The result is an extremely destructive review, as savage a piece of criticism as any I can recall reading outside of Nicolas Slonimsky's *Lexicon of Musical Invective*.[7]

Holland is also insensitive to the pressures a performer feels at a debut. The pianist may have been too scared to play well. In addition, the review says nothing about the difficulty of the pieces that were performed. Perhaps the pianist overextended himself while trying to make a good impression with such big works. The Brahms has some of the toughest technical challenges in the repertory, and the Liszt, Ginastera, and Beethoven are far from easy. Indeed, the Beethoven's combination of musical and technical problems makes it particularly tricky. When pianists tackle works too difficult for them, they frequently stiffen up, to the detriment of their tone and technique, and they may even lose the ability to play a piece well that was once simple for them. By mentioning some of these points, Holland could have shown an ounce of compassion while still reporting the pianist's weaknesses.

Noel Goodwin wrote this account of an orchestral concert for the *Times* (London) of December 15, 1989.

CONCERT
Noel Goodwin
LPO/Tennstedt
Festival Hall

Klaus Tennstedt was toweringly in command on Thursday, as befits a "Conductor Laureate" of the London Philharmonic measuring his players up to Bruckner's Fourth Symphony. He favoured the 1880 edition, and made a powerful case for accepting the composer's second and even third thoughts embodied in this, while excluding later changes instigated by others.

"Romantic" was the sobriquet Bruckner allowed to be attached to the Fourth, and romantic was the expressive style of a performance that surged and glowed without becoming indulgent. This conductor knows that in a work lasting over an hour, pulse and proportion are fundamental aspects.

So the symphonic edifice was given room to unfold and develop, with a sense of epic adventure from the outset, in the pealing brass and smoothly eloquent strings. This sense of adventure was still apparent when it came to launching the finale, after the heady tread of the slow movement had been tempered by a tenderness (almost a sense of nostalgia), and after a jauntily rhythmic hunting-tableau in the scherzo.

Transitional episodes throughout were finely graded, and the orchestral playing was grandly sonorous in the great climaxes, with some delicate transparency in the lighter passages. There were a few rough edges in the ensemble, but particular credit is due to the eloquent legato phrasing of violas and cellos, and to a fervent brass choir of whom the first horn made the most of his solos.

The way was prepared at the start of the programme with a weighty, dramatic account of Beethoven's First Symphony. Tension was seldom allowed to relax and the *cantabile* marking for the andante was more urgent than gracious. For the minuet movement that became the first of Beethoven's scherzos in all but name, Tennstedt found a lingering sense of formality that brought its own

rewards, before he braced the vigorous last movement on
an exuberant rhythmic impetus.

This is a curiously uneven review. To Goodwin's credit, it projects
a reasonably clear image of what the concert was like, though the style
is overwritten and the language often colorful at the expense of logic.
Some passages work, including part of the third paragraph and all of
the fourth, but elsewhere the results seem stuffy—the lead for
instance—or silly and unintentionally comic.

Isn't it a platitude to say (second paragraph), "This conductor
knows that in a work lasting over an hour, pulse and proportion are
fundamental aspects"? Granted pulse and proportion are important in
long pieces, but aren't they in all music? And although one can launch
a ship, it seems a bit forced to launch a finale (third paragraph).

The involved last sentence has two problems: First, it's unclear
how a scherzo—a word literally meaning "joke"—could have "a
lingering sense of formality." A minuet could, which was what
Beethoven called the movement, but Goodwin says this is a scherzo in
all but name. And to brace something suggests holding it fixed firmly
or steadily, whereas the context suggests that Tennstedt pushed the
movement forward.

Sometimes, instead of the usual description of a program, a review
may properly focus on only one aspect of it. For instance, in November
of 1989, Daniel Webster of the *Philadelphia Inquirer* went to New
York City to hear the Philadelphia Orchestra at Carnegie Hall.
Because there had been complaints about the hall's sound after its
1986 restoration, further changes were made in the summer of 1989 to
improve matters. Instead of routinely reporting about the orchestra's
playing of standard music, Webster concentrated on the hall's
acoustics, since that was what was newsworthy.[8] His readers didn't
need another detailed analysis of the Philadelphia Orchestra's playing.

We will now study four reviews of new music to consider the problems that these reviews present to critics. Donal Henahan wrote the first, "Graffman Heard in a New Concerto," for the *New York Times* of April 4, 1968.

> Composers who look at where music is heading these days and decide not to follow are faced with a serious problem: At what point should they try to arrest the flow of musical change? If the decision is to return to an earlier period in sound and esthetics, as Stravinsky and others did in a famous neoclassical about-face of the twenties, and as other composers are now gingerly beginning to do again, how can the old sounds be related to the emotional lives of contemporary listeners?
>
> Benjamin Lees, whose Piano Concerto No. 2 had its first New York performance last night at Philharmonic Hall by the Boston Symphony, took us back to Bartók and Prokofiev of 40 years ago. This particular time was one of tremendous excitement and ferment in music, and the nostalgia of composers who love the great works of the period is understandable. It is certainly possible that excursions into that past may produce new discoveries.
>
> The Lees concerto, at any rate, did not prove to be such a discovery. Although it was played with awesome facility and faceless modesty by Gary Graffman (who commissioned the concerto and gave its first performance in Boston last month), the work impressed one chiefly with its flashy surfaces.
>
> A straightforward, neoclassically oriented composition in three movements, complete with a long, busy first-movement cadenza, the Lees went down in three smooth swallows, presenting few problems to anyone who knew the Bartok First or Prokofiev Third concertos. The slow movement contained some imaginative patches, opening and closing with duets for the piano and timpani. But, unless Mr. Lees was pulling our leg, what was that almost literal quotation from Bartok's Concerto for Orchestra doing in there?
>
> The piece, not surprisingly, sounded extremely professional and playable, but it generated no atmosphere of its own, and not even any fresh sonorities to occupy the attention in place of better things. Erich Leinsdorf also conducted the justly neglected Prokofiev symphony No. 2

in D minor, which was having its first New York performance, and the Beethoven Fifth, which was not.

The speculations of the first paragraph are intriguing, though the
subject is so enormous that the questions raised there remain largely
unanswered. Yet these issues make an admirable introduction to the
report about the concerto, and their concerns pervade the entire
review.

Henahan says the piece impresses most by its "flashy surfaces,"
mentions the period and composers which influenced the work most,
and then classifies it by form. He concludes that though "professional
and playable," it is largely derivative and unimaginative. This stylistic
pigeonholing effectively describes the work in few words, but still
might leave those readers dissatisfied who would prefer more details
about the concerto, even if it meant stealing the necessary space from
the provocative lead.

The witty ending disposes of two big pieces in one sentence.
Fortunately, a standard work, like Beethoven's Fifth, can be ignored
this way when necessary, but consigning the Prokofiev to continued
oblivion with only two words, "justly neglected," is troubling.
Although demands of space often require choosing words, usually
adjectives, that accomplish the most with the fewest syllables,
dismissing an entire piece so lightly is upsetting. The action may be
acceptable here, since it corroborates the verdict of history, but at
times the practice leads to cruel and superficial criticism. Patrick J.
Smith complains about "the current popularity for adjectival criticism
('Beethoven's overrated *Eroica'*) which combines pithiness, subjective
outrageousness, and bogus learning in one neat package."[9]

Michael Kennedy uses a different approach when describing a new
work by the Soviet composer, Sofia Gubaidulina. His report is part of a
multiple review of four compositions which appeared in the *Sunday
Telegraph* (London) in 1989. Although the whole review is lengthy,
the excerpt that follows is relatively brief, probably because the
descriptions of the other works used up most of the space.

> On Tuesday her violin concerto, entitled **Offertorium**, had
> its first public performance in Britain in **Birmingham
> Town Hall**, with Gidon Kremer, the dedicatee, as soloist
> and Simon Rattle conducting the City of Birmingham
> Symphony Orchestra.
>
> It is in one movement and has only a superficial
> resemblance to a concerto as the term is usually
> understood, although other violin concertos, notably
> Berg's come constantly to mind.
>
> *Offertorium* had its origins in Gubaidulina's
> admiration for Webern's transcription of Bach's *Musical
> Offering*. A theme from the Ricercare is the basis of the
> whole work.
>
> And just as Berg, in the finale of his violin concerto,
> commandeered a Bach melody to form a moving and
> elegiac coda, so Gubaidulina draws together all the
> threads to create a closing section in which the soloist's
> Bachian lyrical musing holds in thrall a subdued orchestral
> accompaniment. At this point, one realises that this is a
> religious Soviet work, its title a link with the Orthodox
> Church.
>
> But before this emotional climax is reached, the violin
> is given only restricted chances for such display. Its role is
> that of commentator on the orchestra's treatment of the
> theme, and this results in a dangerously episodic structure
> in which the soloist seems to be bystander rather than
> protagonist. The scoring is often strikingly beautiful, and it
> says much for Gubaidulina's inventiveness that one's
> interest was held throughout. Definitely not non-music.[10]

The details about the concerto's relationship to Webern's Bach
transcription appear gradually, and the reader learns the religious
significance of the work at the same point that realization came to
Kennedy. This interesting technique helps recreate the reviewer's
experience for the reader.

The music is unusual, particularly for a Soviet work, and its
attractive features almost seem to compensate for its weakness as a
violin concerto per se. Kennedy deserves credit for describing it so
sharply, though he leaves us curious about its harmonic style and
wanting to know even more its melodic character. The failure to
describe the performance is excusable since the work was new, space
was tight, and the performers well known. In such cases readers
probably assume that everything went well.

In 1973 John Harbison conducted a program by the Cantata
Singers which included the Boston premiere of his "Five Songs of
Experience." Here is what Michael Steinberg wrote afterwards about
that work:

> It is Blake, the first pair of "Songs of Experience," then
> "Ah! Sunflower!", then the final pair, "The voice of the
> Ancient Bard" and "A Divine Image." The setting is for
> chorus, solo voices, string quartet, and percussion. It is
> simple music. Simple the way Blake's songs are simple
> poems. Don't you believe it. Blake's vocabulary is
> domestic, but out of it he can carve this line: "the Human
> Face a Furnace seal'd." Harbison, with his ostinatos, his
> wailing descants (that sun-flower "weary of time!"), his
> transparent dissonances and strange concords, has found a
> musical voice for Blake. It is set out in powerful
> symmetries. It is concentrated, clear, and, beneath the
> simplicity, rich in vision and technique.
>
> Things are together, but then not quite. Harbison writes
> close imitations, accompaniments which almost duplicate
> what they accompany. You hear that the events are not
> complicated, but it hard to bring them into focus because
> everything seems slightly out of phase. Suddenly the
> chorus enters, filling in and "explaining" the gaps in the
> solo soprano's melody, lines or blocks come together or
> they separate unambiguously, and at those moments
> mystery turns into clarity. But both are there always, the
> mystery and the clarity and to project both, Harbison has
> imagined his exquisite, Schuetzian concerto-like texture
> for his "Songs of Experience."
>
> Harbison notes that the choral writing grew out of "the
> steady musical exchange, both practical and speculative"
> of Cantata Singers rehearsals. His "Songs" are strong
> Blake interpretation, and they are also remarkably "heard"
> writing for voices with instruments (with, I imagine, some
> debt to Schuetz, to the Burning Bush prologue of
> Schoenberg's "Moses and Aron," and the Webern
> cantatas). The soloists sing at different times from
> different parts of the stage in different relationships to the

chorus, adding one more dimension to Harbison's textural vocabulary.

A beautiful work, effectively performed, and received with enthusiasm. The solo parts were written for the standard Cantata Singers quartet, Jane Bryden, D'Anna Fortunato, Karl Dan Sorensen, Mark Baker; they were impressively sung, with extraordinary opportunities extraordinarily grasped by Bryden and Sorensen.[11]

The variety in Steinberg's style matches the thought of the moment. The short sentences in the first paragraph—one sentence is even incomplete—create a dialogue between opposing points of view as an idea is set up and then demolished. Later passages tend to have longer sentences and smoother rhythms.

The second paragraph almost uses a stream-of-consciousness technique as it describes Steinberg's changing responses to the music. Other passages discuss the stylistic influences on the work and give further clues to its harmonic style. The richness of detail and subtlety of allusion may make the review difficult to follow at first, but its many insights become clearer upon repeated readings.

The next example serves a dual function as the last review of new (or almost new music) and the first of opera. Since opera is primarily a staged art form, a critic must also describe the dramatic action, acting, costumes, and sometimes dance as well. Even for a critic who is competent in these areas, writing an opera review can be challenging because of the number of details that require attention. A review can easily degenerate into a report card which routinely grades each participant, including the directors, but bores the reader by presenting so many details in mechanical order. To avoid that fate, a review must generalize about the production in a manner that captures the reader's imagination and yet allows for the inclusion of the necessary information. The three examples which follow show ways to accomplish this goal. The next chapter discusses how critics face the problems presented by the frequently bizarre staging of opera today.

In the first review, Rodney Milnes of the *Financial Times* (London) describes a 1989 performance of Ligeti's opera, *Le Grand Macabre*.

Although the work was given in concert form and not staged, many of the same principles of reviewing apply.

At a time when anything less than 90 per cent capacity in a subsidised theatre spells abject failure in the eyes of our paymaster, the ENO [English National Opera] can scarcely be blamed for failing to revive their 1982 staging of Ligeti's dazzling comic opera; all the more reason, then to welcome and marvel at the Philharmonia's brilliant concert performance on Monday as part of the "Ligeti by Ligeti" series.

In fact, the composer is said to have disliked the Coliseum production, and in the light of the concert (which he appeared to enjoy enormously) one might speculate as to some of the reasons: maybe Elijah Moshinsky over-intellectualized a score that goes mainly for the gut, and indeed the funny-bone, and frequently simultaneously.

Parodies, from Monteverdi to Bach to Donizetti and back again, fall over each other in a cascade of sardonic wit; the cheerful obscenities (those so cravenly cut by the ENO happily restored here) have the audience rolling in the aisles; and then Ligeti pole-axes you with music of bewildering beauty and dramatic power, whether the great Passacaglia, the apocalyptic approach of Nekrotzar-as-Death, the extraordinary final interlude--truly music for the end of time--or the exquisite duetting for the lovers who copulate obliviously as the world comes, or doesn't come, to an end.

And this is truly operatic music, music that manipulates and controls the action and the audience instead of just illustrating or decorating: the fact that the accompaniment to the appalling Mescalina being rogered to death—a daintily macabre Marche Militaire—should strike one as amongst the funniest music written this century shows just how far right and proper reactions have been subverted. In this respect Ligeti is the Offenbach, if not the Rossini, of the 20th century.

The fact that the opera seemed even funnier in the concert hall than in the opera house was due both to Elgar Howarth's straight-faced but glinty-eyed conducting of the alert Philharmonia (the Monteverdi fanfares for motor-car horns and doorbells executed with the most delicious solemnity) and to a superb cast headed by Eirian Davies, truly virtuoso as the coloratura soprano Chief of Secret Police, Ude Krekow and Christa Puhlmann-Richter as the sadomasochistic husband and wife, Kevin Smith wonderfully fatuous as the Prince, and Dieter Well as Nekrotzar himself, more menacing of demeanour, honestly, than of voice.

The full house thoroughly appreciated what seems to me one of the wittiest as well as the most frightening of 20th-century operas.[12]

Milnes is extraordinarily successful in depicting the bitter humor and sophistication of the opera. The writing mixes tidbits of the story, brief descriptions of the music, lists of characters—even these are bizarre—names of composers parodied, and reports of audience laughter, into a mosaic which matches the vivacity of the work. The sophistication of the writing, which matches that of the opera, is aimed toward an audience which can easily grasp the wealth of references.

But something is missing. We're given no coherent idea of the plot, nor even of the number of acts, though some readers may have been familiar with these facts from the previous production. Although this production wasn't staged, this information is important, particularly since the cast projected the parts with their bodies as well as their voices—for example, Dieter Well was "more menacing of demeanour, honestly, than of voice." In any case, after encountering such virtuoso writing, it almost seems petty to quibble about such details.

Virgil Thomson's report about a January 13, 1945, performance of *Die Meistersinger* shows the imagination, irreverence, and insights which made him an important critic.

"DIE MEISTERSINGER," opera in three acts, book and music by Wagner, revival at the Metropolitan Opera House last night. The cast:

Eva	Eleanor Steber
Magdalene	Kerstin Thorborg
Walther von Stolzing	Charles Kullman
Hans Sachs	Herbert Janssen
Beckmesser	Gerhard Pechner
Pogner	Emanuel List
Kothner	Mack Harrell
Vogelsang	Donald Dame

Fairytale about Music

Richard Wagner's "Die Meistersinger von Nuernberg," which was given again at the Metropolitan Opera House last night after an interval of five years, is the most enchanting of all the fairy-tale operas. It is about a never-never land where shoemakers give vocal lessons, where presidents of musical societies offer their daughters as prizes in musical contests, and where music critics believe in rules of composition and get mobbed for preferring young girls to young composers.

• • •

It is enchanting musically because there is no enchantment, literally speaking, in it. It is all direct and human and warm and sentimental and down to earth. It is unique among Wagner's theatrical works in that none of the characters takes drugs or gets mixed up with magic. And nobody gets redeemed according to the usual Wagnerian pattern, which a German critic once described as "around the mountain and through the woman." There is no metaphysics at all. The hero merely gives a successful debut recital and marries the girl of his heart.

• • •

And Wagner without his erotico-metaphysical paraphernalia is a better composer than with it. He pays more attention to holding interest by musical means, wastes less time predicting doom, describing weather, soul states, and ecstatic experiences. He writes better voice leading and orchestrates more transparently, too. "Die Meistersinger" is virtually without the hubbub string-writing that dilutes all his other operas, and the music's pacing is reasonable in terms of the play. The whole score is reasonable. It is also rich and witty and romantic, full of interest and of human expression.

• • •

The first of the successful operatic comedies for gigantic orchestras, like Verdi's "Falstaff" and Strauss's "Rosenkavalier," it is the least elephantine of them all, the sweetest, the cleanest, the most graceful. For the preservation of these qualities in performance George Szell, the conductor, and Herbert Graf, the stage director, are presumably responsible. For the loan of some new scenery, which enhanced the final tableau, the Chicago Civic Opera Company merits our thanks. For careful singing and general musical good behaviour all the artists deserve a modest palm.

• • •

Charles Kullmann, who sang the tenor lead, did the most responsible and satisfactory work, I should say. John Garris, as David Herbert Janssen, as Hans Sachs, and Gerhard Pechner, as Beckmesser (and he didn't ham this role, either) were highly agreeable. Eleanor Steber's Eva was pretty to look at but vocally satisfactory only at the difficult moments. Elsewhere there was a careless buzz in her voice. Emanuel List, as Pogner, sang well but a little stiffly, keeping his voice down to match the others, who are all small-volume vocalists. Mr. Szell kept the orchestra down, too, so that everybody could be heard. The performance all through was charming, intelligible, and a pleasure to this usually anti-Wagnerian opera fan.[13]

What makes the opening of this review so much fun is the reinterpretation of the plot, first as a fairy tale and then as a contemporary story—"The hero merely gives a successful debut recital and marries the girl of his heart." Using this approach as a springboard, Thomson then surveys Wagner's works and arrives at surprising but plausible conclusions. One might ask, though, whether this opera is truly the least elephantine of the three works he compares.

Although this performance was the first of *Die Meistersinger* at the Met since the start of World War II, it's surprising that Thomson didn't expand on this, in view of the controversy during the war about whether to perform Wagner's works.

Thomson's description of the performance lacks his usual richness of detail, perhaps for lack of space, but he delivers the standard report

about conductor, stage director, sets, and chief singers with efficiency
and an occasional surprising image. Expressions like "For . . . good
behaviour all the artists deserve a modest palm," with its clever pun,
keep the writing fresh and add to the reader's pleasure.

Peter Heyworth wrote this description of a revival of Rossini's
William Tell for the July 8, 1990 *Observer* (London). Although what
follows is a fairly spacious report, it's actually only the second half of
a lengthy review whose first half described Michael Tippett's latest
opera, *New Year*.

> More than 100 years have passed since Rossini's
> **Guillaume Tell** was last staged at Covent Garden. Why
> has an opera that was so widely performed in the
> nineteenth century and exercised such a profound
> influence on the course of French opera, not to mention its
> impact on composers as diverse as Wagner and Verdi,
> suffered this neglect?
>
> Perhaps its very success has been partly to blame; a
> work that did so much to determine the conventions of
> grand opera inevitably suffered when those conventions
> fell from favour. Viewed from the far side of the
> Wagnerian revolution, parts of *William Tell*, notably where
> Rossini attempts to depict the natural world, can sound a
> little tame. Burdened with a plethora of choruses and
> dances, it can also seem slow-moving and long-winded.
> The first act alone, which does little more than establish
> the work's dramatic framework, lasts 70 minutes.
> Together with the misguided notion (which to my shame I
> once held) that Rossini's 'serious' operas are not all that
> serious, these are some of the factors that have
> undermined the work's appeal.
>
> Yet sympathetically performed, as it for the most part
> is at Covent Garden, *Tell* can still hold the stage. Rossini
> poured everything he had to give into the only work he
> ever composed from scratch for the prestigious Paris
> Opera. In no other score did he so convincingly work on an
> heroic scale. The big concerted numbers have real
> splendour. The orchestration is far more ambitious and
> varied than in the more hastily written Italian operas. The

music's inventive range is equally impressive; in a work that lasts over four and a half hours, few numbers fail to make their mark. By the end of the evening one understands why Rossini was regarded as the most celebrated opera composer of his day.

Wednesday's performance suffered from the absence of Chris Merritt, one of the few present-day tenors who can measure up to the taxing role of Arnold. In his absence little of the singing aroused the excitement that is an essential ingredient of the work. As the heroine, Mathilde, Lella Cubberli delivered some fine spun legato singing, but lacked dramatic punch. Gregory Yurisich was an appropriately robust but otherwise unremarkable hero.

Some of the best performances came in minor roles, notably Linda Kitchen (Jemmy), Ewa Podles (Hedwig) and Stafford Dean, who made a telling Gessler. Louis Lebherz revealed a rich and solid bass voice as Melcthal. Justin Lavender took over at short notice from Mr Merritt. His voice is, of course, too light for the part, but he sang with notable sweetness of tone and an elegant sense of line. I look forward to hearing this promising young tenor in a role better suited to his vocal resources.

After a disappointingly uncompelling account of the famous overture, the orchestra play under Michel Plasson gained in warmth and attack as the evening progressed. In view of the hash made of the opera at La Scala, Milan, last season, John Cox's traditional and nicely detailed production came as something of a relief, even if the results were sometimes a shade predictable. His designer, Robin Wagner, followed suit with sets of rather variable quality, though his skyscapes were notably successful. The net result was not a performance to set the house on fire. But it was good enough to convey a sense of the work's stature.[14]

The Observer © 1990

In Heyworth's review the music is the main news since the production is a revival of a major but long neglected work. Heyworth's description of what makes it important, both musically and historically, is well done as is his explanation for the opera's long neglect. These issues occupy the first part of the review.

As in Thomson's report about *Die Meistersinger*, developing the themes of the lead takes longer than describing the performance. In both cases, however, the time seems well spent, though one might regret here the absence of word about the plot, since the Rossini is relatively unfamiliar. Many recall the famous incident with the apple, but few remember more about *William Tell*. Perhaps Heyworth felt that untangling the complications of the Tippett libretto in the first part of the review had provided more than enough plot for one day's reading.

The writing has a few other problems, too. The comments on the singing are clear but somewhat bland and general, and the remarks about the sets and staging, although more specific, fail to paint a sharp picture of the production. It's also confusing to discuss a singer *not* present and then wait a while before mentioning his replacement. Despite these complaints, however, Heyworth deserves praise for writing an engrossing report.

A concert with many sharply contrasting pieces by different composers and performers is hard to review. The writing, like the program, tends to seem fragmented because of the need to report about so many composers and performers. This problem arises in a variety of contexts but most often with concerts of new music or student recitals with many soloists.

One way to give the writing a focus is to describe the best performers or works first and at greatest length and then to divide the unused space among the remainder. Another technique is to find an overall theme to unify the review. Will Crutchfield uses both approaches in this example from the *New York Times* of April 17, 1985, entitled "11 Opera-Audition Finalists in Concert at the Met":

> The Metropolitan Opera National Council no longer names winners for its celebrated annual auditions; instead, each finalist wins $5,000, and they all gather for a friendly concert of arias and ensembles at the Met. But if audience response could have awarded a first prize Sunday afternoon, it would have gone to Julia Faulkner, 27 years old, of Ames, Iowa, and she would have deserved it.
>
> •
>
> Miss Faulkner sang Marietta's song from "Die Tote Stadt" and trios from "Rosenkavalier" and "Don Giovanni" with a creamy, clear and apparently effortless soprano sound. May she soon discover a further degree of

expansiveness; she seemed a bit shy of full voice and broad phrasing. But then an odd air of caution hung over the proceedings all afternoon, and the concert never took fire.

This year's crop of 11 finalists included six sopranos, two mezzos and three baritones, ranging in age from 23 to 32. Several seem poised to make useful contributions on the regional opera circuit.

•

Karen Williams, a soprano from Brooklyn, sang "Come scoglio" with evenness over a wide range and a better-integrated low register than many young sopranos. Philip Cokorianos, a bass-baritone from New York, has sturdy Mozart in him. Donna Zapola, a soprano from Pennsylvania, showed some shimmering tones in the "Rondine" aria, but let the high note just sort of go by and couldn't ride the climactic phrases in so big a house. Richard Cowan, a bass-baritone from Ohio, has a basically impressive sound that he forced and pushed into hollow stiffness.

The young Californian soprano Deborah Voigt was tentative and not fully on top of things in the big "Freischütz" scena, but a nice full voice is in there waiting to blossom. Margaret Jane Wray, a mezzo from Illinois, gave an unadventurous reading of Cenerentola's final aria, with a good basic sound that seemed not yet ready at 23 for the work's extremes of range. Victoria Livengood, mezzo, from North Carolina, has an intriguing vibrato, but pushed mercilessly and paid for it in uncontrolled releases. Anne Johnson of Scarsdale, N.Y., floated some lovely top notes, including a genuine diminuendo on high D, but has not yet got the knack of singing intimately without fading into the background. Stephen Biggers, a Texan, who has a clearly defined baritone sound, produced only a gurgle for his big high note in "Avant de quitter ces lieux." (Don't worry, Mr. Biggers, it happened to Lawrence Tibbett, too).

•

But how to account for the pervasive dullness? Of course they were all nervous; who wouldn't be? But nerves can light a fire as well as damp it, as anyone remembers who heard Ashley Putnam's performance in the finals a few years back. Sunday, no one swept on and took the stage; no one electrified the audience with virtuosity or bravura; no one—except Maryte

Bizinkauskas, a soprano from New Jersey, in the "Rusalka" aria—went for the main chance on a high note.

One can't help suspecting that these singers struck more sparks on their way here. Perhaps the uncompetitive democracy of the event was an anticlimax. A stage director and elaborate coaching staff were credited in the program; perhaps it would have been better to leave the singers alone with the performances that got them this far. Perhaps the conductor Thomas Fulton's insensitivity to balance daunted them.

At any rate, it was a bland concert. "Show off!" one wanted to tell them. Sock it to us! Go for broke! Act like a star! Compete!

The most valuable aspect of this review may be Crutchfield's many criteria for evaluating singers. The writing reflects his interest in and vast knowledge of the voice, an interest so intense that toward the end of 1989 he gave up full time reviewing to become a voice teacher and opera conductor.

The review also shows how a concert with eleven soloists can be reviewed coherently and with a seemingly casual and spontaneous manner that is refreshing. Observe how he avoids cluttering the page with names of pieces and composers, though at the price of having an incomplete listing of works which may bother those not knowing the repertory.

A main theme, the dullness of the program and speculation about what caused this, holds the sections together. Since the lead draws attention to the best singer, this theme first appears at the end of the second paragraph and returns after the description of the singers. The last paragraph imaginatively restates the theme using slang, a freer and less reserved language which matches the way Crutchfield wishes the singers had performed.

Chapter Seven

Writing the Concert and Opera Review

Chapter six emphasized the public aspect of criticism, the printed review, where the thoughts of a critic appear as filtered by the medium of words. This chapter, though, studies a more personal side of criticism, how critics prepare for a program, listen to the music, and then write up the review. What follows largely relates to these concerns, even though the topics are varied.

After a brief survey of the work habits of critics (which builds on what was mentioned in chapter three), comes a discussion of how they evaluate the visual interest of performers, any memory slips that occur, the audience response, and the staging of operas. Next these pages consider how critics use their knowledge of performance practices when reviewing. A summary follows of what they expect from performers, and a reflection upon the personalities that critics project in their writings concludes the chapter proper. Afterwards, a postscript in outline form summarizes what critics keep in mind when reviewing.

THE WORK HABITS OF CRITICS

Because some concerts require advanced preparation, the work of critics may begin long before the program. Often, the impresario or concert manager provides material for study—perhaps some biographical data or an advance copy of the program and notes. And as we saw in chapter three, if a piece or its musical style is unfamiliar, a critic may examine scores and listen to recordings.

Still, no cram session may be enough to fill in the gaps in a field like ethnic music, and a desperate critic could ask a specialist to come to the concert and provide help. Ideally, the review would then mention that person's name, but a critic who often admits to needing help soon looks incompetent. To avoid that fate, some critics may use a helper and say nothing about it, but most probably review the program alone regardless of how insecure they feel. In such cases experienced critics try to talk about what they know, keep silent about what they don't, and avoid using terminology which they haven't mastered.[1]

Besides using the score for preparation, critics often follow one during the program. Doing this helps a critic spot memory slips and (more important) tell whether the performer observes the composer's markings and projects the subtleties of the work. Following the printed music also helps a bored or sleepy critic stay awake.

Yet listening with a score has its drawbacks, for one hears music differently than the rest of the audience, which makes it harder to sense how others feel. One can also miss the overall sweep of the music and the pleasure of listening. Granted, this last problem can also arise when listening without a score, but the danger may be greater with one. Critics sometimes compromise by using the printed music for some movements but not for others. Another approach, if the performance is repeated and the review can wait, is to hear the program twice, once with a score and once without.[2]

The concern about listening differently also affects the reviewing of first performances of new works. Many composers say that a critic who studied the score beforehand and attended rehearsals would write a fairer review. Some critics try to follow that pattern, as Edward Rothstein did when he attended both the dress rehearsal and opening night of Hugo Weisgall's new opera *Esther*.[3] (It should be noted, though, that dress rehearsals of operas frequently resemble performances and may even have audiences.) Some critics believe, however, that attending rehearsals spoils the virginal experience of a first hearing and keeps them from sensing how others might like the piece. Still, the entire debate seems academic at times, because the critic may have little time for preparation or the score may not be available. Besides, the critic is often the last person anybody wants at a rehearsal of a difficult new work.[4]

VISUAL INTEREST OF PERFORMERS

No performer has ever suffered from being interesting to watch. Leonard Bernstein is a prime example of a conductor whose career was helped by a flashy stage manner. (Bernstein, though, also had something important to offer musically.) Yet many other conductors, including Monteux and Reiner, achieved artistic and commercial success without such flamboyance. Critics also tend to keep in mind that being interesting to watch doesn't always produce good music. Consider what Michael Steinberg says about Eugen Jochum conducting the Boston Symphony:

> I often felt a weird discrepancy between what I saw and what I heard.
>
> What I saw was someone extremely active on the podium, often in highly descriptive gestures, constantly engaged in urging on, stirring up, leaning far over and twisting into S-shapes, smiling, making confiding or beckoning motions with his index finger. . . . What I heard in Handel's overture [Agrippina], for all but the minuet of the Mozart ["Jupiter" Symphony], and for many pages of the "Unfinished" was flat, square, unmodulated playing of notes, one after one, on and on. I could find no connection between the animated attentiveness in the visual performance and the dull, colorless playing the orchestra produced in response to it.[5]

MEMORY SLIPS

What do critics say when confronted by a memory slip? No simple answer is possible, because the problem is many sided. It's often difficult to tell whether a slip came about from nerves or from not knowing the work well enough. Memory slips are important because they disturb listeners and reflect unfavorably on a performer's reliability. They often are worst in a concerto, since it's harder for a soloist to cover up a slip with an orchestra than when performing alone.

Some gifted performers memorize with ease—the skill is an aspect of musical talent—but the less fortunate may be haunted by the fear of forgetting. Today's social customs are roughest on pianists in this regard, since they are generally allowed to use music only for those twentieth-century pieces which are hard to memorize. At times, though, the emphasis on playing by heart appears exaggerated, because it seems silly to complain if a more traditional program is superbly played while using music. Still, it must be admitted that memorization often helps bring about a better performance.

Even great artists in their primes are sometimes afflicted. When Artur Rubinstein played in Rochester, New York, in 1959, he floundered in one section of Chopin's A-flat Polonaise, a work he played frequently then. Fortunately, he was able to avoid a complete breakdown. Birgit Nilsson was less lucky in a 1971 solo recital in Los Angeles, for she got lost in "Pace, pace mio Dio" from Verdi's *La Forza del Destino* and had to stop.[6] Yet neither performer was having an off night aside from the memory slip, and I remember hearing magnificent things from both.

What critics say about memory slips is likely to depend upon their frequency and severity. A lapse covered up gracefully without a stop may receive only casual mention, perhaps even commendation for the way it was covered up, but a complete breakdown, or a skip in panic to a different section generally merits more attention. Still, some slips aren't mentioned at all, perhaps because they seem too trivial, or because reporting them doesn't fit the structure of the review, or because the critic didn't hear them.

AUDIENCE RESPONSE

When people complain that the audience loved the performance or music but the critic hated it, they are implying that the critic is out of step. Fortunately, most critics aren't intimidated by such remarks and continue to say what they think, even when they report the audience response. Critics often have good reasons for discounting its significance. Gauging the response can be harder than many people realize, particularly in a large hall with many balconies, because the applause may vary from one section of the hall to another, and nobody can see or hear what happens elsewhere. Then, too, an audience may begin with a bias if composed of friends of the performer or composer. The reception can also be the result of a paid claque hired to applaud (or boo) a performer, something opera houses have long endured and at times actually encouraged.[7] Even standing ovations, those demonstrations of audience feeling supposedly reserved for the truly outstanding, memorable, and unusual events, are partly the result of peer pressure, since a reluctant concertgoer may also rise when others stand, in order to avoid looking cold and unresponsive.

THE STAGING OF OPERAS

Critics often differ sharply about the staging of operas from the standard repertory. Such disagreements are inevitable since the same kinds of controversies exist in the world of spoken theatre. Plays by Shakespeare, Molière, and nineteenth- and even twentieth-century writers are often revived in ways that contradict both the stage directions and what the lines have to say.

Granted, it's impossible to reproduce a play exactly as it was first done, and attempts to do that usually seem stilted. Today's casts and theatres are different from those of the past as are the attitudes of today's audience. Still, a critic must report what works and what does not, even when there is no consensus about what is right.

At times stage directors (and set and costume designers) seem out of control because they impose such bizarre conceptions on a play or opera. The tolerance of opera companies for these absurdities is amazing, but the managers may feel that a subscriber who has seen the same work time and time again may welcome something different, regardless of whether it makes sense. (Some critics may feel the same way, too.)

But doesn't the opera company have a responsibility to someone seeing an opera for the first time? Shouldn't the company present a version reasonably close to what the composer and librettist intended, so that the first-time viewer can get a reasonable impression about what the work is like?

Productions which blatantly violate the text seem designed for people who don't know the language. Supertitles, however, are overcoming the language barrier, though their translations can be inaccurate. The words can be equally incorrect when opera is sung in English. For instance, in one scene of Verdi's *Rigoletto*, the title character tells a servant to make sure the door is closed in order to protect his daughter, Gilda. But in a 1985 English-speaking production which I saw, the non-realistic sets lacked true walls, and the text was changed, presumably to avoid seeming absurd or even comical.[8] One may ask, though, whether an audience is really seeing *Rigoletto* when an open set destroys the character of a scene in which a father wants his daughter shut in tightly for her protection.

To be fair, it must be noted that some of the most publicized and influential experiments in the staging of opera took place in Bayreuth after World War II, for an audience that largely knew when the sets and production didn't match Wagner's lines. (Why this situation was tolerated is too lengthy and complicated a story to present here.) Sometimes, too, the alterations even seem to work. In a 1975 staging of Donizetti's *The Elixir of Love* that was sung in English, the scene was shifted from a nineteenth-century Italian village to Texas in 1845, and the farmers and peasants of the original became ranchers and cowboys. The new setting fit the playful mood of the opera, and the ease with which a quack doctor dispensing love potions was transformed into a medicine man of the Old West may have added to my pleasure.[9]

A 1994 review by John Rockwell of three French productions of Strauss operas touches on these issues. About *Salome* he comments, "Here Mr. [André] Engel chose that increasingly annoying cliché, to update the action to the fin-de-siècle, when both the play and the opera were created." Later, after describing a performance of *Ariadne auf Naxos*, Rockwell says:

> But neither of these stagings came close to the Chatelet's "Frau ohne Schatten," which ran throughout March and which was far and away the best production of this vast allegorical epic of an opera that this "Frau" veteran has ever seen.
>
> The problem with most "Frau" productions has been the complexity of the scenario, the shifts between levels of existence and the specificity of Hofmannsthal's stage directions. Andreas Homoki, the director, and Wolfgang Gussman, his designer, solved these problems by simplifying much, by retaining a few key props (for example, the pan of frying fish) and by creating an entirely plausible, ravishingly beautiful parallel symbolic universe. This consisted of a stage covered with mysterious, vaguely pubic runic squibbles in black and white; gigantic phallic red arrows, yellow boxes and cloths for the Dyer's world, and rich purple cloaks as the Emperor and his once-shadowless wife took on the warmth of humanity at the end.
>
> It may sound simplistic; in practice, it worked to near-perfection with choice after dramatic and scenic choice solved in an utterly convincing and visually seductive

way. . . . The young Mr. Homoki, whose first major
production this was, is a talent to watch for eagerly.[10]

The task of visualising the scene was made easier for readers by a
photograph, striking even in black and white, of the parallel universe
from this production.

Note that Rockwell condemns the *Salome* production for tampering
with the time period in which the story is set because the change
(presumably) adds little to the opera. He accepts, though, the
alterations in *Die Frau ohne Schatten* because they work and because
they solve some staging problems. I suspect that most critics would go
along with these positions, at least in theory.

Unfortunately, for many directors and designers, the urge to create
something different crushes their obligation to project the character of
the text and music. Such behavior continues to create problems for
critics and others. One can only hope that staging the many new
operas which invite innovation will satisfy the wilder creative impulses
of some of these directors and designers, so that when they return to a
more traditional work, they can present it without distortion.

PERFORMANCE PRACTICES

The field of performance practices tries to decipher what the
musical notation meant when a piece was first composed and
performed. This information is needed because the signs have changed
meaning throughout the years, and the degree of detail with which
composers notated their wishes varied from period to period. Studying
performance practices helps a musician play in a way that is more
historically authentic and, in the opinion of many, artistically better.
Critics must also know the subject in order to judge whether a
musician is doing a good job.

In the nineteenth century these concerns were less important, for
musicians worried little about authenticity, and performances of Bach
resembled those of Brahms, Liszt, or Cesar Franck. Though pockets of
today's public still embrace such Romantic sounds, performers are
now generally expected to play all music in a style nearer to the
original.

How close they can get is debatable, however. A completely authentic performance may be impossible today because the conditions that prevailed when a work was first performed can't be reproduced.[11] The search for an authentic performance also suggests that there was only one proper way to play a work when it was first written, whereas in reality there may have been more than one.[12]

Yet some degree of authenticity is desirable, though deciding how much or even saying what authenticity means in this context is difficult. Does it mean being faithful to the period, or following the specific intentions of the composer as marked in the score, or some combination of the two?[13] The answer probably varies with the period under consideration, since what is right for Bach could be wrong for Stravinsky.

The emphasis on authenticity has produced the growing preference for music played on original instruments or their copies rather than on modern ones which differ from those for which the music was written. Still, though the proponents of original instruments have gained ground, the battle isn't over, and one regularly hears performances today on both types of instruments.

This situation presents critics with some difficult decisions. Although a handful of critics may condemn any performance on modern instruments for music written before the middle of the nineteenth century—roughly the time when the change to modern instruments was completed—most critics are likely to prefer a lively and exciting performance on modern instruments to a drab one on original instruments. The same tradeoffs apply to other aspects of authenticity in performance.

Critics are challenged by the field of performance practices, for the subject is vast, the body of knowledge ever growing and changing, and scholars disagree on many key issues. Besides, an intellectual grasp of the concepts is not enough, for critics must recognize the differences in sound between different types of performances in order to tell whether a performer is playing stylistically. With so much to master, it's no wonder that critics make mistakes at times.

WHAT CRITICS EXPECT OF PERFORMERS

What do critics ask of performers, besides the fundamentals of tone and technique and of basic musical training? In other words, what criteria do they use to separate the good players from the mediocre, the inspiring and great from the merely good? Here are some possible answers:

First, a creative imagination which makes the playing seem fresh at all times and not routine. Second, an intensity of feeling which infuses the performance with radiance and vitality. The ability to project the notational markings of the score comes third, though it must be accompanied by an understanding of the performance practices of the time and an awareness that the composer's conception may not be the only valid way to play the piece. Fourth, dependability, which means more than playing routinely every day, but playing magically whenever in front of an audience. (No critic can learn this about a performer from only a single concert.) A fifth trait is the ability to give performances that vary from concert to concert and from year to year without distorting the music. A listener who hears the artist play the same work again should still be able to find the playing fresh. Sixth, in works where it's fitting, a willingness to take risks and the ability to survive them, almost like a tightrope walker, thus stretching music beyond its usual limits. (A performance of a brilliant piece shouldn't sound cautious.) Some of the excitement of Horowitz's piano playing came from this characteristic.

Some critics also mention a seventh point, that a great musician must have a distinctive quality which is relatively easy to spot. If nothing else, such a trait helps as a marketing tool to separate the performer from the crowd. Probably, such a quality is more readily found today in singers than instrumentalists, since voices vary greatly.

An eighth point may be expected less by critics than by agents and those doing the hiring: In order to have a big career, a performer must learn music quickly and command a large repertoire. These skills may be particularly essential for pianists who must know many concerti to get frequent engagements with orchestras.

Obviously, only the finest artists meet all of these standards, people with strong personalities, though not necessarily flamboyant ones. Some musicians achieve critical and popular acclaim in a repertory which demands sensitivity rather than bravura, introspection rather than overt showmanship. A major performer needn't appeal to everyone.

THE PERSONALITY OF A CRITIC

One last topic remains: the personality of a critic as expressed in print. A great variety can be found ranging from the quiet and neutral to the eccentric and flamboyant. Often, though, that personality is less a product of the individual than of a controlling editor. Editors who favor a grey prose with a stance of objectivity choose critics who write that way, and when confronted with someone who writes differently, try to reduce that person's writing to the same blandness as everyone else's. Fortunately for readers, some editors still welcome a writer with a distinctive personality.

One could argue, though, that this portrayal is exaggerated, since all editors aren't flagrant manipulators and most writers fall somewhere between the two poles of blandness and flashiness. Besides, a neutral prose which conveys a clear picture of a program is preferable to showy writing which tells little about the music.

Perhaps if we look in different directions, the personality of a critic may emerge. Some are easy-going, others grouchier. Some emphasize the sociologic or cultural ramifications of a program and make broad and even Spenglerian interpretations of where music is going, while others stick strictly to the music. Some project a dignified patriarchal image, but many are brash youngsters with a cause. Some make frequent comparisons with the past, while others stay close to the present. A very few, like Virgil Thomson at his best, can peel away the layers of stale thought and habitual response which accrue to a piece after many years and inhibit our enjoyment of it. And a genius like George Bernard Shaw could attract a public by flaunting his colorful eccentricities and rapier wit and then proceed to give readers something worthwhile and original to consider.

Often, the personality of a critic comes from a vividness of image and a distinctive way with words. Look back some pages in this chapter to Michael Steinberg's review of Eugen Jochum conducting the Boston Symphony. Steinberg's interesting choice of vocabulary, the sensitive rhythm with which description is added to description, and the effective contrast between the vitality of the visual picture and the drabness of the sound—a point made twice in different ways—add interest to his writing. Readers who look closely can find other means by which critics fix a personal stamp to their writings.

POSTSCRIPT

A SUMMARY OF WHAT CRITICS CONSIDER

The following summary of what critics consider when reviewing a program doesn't pretend to be complete, because it's impossible to anticipate every eventuality. Even so, every review can't cover each item given below, because a particular point might not apply to the program. Besides, lack of space would usually preclude it. Please note, too, that an occasional topic, like "Conductors," stretches the boundaries of this outline and goes beyond the scope of a single concert to consider the entire work of a musician.

The Performer

1. Rank: whether an unknown, artist on the way up, or established musician
2. Personality
   a. Type of feeling and temperament
   b. Whether striking or unusual
   c. Variety of color and imagination
   d. Ability to maintain interest upon repeated hearings
3. Stage manner and appearance
4. Breadth of repertoire
5. Technique

The Performance

GENERAL CRITERIA

1. Amplification (if used) and its quality
2. Articulation
3. Attacks and releases, clarity of
4. Balance
5. Contrasts (presence or absence of the appropriate ones): lyricism vs. drama, dynamism vs. restraint, and so on[14]

6. Dramatic continuity, including transitions between themes, ideas, and sections
7. Dynamics
8. Ensemble
9. Form, projection of
10. Harmonic change and structure, projection of
11. Interpretation, including whether the conception fits the music
12. Intonation
13. Memory
14. Notes, accuracy of
15. Performance practices and stylistic authenticity
    a. Composer's intentions. Were they followed?
    b. Instruments. Were the appropriate ones chosen—for example, a harpsichord, Baroque violin, or recorder, if needed?
    c. Ornaments, cadenzas, and other improvised passages
    d. Performance style, authenticity of
    e. Score. Was an authentic one used?
16. Phrasing
17. Rhythm and tempo
    a. Continuity
    b. Liberties: rubato and tempo changes
18. Style, nature and consistency. Does the same conception appear throughout the piece?[15]
19. Technique and virtuosity
20. Texture and inner parts, clarity of
21. Tone
    a. Projection
    b. Variety and quality

SPECIAL CRITERIA FOR SOME INDIVIDUALS, GROUPS, AND GENRES

1. Conductors
    a. Appearance
    b. Baton technique
    c. Orchestras, skill at building a good one
    d. Rehearsal technique
    e. Soloists, ability to accompany them. Are they allowed enough freedom? Is the ensemble good?

2. Harpsichordists and organists: registration (the choice and combinations of strings or pipes)
3. Choruses
    a. Balance between sections, e.g., altos and sopranos
    b. Blend of voices within a section
    c. Pitch and intonation when singing *a cappella*
4. Orchestras
    a. Balance between instruments
    b. Blend of instruments within a section, say, the cellos
    c. New works, ability to learn quickly
5. Opera—acting, ballet, costumes, libretto, lighting, sets, staging
6. Pianists—pedaling
7. Singers
    a. Diction
    b. Projection of feelings and drama of text
    c. The voice: attacks and releases, breath control, classification (type), ease of production, dynamic range, evenness of registers, flexibility, freshness and state of development, legato, pitch range, size and carrying power, tone quality, variety of tone color, vibrato

Programming

1. The music, including an evaluation of choices
    a. Balance between works. Is it good?
    b. Difficulty for performers
    c. Ease of appreciation by audience
    d. Emotional depth and degree of seriousness
    e. Heavy or light, or a mixture
    f. Mood and character
    g. Order of works. Was the best one chosen?
    h. Quality
    i. Standard or unusual works
    j. Style(s)
2. Any theme or pattern to the programming?
3. Does the choice of music show off the players to their advantage?

Extra-Musical Factors

1. Historic, sociologic, and economic influences on the concert
2. News value of the program
3. Program notes, quality of
4. Relationship of music to other arts and to culture—particularly important for ethnic music and for multi-media works

The Audience

1. Response
2. Size
3. Sociological makeup

The Auditorium

1. Acoustics
2. Appropriateness of size and character to the program
3. Comfort
4. Lighting
5   Sight lines
6. Stage: size and flexibility

Chapter Eight

Intentions, Program Music, and the
Expression Theory

Before our discussion of the concert and opera review is complete, we must consider some important issues regarding the intentions of composers and performers. These concerns have played key roles in the lengthy, colorful, and frequently controversial history of musical aesthetics.

Critics sometimes discuss the intentions of performers, just as William Mann did in a 1973 review for the *Times* (London). The following excerpts describe Roger Woodward's playing of the Tchaikovsky B-flat Minor Piano Concerto with the Royal Philharmonic Orchestra:

> Those of us who have admired Mr. Woodward's playing of Stockhausen or Takemitsu or Barraqué could suspect that his pianistic qualities are just right for the most popular of all Russian piano concertos. . . .
> As a whole the performance did not quite live up to expectations. . . . The effects did not all come off and the thought-connexions were not held together until the end. A thoughtless virtuoso would not have let this happen. Mr. Woodward thinks about what he plays: he dared to delve deeper into the music than he is yet able to reveal in its entirety. The concerto will repay such interpretive investigation and Mr. Woodward's shortcomings (let alone his sustained flashes of insight) could cast doubt on easier successes in the music's glamorous bravura.[1]

How can Mann know Woodward's thoughts, particularly when the issues are so subtle? When Mann says, "Mr. Woodward thinks about what he plays: he dared to delve deeper into the music than he is yet able to reveal in its entirety," the writing makes claims that Mann can't justify. Indeed, the way he makes excuses for Woodward suggests that Mann is prejudiced in the pianist's favor. For instance, he says, "A thoughtless virtuoso would not have let this happen." Isn't it irrelevant, though, whether Woodward is thoughtful or thoughtless, for what counts is how well he plays? Other reasons besides Mann's could also explain what went wrong, including that Woodward had just learned the piece and needed more experience playing it.

As this example suggests, it's inappropriate to refer to a performer's intentions in a review.[2] Not only are the intentions usually unknown to a critic, but even if they could be known, say, from an interview, what counts are the results, not the intentions. When a critic talks about the performer's intentions, those who read between the lines may suspect that the intentions weren't realized and the playing wasn't good.[3]

Intentional writing also produces circular reasoning. If one must analyze the performance to discover the intentions, it's unsound to turn around and use that newly discovered information to evaluate the performance.

Still, intentional writing is commonly found, perhaps because many of its authors are unaware of the problems. And sometimes intentional writing serves as a convenient way to pad a review. Saying "The pianist conceives the work as a conflict between opposing forces, full of tension and drama," for example, uses more words than merely stating, "The playing was dramatic with many sharp contrasts," which is what the listener can hear. Because it's so verbose, an intentional style of writing helps a critic fill up the page when pressed by an immediate deadline.

Monroe C. Beardsley says, "The recurrent key terms of intentionalist criticism are such terms as: 'sincere,' 'artless,' 'spontaneous,' 'facile,' 'contrived,' 'forced,' 'subjective,' 'personal,' and 'authentic.' "[4] When one appears, it should serve as a red flag that warns readers to check whether the statements are about the intentions or the music.

The intentions of *critics* are fair game for readers, however, because a critic is primarily a reporter providing information, and a review contains factual information which can be either true or false. If this information seems inaccurate or biased, it makes sense to question the critic's motives, as I did when discussing Mann's writing.

A non-verbal work of art, though, such as a dance, symphony, or painting, is in a different category since questions of its truth don't arise, unless a person uses "truth" in a metaphorical way that can't be checked. A composer might write a good or bad symphony, one that is original or derivative, but not one that is either true or false.

In short, the intentions of composers are as irrelevant as those of performers, for what counts is what is in the music and not what the composer intended to put in. Still, this principle has three possible exceptions, all of them important. We discussed one earlier in regard to performance practices: the propriety of considering what a particular marking meant to the composer. Another exception arises when discussing the psychology of the artist, since one is now talking about the composer or performer as a person and not about the piece or the performance. The last exception may be program music.

PROGRAM MUSIC AND THE EXPRESSION THEORY

Though the many borderline cases make it difficult to define the subject precisely, a program is basically a narrative attached to a piece of music which the music is supposed to illustrate. Society generally grants composers the right to attach a program—an interpretation of the meaning of a work—to their music. Indeed, it's impossible to stop the composer, though nobody can force an unwilling listener to take a program seriously regardless of who wrote it. Some listeners also attach programs to a piece even when the composer doesn't.

This topic and some related concerns surfaced in a review by Joseph Horowitz, which appeared in the July 17, 1980, *New York Times* with the title, "Disks: 'Pathétique' in Furtwängler's Interpretation." Among its interesting features is the discussion of Furtwängler, a man whose recordings exerted a dominant influence on many conductors.

TCHAIKOVSKY: Symphony No. 6 ("Pathétique"). Berlin Philharmonic, Wilhelm Furtwängler conducting. DG Privilege 2535165-10 (mono only).

By the time he wrote his "Pathétique" Symphony, Tchaikovsky was prone to spells of shattering melancholy. He thought it his most honest work. The premiere took place Oct. 16, 1893, and was not a success. Nine days later, he died of cholera as a result of drinking infected water, perhaps intentionally.

The present recording of the "Pathétique" was made in concert in Cairo in 1951. For Furtwängler, it came in the wake of a cataclysmic war, as well as the vilification he suffered for refusing to flee Hitler's Germany, where he had tried to play an apolitical role.

•

Furtwängler's vision of the "Pathétique" is purged of
sentimentality or charm. He mainly finds a wrenching
psychological document, chronicling episodes of
lonesomeness and vehement grief, culminating in
illimitable despair.

His startling treatment of the opening measures
encapsulates what follows; the scorching sforzandos and
crescendos, unrestrained ritards and distended silences
would be ruinous if for a moment the motivating pathos
seemed less than genuine. Later in the first movement, the
famous theme for muted strings, marked by Tchaikovsky
"teneramente, molto cantabile, con espansione," is sung
with such patience and affection it would seem certain to
disrupt the larger structure; instead, Furtwängler's
immersion in the emotional flux is so complete that, for
once, the tune seems integral to the unfolding drama rather
than a saccharine sideshow. The climax of the movement,
marked "largamente" and quadruple-forte, brings an
avalanche of lamentation.

Tchaikovsky apparently conceived the two middle
movements of the "Pathétique" as bright interludes, but in
Furtwängler's reading they are swallowed up. The
swirling second movement seems shocked into
resignation. The third movement's triumphant march
seems not to fit.

•

The Adagio finale states Tchaikovsky's meaning in its
starkest form. Here, Furtwängler fashions a psychic
landscape so bleak the cathartic power of the symphony is
called into question. Is there, one wonders, a comparably
hopeless declaration of defeat in all of music?

The Schwann catalogue lists one other Furtwängler-
Berlin Philharmonic "Pathétique" (Seraphim 60231) a
studio recording from 1938, before Hitler bared the full
measure of his savagery. The conception is the same, but
the anguish of the 1951 performance is rawer and more
constant—as if the tragedy it enfolds were that much less
answerable.

Horowitz's writing is effective, for his words capture the intensity
and commitment he finds in the performance. Nevertheless, these

pages must question many of the assumptions underlying this review, assumptions that are sometimes alluded to rather than overtly stated. Horowitz suggests that the feelings of composer and conductor are communicated by the music to the audience. For example, Tchaikovsky's melancholy is present here in "his most honest work," as are Furtwängler's sufferings during and after World War II, and the audience can feel the depths of their turmoil. (A 1938 recording, made "before Hitler bared the full measure of his savagery," lacks the same intensity.)

Horowitz's position, which holds that the composer's feelings are embodied in the music and then transmitted to the audience by a performer with the same or similar feelings, is a form of what is called the *expression theory*. This highly romantic belief is often associated with such highly romantic music as the Tchaikovsky and is reflected in an old saying about performers, "They won't play with true feeling until they have suffered." That saying, however, is as hard to prove as the expression theory itself. The techniques of expression in performance can be taught, as any good instrumental or vocal teacher knows, and the ways students learn them show little relationship to their personal lives. Indeed, an alternate saying of mine probably has more validity: "Until performers learn to play with feeling, they will suffer, because few people will want to hear them."

Besides the primary evidence (what is in the score), Horowitz uses secondary or indirect evidence to make his points—letters and comments by Tchaikovsky about the work, and biographical data about Furtwängler. Although such information can be interesting and helpful, it may also be questionable or inaccurate.

Tchaikovsky's statement that this is "his most honest work" must come from such a source. But what can that statement mean? What is honesty in music? An honest work presumably tells the truth, yet music cannot be literally true or false. If composers express truth in music, that truth must be a different, almost metaphorical, kind of truth. Perhaps, though, Tchaikovsky meant that the work embodies his feelings more accurately than does any of his other pieces. Such an explanation makes sense in one respect, for music can have emotional qualities. Its harmony, tempo, rhythm, and articulation can make a passage cheerful, gloomy, mischievous, or melancholy. (The piece isn't literally melancholy, however, for if it were, as E. F. Carritt said, we would have to cheer up the poor thing.)[5]

Still, even if Tchaikovsky called it "his most honest work," the "Pathétique" may not be a musical autobiography. Indeed, there are at least two problems with saying it is one. Not only doesn't the triumphant march fit this picture of melancholy, as even Horowitz observes, but when composers are depressed, most can't write music at all.

It could be argued, though, that an autobiography is not written in the heat of the battle. The picture of melancholy could be a recollection of that feeling, painted when its creator has returned to a more cheerful state. Tchaikovsky could do this because he was a skilled opera composer who could turn out music to match the changing moods of his text without having to experience that feeling while writing. Otherwise, he would have burned up from the task.

When Horowitz says that Furtwängler "mainly finds a wrenching psychological document, chronicling episodes of lonesomeness and vehement grief, culminating in illimitable despair," the words suggest that Furtwängler thinks the work is an autobiography. One might ask, though, how Horowitz could know the conductor's feelings, thoughts, or visions of this work except through the music? The intentionalism is bothersome though not surprising, since most forms of the expression theory are intentionalist.

It is also an interesting question whether a piece can "chronicle episodes of lonesomeness and illimitable despair." If "chronicle" means to relate a narrative, two factors make it doubtful that this work can. First, without sung words, music has difficulty giving the who, what, where, when, or why of a story. A referential (symbolic) clue can fill the gap—in *Madame Butterfly* listeners learn that the *Star Spangled Banner* stands for the American, Lt. Pinkerton—but this symphony lacks that kind of evidence. Another problem with saying that any piece is an autobiography is that musical themes change, develop, disappear, and return according to the laws of musical form, and the resultant structure seldom matches that of a narrative unless both music and narrative are simple. As a result, if the "Pathétique" is an autobiography, it must be a very general one which doesn't attribute specific meanings to each musical episode.

That could be enough, though, for those advocates of program music who hold that the correspondence between the music and story need not be exact. It's sufficient for them if the music reflects a story without literally illustrating it. Perhaps Tchaikovsky would have gone along with this position. Since one of his letters indicates that he had a secret program for his Fourth Symphony,[6] he might have accepted a suitable one for the "Pathétique," although he gave that work only a name.

Another complication is that programmatic language can be used metaphorically to convey the character of a passage without being meant literally. Hanslick, who was largely opposed to programmatic interpretations, allows for that possibility in this passage from *The Beautiful in Music*:

> As music has no prototype in nature, and expresses no definite conceptions, we are compelled to speak of it either in dry, technical terms, or in the language of poetic fiction. Its kingdom is, indeed, "not of this world." All the fantastic descriptions, characterizations and periphrases are either metaphorical or false.[7]

These remarks may help explain what Hanslick wrote in 1862 about a recital by the twenty-one-year-old pianist Carl Tausig:

> Tausig had assembled an interesting programme. Beethoven's Sonata in E major, opus 109, is among the most rarely played sonatas, and was welcome if only for this reason. Every work of the master, even if not one of his important ones, exercises a magic fascination. At worst, we accept it as a memorable page from Beethoven's autobiography. This sonata—it was composed in 1821—tells of unhappy days. Melodies full of proud rapture and noble grace are impulsively interrupted by bad humour and a weary lowering of the wings. Lenz, the foremost of Beethoven's admirers, calls the first movement of the E major sonata *'faible, diffus, et maigre dans sa diffusion.'* It is certain that this Allegro, interrupted twice by an Adagio, has no proper centre and resembles rather a free improvisation than a sonata.[8]

This description isn't easy to interpret. One possibility is that the writing is truly programmatic, which would suggest that Hanslick didn't always practice what he preached. Another interpretation, though, is that Hanslick is using metaphors to describe the music. He may feel that the music was not cheerful, hence a tale of "unhappy days." And the description of melodies "interrupted by bad humour and a weary lowering of the wings" could depict the abrupt changes in theme and tempo that characterize the first movement. Incidentally, although that movement is more tightly organized than Hanslick realizes, it does have an improvisatory character.

Program music, with its concern for the interrelationship of the arts, particularly music and literature, seems particularly at home in the nineteenth century. Yet program music was controversial even then in its heyday, as we have seen. Its advocates and opponents fought fanatically with no more common ground than a devout believer and an atheist in a religious debate. Logic seems almost irrelevant when faced with such intense feelings.[9]

Although this century's scientific attitude is less congenial to program music, some composers, listeners, and even critics still attach programs to works, or describe them with elaborate metaphors. Indeed, in chapter five we read a spectacular example, Paul Rosenfeld's flights of fancy over Ernest Bloch's violin and piano sonata. The points of view displayed by this chapter's examples regarding intentions, the expression theory, and program music are still very alive in music criticism today.

Chapter Nine

Reviewing Recordings

After listening to a recording, a critic usually produces a different kind of review than after hearing a concert. A record review can't describe the audience, hall, or appearance of the performers, nor can it convey the excitement of being present at a live program. Yet a record review can still be interesting by discussing a host of topics not available for concert reviews and by depicting the beauty of a wonderful piece or performance.

In some ways it's easier to review recordings than concerts, for recordings can be heard again if needed and can be reviewed anywhere. Although one must usually live in or near a major metropolitan city to hear a broad array of live music, the record critic in a remote town isn't similarly deprived. It's true that buying recordings in far-off places is harder—though some are difficult to find anywhere—but many can be ordered by mail, and editors can forward them to critics.

A critic can be certain how well a performer plays a piece after hearing it live but not after hearing it on a recording. Indeed, without further evidence only naive critics predict that the performer who is marvelous on a CD will be as good in concert. Recordings often make performers sound better than they really are, because the sound can be manipulated and improved in ways to be described later.

Critics who are not naive but lack the background needed to review recordings well often conceal their weaknesses by talking about what they know, saying little about what they don't, and by choosing another recording if the first one presents a problem they can't handle. This approach isn't foolproof, however, for a sharp reader might see through the critic's defenses if the review complains, for example, that the sound is poor but then gives only a lame description of what is wrong.

Journals that specialize in reviewing recordings tend to do a better job than newspapers. Not only do most newspapers fail to give enough space to recordings, but they make poor use of what little they grant, because they lack a coherent philosophy about what to review. The number of new releases is too great for them to be comprehensive, yet most have found no decent alternative. Perhaps to compensate for this weakness, some newspapers try to make their offerings more attractive by combining several reviews into one article and attaching a lead whose theme supposedly ties them together. This format works if the recordings have enough in common to form a natural unit but seems artificial when they don't.

Incidentally, record reviewers usually talk only about recordings and leave the discussion of CD players, turntables, speakers, and the like to the reviewers of stereo equipment.

WHAT A RECORD REVIEW SHOULD INCLUDE

The content of record reviews varies greatly, but the best ones usually discuss the quality of the music, performance, and sound, and if the work is new or little known, its style. Less important but still helpful is an evaluation of the accompanying notes. Most readers also want to know whether the recording is worth buying and, if several performances of the same piece are available, which one is best. (Unfortunately, some reviews mention only the new recording.) When a comparative review appears, it usually describes the latest release in detail and mentions the others only briefly.

Various factors, some non-aesthetic, complicate making comparisons. If the best recording costs more than one almost as good, no recommendation is obvious. (Comparing prices is difficult, however, since list prices are discounted at percentages that vary with the store and record label.) Then, if the major work takes up only part of the recording, the quality of the remaining pieces may be a determining factor. And last, if the conductor with the best interpretation recorded with an inferior orchestra, it may be hard to say which performance is better. When there is no clear-cut choice, a critic may list the options and let readers choose. If a recording is clearly the best but appears on a hard-to-find label, a critic might also suggest an alternative.

A heading to a record review often gives such basic information as the title, contents, names of performers and record company, catalog number, list price, and the formats in which it comes, particularly CD and tape cassette. In addition, if the *Schwann* catalog doesn't list the record company, readers welcome its address or that of its distributor.

Of course, some reviews follow their own agendas and disregard most of the concerns expressed in this chapter. An example would be the highly personal review of Tchaikovsky's Pathétique in the last chapter.

THE SOUND OF RECORDINGS

Choosing the best sound for the recording from the wealth of options can be a difficult decision for producers and engineers. They usually favor the sound of a good concert hall for soloists, if only because unwanted noises such as the scratches of a violinist's bow and the sounds of fingers hitting the fingerboard don't project far in a concert hall and remain inaudible to most listeners. Still, this sound ideal is flexible and requires further choices, since no two auditoriums are alike in their acoustics, and the sound can vary from seat to seat within the same hall.

The number of options becomes greater when recording an orchestra, and producers and engineers split into two opposing camps about how best to do it. Those who want the blended, warm sound of a seat in a good concert hall favor using a limited number of microphones. Their opponents prefer many microphones, fearing that otherwise the individual instruments will not project with sufficient clarity.[1] The sharpness and clarity of this last sonority is often considered to be the typical high fidelity sound, though many dislike it.

The engineers have enormous power throughout the recording process. First they catch the performance on reel-to-reel tape, and then, following the directions of the artists, cut and splice the tape to choose the best part of each run-through (take). The engineers also filter out unwanted frequencies, alter the dynamics and balance, and change the placement of microphones before making another take. And if more than one microphone is used, they control the balance by altering the percentage each microphone contributes to the final version.

The engineers can also change the dynamic level of a passage or instrument, sometimes even to the point of producing an unnatural sound. A clarinet, for instance, has one quality in piano and another in forte, but when an engineer significantly raises the volume of a soft note, the recording has a tone color that's impossible to create live.

Sometimes the engineers record the accompaniment to a vocal part and later dub in the voice when a singer, for illness or other reason, isn't present at the first recording session. They can also record the high notes first while the voice is fresh and then insert them into their proper places. Erich Leinsdorf properly derides both procedures, however, because the give and take between performers, which is so essential to creative music making, is lacking when one part is already frozen, even though singers hear the orchestra over earphones when dubbing. In addition, a high note recorded out of sequence can't grow out of the preceding phrase and reflect its color, tension, and direction.[2]

The ability to recognize when engineers tamper with the sound, plus an extensive knowledge of the Wagnerian repertory helped critic David Hamilton uncover a curious fraud. He spotted that two disks claiming to be Bayreuth performances of *Parsifal* and *Die Götterdämmerung* were phony, because music from different performances had been pieced together. In one scene alone Hamilton counted at least nine splices![3] (When splices are noticeable, the tempo, pitch, dynamics, or tone color don't match between sections, and a click or other noise may accompany a particularly clumsy splice.) Fortunately, such flagrant fakery appears to be rare.

HOW RECORD CRITICS WORK

Record critics generally prefer to use the same playback system each time they listen. Otherwise, if the sound of a disk is bad, they may not know whether the fault is the record's, the system's, or their unfamiliarity with the sound of the system.[4] Unless they must hear a library recording, most record critics also work at home, not only because they know the playback system but for the convenience.[5]

Still, that convenience is small consolation to a critic who must review a new recording when twenty or thirty performances of the same piece are already in print. How many critics would have the time or patience to listen to them all, assuming that number of versions is readily available? One might eliminate some examples after a brief sampling because of a bad conductor, sound, or orchestra, but one must hear others in entirety for a fair judgment.

David Hall had a practical solution for some problems. When critics are pressured by a deadline, he suggested (without naming a specific work) that they at least check the tough syncopated passages in the last movement with those in other recordings. At times, though, the task is simply impossible. What do you do, asks David Hamilton, with sixty recordings of live performances of the same Wagner opera?[6]

Because of the sheer number of recordings available, some critics compare a new release only with their past favorites, which makes the task more practical but eternally rejects a slighted disk. Still, critics are taking a chance if they rely on their memories or notes of a recording without hearing it again, because their tastes may change after a number of years.[7]

Editors often screen recordings before assigning them for review to avoid wasting space on what isn't worth buying.[8] This practice helps produce a higher percentage of positive reviews of recordings than for concerts. Another factor also contributes to this phenomenon, however: Disks have fewer mistakes, since performers can correct them when recording.

Even so, some recordings still get bad reviews, if only to maintain a critic's credibility. After all, who can trust a critic who only says good things? Besides, buyers must also be steered away from the well-publicized but atrocious recordings. A review also functions as more than a purchasing guide, and a description of a bad disk can be both interesting and informative.

RECORDINGS AND CONCERTS: THE AESTHETIC DIFFERENCES

Critics often complain that performers are more exciting when heard live than on recordings made in the studio. One explanation may be that performers cautiously adopt a neutral, middle-of-the-road approach when recording for fear that an extreme and daring interpretation would wear badly on repeated hearings.[9] (Though one might argue that performers could be more reckless when recording because they can correct any slips later.) In any case, another and probably more important reason for dull recordings is the practice of splicing a passage from one take to another. Because each take has its own character, a performance created from bits and pieces may lack a sharp and coherent personality. Even so, some artists, like the late Glenn Gould, enjoy using all of the resources of the recording technique.[10] One of Gould's obituaries emphasized, however, that he resorted to multiple takes and splicing because of an interest in the possibilities of the medium and not because he couldn't play the notes correctly the first time.[11]

Live performances have other advantages, too. Some artists are inspired by the audience and perform better in concert than when recording. In addition, wrong notes and minor slips, which are generally unacceptable on recordings, seem less objectionable in an exciting live concert. Erich Leinsdorf gives an example when describing a series of programs he conducted for the London Philharmonic:

> Another somewhat tragic part of that engagement was a recording for Decca of the Immolation Scene from *Götterdämmerung* with Marjorie Lawrence singing the part of Brünnhilde from her wheelchair. She had made a most courageous comeback [from polio], and one of my first concerts in that particular series was with her as soloist. She was wildly applauded, and while she had never been a faultless vocalist, I thought that it all came off remarkably well. The microphone, however, is a merciless thing, without the critical faculty of the human ear. We can edit out what may be unpleasant and disturbing; we take the whole personality rather than the imperfect detail, but not so the mechanical pickup.
>
> The sessions were quite a sad story. For several days we tried to get something usable, but in the end the engineers, the producer, and I (and perhaps a lot more people with whom we did not exchange views) realized that nothing of these efforts could be utilized in a commercial recording and nothing was ever published.[12]

In recent years a number of artists have started recording their concerts live, in the belief that tape-splicing saps the vitality of a recording. The results may come closer to concert hall ambiance, to the sensation and excitement of being present at the concert. Paradoxically, though, some producers then remove the sound of someone opening a candy wrapper or the applause at the end of movements,[13] or allow themselves the luxury of a later "touch-up" session to correct any glaring errors.

If an orchestra is recorded when playing the same program several times, the conductor and producer often choose the best example of each movement to make up, say, a symphony, but do not splice within a movement. This practice maintains the excitement of a live concert and gives some choice but without the loss of coherence and intensity that afflicts some studio performances.

People sometimes spot a curious phenomenon: A concert that was extremely exciting when heard live loses vitality when released as a recording. Three possible explanations for this come to mind. First, we frequently feel disappointed when we return to something we loved the first time. Perhaps memory exaggerates the intensity of the first experience, or what was fresh and unusual at first loses novelty and excitement upon repetition. Another possibility is that some of the initial excitement may have come from being in the hall during the marvelous playing. Such a personal, almost metaphysical, feeling is a major strength of a live concert and cannot be measured scientifically nor captured in a recording. A third explanation is that the recorded sound might have been inferior to the concert's, perhaps because of poor microphone placement or because the recording failed to preserve the full dynamic range of the live performance.

THE RECORD BUSINESS

Many aspects of the record business are bewildering, but the way it ignores the ordinary rules of supply and demand is particularly strange. When forty copies of, say, Tchaikovsky's Sixth are available, it makes no sense to release another, yet new versions keep appearing. What can account for this curious behavior?

There are many answers to this complex question. David Hall pointed out one of them when he said that the record business is a gambler's business and therefore wasteful. (Presumably, producers hope to make a killing and therefore take chances, even seemingly illogical ones.) Hall also observed tartly that if you think there is overproduction in the classical field, look at the popular.[14] Another factor leading to superfluous recordings is that many record companies have large groups of musicians under contract whom they must keep busy and who want to record works already on the market. A producer may also feel that the public wants to hear what a brilliant young conductor does with a particular work regardless of how many times it's been recorded. In addition, producers often become emotionally involved in producing a recording, and want to satisfy their interests and egos regardless of what the public wants. This practice isn't always bad, however, since many works of great musical value but little commercial appeal have appeared only because of the dedication of such individuals.

Recordings of contemporary music often appear under different circumstances and may be issued by non-profit companies. An important one, Composers Recordings, Inc. (CRI), resembles a vanity press because the composer, possibly aided by a grant, must pay for the bulk of the project. Unlike a vanity press, however, its editorial board rejects 90 percent of the composers that apply.[15]

Many recordings also come from clear-cut vanity presses, including disks that performers make, often at considerable expense, to help launch their careers. A recording may now fill the role once taken by a New York debut. Despite the poor reputation of vanity books, vanity recordings are often good.

Critics usually don't discuss the financing of recordings, perhaps out of kindness to musicians. When a recording is good, saying it appears on a vanity label could hurt sales, and when it's bad, there's no need to hit harder by describing the funding. Besides, the critic may not know the details. The money could have come from a foundation or university grant rather than from the performer or composer.

PIRATED RECORDINGS

Pirated recordings—those released without the permission of the performers or the original producer—are another oddity of the record business. Although it seems strange that such recordings appear commercially, they are commonly found and will continue to be issued if only because it's hard to prevent their sale.

The original tapes are usually made from broadcasts or by equipment smuggled into a concert hall. Making a tape from smuggled equipment is questionable ethically, but releasing such a recording commercially is more so. Even if one overlooks the legal and moral issues, one might ask why the public would want anything whose sound was likely to be inferior because of the poor conditions under which it was first taped.

The answer seems to be that such recordings preserve magnificent performances and music that would otherwise be lost. Indeed, a pirated recording may be the only one in the catalog. In the past such recordings satisfied the public's curiosity about a celebrity like Maria Callas, whose name alone could justify a release even if better versions of the same work were available. Pirated tapes also serve other useful purposes. Singers circulate them to display what they can do, and critics use them to check whether the supposedly "unedited" recording of a concert is what it claims to be.

How can pirated disks and tapes be sold legally? A complete answer would be lengthy and complex, but one can simply say that differences in copyright laws between countries make it hard to stop their sale.[16] Some pirated recordings are probably sold legally, some are not, and the status of the remainder is shady.

Perhaps reputable journals shouldn't review such recordings, but if they don't, they would shirk their responsibility to the public and risk having other journals fill in the gap. Besides, the field of pirated recordings presents a fascinating array of topics to enliven a review. One case described in *High Fidelity* centers on their frequently inaccurate labels and notes. A California firm had released some worthwhile and otherwise unavailable symphonies by a British composer, Havergal Brian. (The BBC, which held the legal rights to the performances, had kept them buried.) When the works appeared, instead of giving the true names of the conductors, the record company gave a fictitious one that was easily confused with that of a well-known conductor, apparently in the belief that the false name would help sell the recordings better. John Canarina, one of the slighted conductors, rightly says, "What we are really dealing with here is the equivalent of stolen goods, stolen services."[17]

HISTORIC RECORDINGS

Defining what is a historic recording can be difficult, for everything has historic interest in one sense, even trivia. A poor recording can also be useful to show why another one is better. Still, a definition that includes every older recording would be too broad to be practical, and so I now present one that is more restrictive: *A historic recording is one made before 1939 with a now-dated technology, which has been reissued in a new format.* (I chose 1939 because the sound of earlier recordings was generally inferior by today's standards. The exact year is arbitrary, but some cutoff point is needed and this one seems reasonable.)

An older recording is usually reissued for its beauty or historic importance, perhaps as a momento of a major performer or of a composer conducting his music, or a monumental initial attempt that is still worthwhile today, such as Schnabel's—the first ever of the thirty-two piano sonatas by Beethoven.

In the original versions of older recordings, it's often difficult to hear the music over the background noise. Granted, with experience some listeners learn to ignore the interference, but others can't. Although modern technology can remove most background noise, part of the music may go with it. One possible solution would be to filter out the noise in a record directed to the general public and leave it in for one aimed at professionals. But does any classical recording have such a simple, clearly defined audience? Probably not. A recording of Caruso's, for instance, which eliminates background noise at the expense of distorting the sound of the voice would be unacceptable.

Here are examples of two different techniques that brought good results. (It would be fun, though, to see what would happen if the two critics swapped disks, for they may have very different tastes.) In the first example, Peter G. Davis describes the releases by the Rubini Company of England of vocal performances made from 1902 through the 1920s:

> The transfers are honest ones without filtering, equalization and the like—the sound of the original is faithfully reproduced, warts and all, in the interest of presenting the recorded voice as truthfully as possible.[18]

Steven Smolian says about another set:

> We now have a good, clear, background-quiet, full-voiced Enrico Caruso on LP. The record, which succeeds where all before have failed, uses computer technology to achieve its surprising results. . . .
>
> The computer adds a couple of features, the most important (given the proper program) being the ability to discriminate between the desired signal and the unwanted background noise mixed in the same narrow frequency band, which after processing leaves the former in the clear and sharply reduces the second. It also removes the random distortion caused by the casual variations in old acoustic recording equipment.[19]

When transferring a recording made in the first quarter of the
century to a modern technology, a problem arises because the speed of
recording was not standardized. Record companies preparing a reissue
must seek the right speed, or the pitch and tempos will be wrong.[20]
Historic recordings often contain wonderful music and merit
attention for that reason alone. The evidence they provide of vanished
performing styles has also influenced many of today's artists. Still, one
must interpret their significance with care. At a session of the 1979
Carnegie Hall conference on music criticism, some participants went
on at length about the glories of pianists of the 1920s compared with
those of the present. After a while the moderator, Michael Steinberg,
interrupted them and stopped what he called "this melancholy story of
the decline of the West." Steinberg said it was a matter of
historiography. He noted that recordings which have survived from the
1920s are the most striking, while the lesser ones are largely forgotten.
A filtering process has taken place which makes it difficult today to
say what piano playing was like in the 1920s.

Recordings of a player piano performing old piano rolls are another
type of historic recording. (The rolls were of thin cardboard with
punched holes that told the mechanism of a specially equipped piano
what to play.) Harold C. Schonberg's interview with Dr. Michael
Stein, a dentist and collector of piano rolls, gives interesting
background about them:

> Pianists started making piano rolls for Welte-Mignon
> around the turn of the century and later for the more
> sophisticated Duo-Art and Ampico processes. The piano
> rolls sound much better than disks made by the same
> artists in the 1910-30 period. They are played on well-
> regulated instruments, and if a 1925 roll was recorded
> today it would have the fidelity of any modern piano
> recording. On the other hand, flat disks made in 1927
> sound dim, scratchy and limited in frequency response. . . .
> [Dr. Stein] agrees that the piano roll process could not
> fully capture the nuances of the pianist. At least flat-disk
> records in the early days, before the advent of tape were
> completely honest. There was no possible way to do any
> editing [unlike piano rolls]. . . .
> So piano rolls have to be approached with caution. On
> the other hand, some great pianists who were never
> recorded on flat disks made many rolls.[21]

One problem with piano rolls is often overlooked. Since even the best pianos vary greatly, in order to get the desired shadings in a live performance, pianists adapt their touch and pedaling to the instrument. Such adjustments are impossible, however, when replaying a piano roll. As a result, the pedaling, balance, and clarity of sound suffer because the new instrument doesn't match the one on which the music was recorded. Therefore, what we hear today often isn't the sound that the pianist intended.

REMASTERED RECORDINGS

Reissues of recordings first made after 1939 also raise troubling questions for critics, particularly now that so many performances have been transferred to CD. Many of these same concerns affect historic recordings, too, though the changes in technology introduce some new wrinkles.

In the 1950s, the dynamic range of records was constrained because the playback equipment could not handle a larger range. But by the early eighties, even before the CD era, the playback equipment had improved, and records could use more of the dynamic range available on the master tapes.[22] Listeners using better playback equipment could also detect on older recordings what earlier listeners couldn't spot, for instance, a moment when the engineers had raised the volume of the woodwind sound.

To remedy this sometimes disturbing effect and to take advantage of the greater dynamic range now available, some producers and engineers decided to redo older recordings.[23] (The later conversions of performances from LP to CD continued the pattern of change.) Remastering is relatively easy to accomplish, particularly for orchestral recordings made with many microphones. During the initial recording sessions, each microphone is recorded on a separate track of the tape. When remastering, the engineers return to the original tapes, which preserve the exact input from each microphone and then alter the balance between them.

The differences in sound between the two versions are usually subtler than those between the original and the reissue of a historic recording. Still, any such change raises some disturbing concerns, partly because the original conductor and soloists often aren't consulted about what is being done. (Frequently, they aren't even alive.) One might wonder, though, whether they would endorse the new version or prefer the older. It's also disquieting to learn that a re-release of a highly praised recording sounds different from the one that earned the compliments.

Consider what could happen if a critic compares two recordings of a Mahler symphony—a new CD by a contemporary conductor and the critic's own LP by Leonard Bernstein. If the critic preferred Bernstein's, the comparison might be misleading if that performance had been recently reissued on CD. The critic's version differs from what readers could buy and hear, even though both claim to be the same performance by Bernstein.

There is no way to avoid such problems. By using a new technology, some producer will always try to improve an old recording or find another way to market it again. Critics may grumble that the new version really isn't the same performance as the old, but producers will ignore their complaints as long as the remastered disks continue to sell.

Chapter Ten

Reviewing Ethnic Concerts and Recordings

Although much of the ethnocentric bias is fading from our culture, the American press often neglects concerts and recordings of ethnic or non-Western music or else treats them shabbily. Too many reviews are bland and uninformative at best, misleading and inaccurate at worst. Frequently, the cause is the critic's failure to "hold up a mirror" to the music or the performance, as Oscar Thompson requires.[1] When that happens, the descriptions don't give readers enough detail for them to envisage what the program is about.

Still, other reasons are also needed to explain why the criticism of ethnic music is often so unsatisfactory. One major problem is that the music is frequently combined with theatre, ritual, dance, poetry, and the visual arts, which is a lot to discuss intelligibly. And to make the critic's task even harder, ethnic works appear in often-unknown languages, in excerpts which distort and obscure the meaning of the original, and frequently with inadequate program notes. Besides, ethnic programs are closely related to the culture from which they come, and a critic must understand the culture to comprehend the art. Although many renowned ethnomusicologists cautiously write only about their specialties, a music critic may have to review all kinds of ethnic music. Pity that poor individual who must be a generalist in such a risky field!

In the following excerpt from a 1977 review, John Rockwell shows one way to survive. After confessing his lack of expertise in South Indian music, he gives his reactions as a person untrained in the culture:

> This listener can only take it on faith that Miss Subbulakshmi is a conscientious upholder of Carnatic tradition and a sensitive exponent of its traditions. In more absolute terms, however—in her ability to communicate emotion through musical means—she is a great artist for any sympathetic listener.[2]

Rockwell's approach works well, for his warmth and enthusiasm convey the way Subbulakshmi's performance crosses the boundaries of style to communicate to someone from a very different background.

It's also worth noting that he admits his ignorance, though admittedly about a difficult and complex style. Even so, a critic who does that often risks losing the confidence of readers.

DESCRIPTIVE VERSUS JUDGMENTAL REVIEWS

Writing a largely descriptive review with little overt evaluation is another useful technique for reviewing an unfamiliar kind of music. Jon Pareles, who generally reports about popular music and jazz, follows that approach in "A Glimpse of Azerbaijan," from the *New York Times* of January 15, 1990:

> Nisim Nisimov came to New York to visit relatives, but when the World Music Institute found out he was in town, it booked him for the concert he played Friday night at the Washington Square Church.
>
> Mr. Nisimov is the head of the music school in Kuba in the Soviet republic of Azerbaijan, and he has won prizes in folk-music festivals in the Soviet Union. He plays the tar, a lute with a banjolike tone, and sings in a supple tenor voice that can be tender or impassioned; he was accompanied by Jeffrey Werbock on the gaval (tambourine) or kamancheh (upright fiddle). The program of classical mugham improvisations and folk songs offered both a chance to hear a vital tradition and a glimpse of the nationalistic pride that has recently brought Azerbaijan into international news.
>
> The choruses of many songs (with lyrics in Azeri and Farsi) included the word Azerbaijan as they praised the beauty of the land. Mr. Nisimov drew an emotional response from the audience when he sang about the river Araz, the border between the Soviet Union and Iran, which divides the Azerbaijani people.
>
> •
>
> The music is related to Turkish and Persian music and to the broader sphere of Arabian music. It is both stark—just a single line of vocals or melody on the tar, accompanied only by a drone—and intricately embellished, with quavers, trills, slides and ululations. Mr. Nisimov explored all the music's subtleties. His tremolos on the tar could be percussive or sustained and

glimmering; his voice was filled with longing or sadness or triumph as he stretched words into elaborate curves or sang out unswerving sustained notes.

The mugham pieces, based on ancient poems and melodic modes, began with annunciatory phrases from the tar, which expanded to ruminative improvisations, impassioned songs and gentle conclusions. The folk songs were shorter and more basic, with paired phrases and recurring choruses. Their steady rhythms had the audience clapping, and sometimes dancing, along.

Although Pareles gives high and unqualified praise to the performer, his compliments appear almost in passing, for example, "a supple tenor voice that can be tender or impassioned." Indeed, Pareles never gives an overall evaluation of the program, which may have been wise since he is probably not expert in its culture, though he compensates by noting the warm response from an audience attuned to the music.

Some critics, though, don't like non-judgmental reviews. Paul Hertelendy of the *San Jose Mercury News* complains that a non-judgmental review is as colorless as a pen-and-ink drawing.[3] It's also questionable whether anyone can even write a review without judgment, since a writer's choices about what to say become an indirect form of judgment.[4] Perhaps the difference is more one of emphasis than of kind. A review like Pareles's can lean toward the non-judgmental without being totally devoid of judgment.

Many ethnic performers share Hertelendy's dislike of non-judgmental reviews for more practical reasons. Local groups need favorable reviews to renew a grant from the National Endowment for the Arts. And when international performers return home, they want a positive review to display to their governments and colleagues as justification for having made the trip.[5]

Writers of judgmental reviews must be cautious, however, because many such programs, including those of Indonesian gamelan and African dance and music, are at least partly religious in nature. If a critic is careless, the review might criticize a religious ceremony in a way that offends those practicing the religion.[6] Indeed, any ethnic program must be reviewed with tact since the sensibilities of ethnic communities often differ from others, and a naive critic could easily offend someone unnecessarily.

ENTERTAINMENT VERSUS AUTHENTICITY

Ethnic programs often reveal a conflict between being entertaining and being authentic. Should a performance be primarily entertainment for Western audiences, or should it present an authentic picture of a country's art? And if an audience prefers entertainment to authenticity, is it ethical to distort a people's art for the sake of a lively show?

In an ideal world there would be no conflict, for a performance would always be both entertaining and authentic, but real life seldom is so accommodating. In the past, commercial productions favored the theatrically effective—sometimes to the point of shameless commercialization—but the level of authenticity may have increased in recent years with the rise in multi-cultural understanding.

Some viewers may complain, though, that authentic performances can be less than exciting at times. An audience is not a monolithic block, however, and what seems dull to one person might fascinate another. Since some listeners prefer works that are quieter and more profound while others favor the flashy, a largely descriptive review lets each group decide whether the program is for them. (Of course, a bad ethnic concert may not be worth recommending to anyone.)

Sometimes a critic who knows nothing about the cultural background of a performance can spot something that suggests that the work is not completely authentic—perhaps an inconsistency of style or an overly theatrical display. Often, though, it is difficult to decide what is authentic or even to define what that word can mean in a particular situation. The very act of transforming a five-hour temple ritual into a two-hour performance on a Western stage involves distortion. And the art of some countries is in such a state of flux because of acculturation—the process and result of adopting the culture traits of another group[7]—that nothing seems authentic. Defining authenticity in this context can be as difficult as in the field of performance practices.

Would it be best if the public and critics preferred uncontaminated works reflecting a long artistic tradition over acculturated works which seem less pure? Perhaps, but such a preference might reject much vital contemporary art. When two cultures combine, the initial results are often a hodge-podge, yet magnificent new styles and works often emerge from the fusion. For example, jazz combines elements from European traditions with those of African origin.

Even so, a description which points out any foreign traits introduced into a style, regardless of whether they weaken it, sharpens the picture for readers. When reading about a concert of Middle Eastern music, most readers would welcome learning that the use of microphones coarsened the sound, that the singer employed an echo chamber effect derived from popular music, or that the intonation was modified to conform to Western standards.

Performers who choose music from cultures other than their own also face the conflict between authenticity and entertainment. In 1980 Robert Palmer wrote in the *New York Times*: "Peter, Paul and Mary are an institution, and one supposes their creation of an utterly homogenized brand of 'folk' music that's had any ethnic peculiarities removed is an accomplishment of sorts."[8] Palmer's irony shows that he could not stand an interpretation which robs a song of all its ethnic traits, a point that the rest of the review reinforces. Yet this scruple apparently doesn't bother the group's many admirers.

Singers who copy the performance style of a country's folk music differ sharply from Peter, Paul and Mary. The conflict between the authentic and the appealing may remain, however, though in a different guise. Here is what Tom Johnson wrote in 1978 about a vocal ensemble called Zenska Pesna (pronounced SHENska PESSna):

> Another reason I am so fond of Zenska Pesna is that they are so true to Balkan traditions. Actually, they are generally truer and more authentic than present-day performers right in Bulgaria and Yugoslavia, where occasional Western European influences and frequent Soviet influences have corrupted many village folk customs. They are also better performers than most Balkan villagers, despite the fact that they grew up in America. . . . But there are sometimes advantages in learning things the hard way, and I think these singers are especially fastidious about finding just the right pronunciations, just the right rhythms, and just the right melodic inflections. If they had grown up in a Bulgarian village, they might tend to take such things for granted.[9]

Observe that Johnson prefers the older, more authentic, tradition to the modern, more acculturated one. In the same article he notes that performers working in a style foreign to their culture may find their creativity and imagination hampered by the search for authenticity and the need to observe the basic notes and rhythms of a song. A group from within the culture, however, could feel free to change almost anything. Johnson, doesn't think, however, that Zenska Pesna found this a problem.

In practice, many performing groups blur the boundaries between ethnic, folk, and popular music. For instance, on August 12, 1990, the *Observer* (London) reviewed four recordings under the heading, "World Music," of which only one, of Chinese music, adheres to traditional practice. The others include an English folk group seeking its own style and performing European folk tunes on a mixture of old and modern instruments including saxophones, an African record showing the influence of reggae, and another from that continent which blends traditional music with African jazz.[10] Since these stylistic crossovers often place ethnic music close to popular music and jazz, newspapers sometimes assign a popular music critic to review ethnic programs.

ETHNIC RECORDINGS

The basic principles for reviewing ethnic concerts apply equally well to reviewing ethnic recordings but with one major difference: Unless a recording mixes styles like those just described, authenticity is a more significant criterion for judgment. Since recordings last longer than concerts and are important historical documents, a recording which distorts a culture and its music may do more harm than an equally misleading concert.

It requires an expert in that music to judge its authenticity properly, and what the expert writes is often too technical for the popular press. That explains why the best reviews of ethnic records tend to appear in specialized journals like *Ethnomusicology* and is the reason why most examples in this chapter are about reviewing concerts, not recordings. Still, it would be too extreme to say that the daily press shouldn't review ethnic recordings unless they involve stylistic crossovers, for that would deprive the general public of word about much marvelous music.

It's not clear, though, how such reviews should be written. A report about a live performance can attract readers by describing any colorful activities taking place on stage, but that option isn't available to the record reviewer. An essay-review which combines elements of a review with descriptions of the cultural background might work, however. And if the beauty of the music communicates easily to a person from another culture, that point is worth emphasizing. A largely descriptive review may be another good choice. The problem of choosing authentic recordings remains, of course, but a reviewer might solve it by selecting those that have already passed muster in a scholarly journal.

Since most critics write their reviews before seeing what others say, following this proposal would break with the usual practice. Even so, a critic would still have important decisions to make when choosing what to review and deciding what to say. A recording that was highly recommended to the readers of *Ethnomusicology* might be ill suited for the general public.

PROGRAMS MIXING NEW AND OLDER WORKS

Some programs using traditional instruments include new works alongside of older ones. Here is what Paul Griffiths wrote about such a concert in 1978 for the *Times* (London):

> The stage is darkened. A spotlight falls on a solitary drummer at the back, dressed in severe Japanese robes, who beats at his slow, steady rhythm, one harsh attack followed by several gentle strokes, each measured and intended. Other musicians enter one by one: a group of women to attend to their kotos, lying ready on tables, as well as players of string instruments, percussion, a little flute and a larger recorder. When the whole ensemble of a dozen or so is assembled, the music proper begins with the dry metallic clattering of the kotos, joined by the strings and later by flute and percussion in episodes whose ferocity contrasts with the generally sombre taste.
>
> This was the ceremony of a performance which opened last night's concert by Nihon Ongaku Shudan. The music was a modern arrangement, but based on an ancient piece and on the classical traditions of Japanese music. It was frozen music, music to be heard without expectation, filled

with the most subtle and intense pleasures of sound, from the sour resonances of the lute to the formal but still physical exertions of the chanting percussionists.

Yet I wonder to what extent a European can understand such art right. The question became particularly significant in a duet for the recorder-like shakuhachis, which according to the programme "give the feeling of the lovecalls of two deer," although to me there was only bitter plaintiveness in the echoes, due to their drooping phrases, stretched tempi and strange intervals. One cannot forget the conventions of one's own heritage.

Even so I enjoyed these examples of classical Japanese music very much more than I did the modern works, which used traditional instruments with a western sense of pace, form and phrasing. For the classical pieces offered a kind of homecoming: here was the timescale of a Messiaen, the solemn gesture of a Stockhausen, the fragrant sonority of a Boulez. The contemporary works by contrast, reminded me rather of film music for travel documentaries.[11]

The rich, sensuous language of the review vividly depicts the more traditional Japanese works. Particularly impressive is the reenactment of the opening procession, almost entry by entry. Unfortunately, language alone cannot recreate the sound of a shakuhachi for readers who don't know it beforehand, despite Griffith's careful choice of words. Yet his brief comment which consigns the contemporary pieces to a commercial Western style succeeds in painting a clear picture of them, though some mention about how the instruments adapt to the style would have been welcome.

The statement, "One cannot forget the conventions of one's own heritage," is troubling, however. Although not completely false, such a strong position is even less acceptable now than in 1978, and shows that Griffiths failed to realize how well a person can be trained to understand another culture.

WHAT CRITICS SAY ABOUT REVIEWING ETHNIC MUSIC

In 1990, Robert Browning, whose World Music Institute presents performances of ethnic music in New York City, interviewed four critics of ethnic music, Robert Palmer, Jon Pareles, Peter Watrous, and John Rockwell. All were writers for the *New York Times*, either currently or in the past. Browning said they agreed on three basic points about reviewing such programs:

1. A review should relate the music to other kinds of music that readers know, to help them understand better what the program was about.
2. "The performers [should] be treated as human beings and their music [should] be treated as a human activity rather than a mystical or mysterious phenomenon."
3. The review should show an understanding of the music's cultural background and intentions.[12]

Browning thinks that the presenter of the program should supply critics with information about the cultural background and should be prepared to introduce critics to ethnomusicologists and members of the appropriate ethnic community for further help. Unfortunately, though such contacts can be useful, they can also create problems if community members or even ethnomusicologists try to manipulate a critic for their own ends.[13]

Implicit in all that Browning says is the assumption that the press should support minority and ethnic arts. This viewpoint is admirable provided the press doesn't go too far and relinquish its objectivity. When that happens, the press could appear biased toward minorities and lose credibility.[14]

WHO SHOULD CRITICIZE ETHNIC MUSIC

Another controversial subject crops up occasionally, the question of who should review programs of ethnic music. (This topic continues chapter three's discussion of the qualifications of and training of critics.) Two crucial concerns lie behind much of the discussion:

1. Can a person who is not of the ethnic group do justice to its music?
2. Should a critic of ethnic music belong to a minority ethnic group?

Although an ethnic might often be more sensitive to the feelings and the work of other ethnics in the English-speaking world, ethnomusicologist Gertrude Robinson, who was African-American, said in 1990:

> There are some white critics who have managed to write sympathetically about non-white groups and they are able to communicate that kind of non-verbal knowledge that is so important. There are very few who are able to do that but I know of a couple of articles I have read that are able to accomplish that. It's not a racial statement.[15]

Using ethnics as critics is made difficult by the fragmentation of the so-called ethnic community. Would a Puerto Rican have a better understanding of the psychology of visiting Indonesian musicians than a white Anglo-Saxon? The answer is uncertain, but a person of Indonesian background might be best of all. Yet, if each ethnic program needed a reviewer from its own minority group, the number of critics required would be enormous. Finding and training them would be a Herculean task, since many would be inexperienced. A newspaper which wanted to review a local group might also discover that the only critic qualified for the job was too involved in that same community to be objective.

Ethnics should be encouraged to enter the profession because they can bring valuable insights to the criticism of all music, not just ethnic music. Their careers are likely to be better, however, if they can also review classical music or popular music and jazz. Because of the difficulties in using part-timers from ethnic communities, it's likely that many papers will continue to use full-time professionals, regardless of their ethnic background, for reviewing ethnic programs.

Chapter Eleven

Radio and Television Criticism

Although relatively little has been written about the relationship between music criticism on the one hand and radio and television on the other, this neglect should come as no surprise, since it reflects the way these two groups tend to ignore each other. Not only does the printed press usually slight the classical music played over radio, though it does better by what is heard over television, but these media broadcast little criticism. The following pages consider what criticism has appeared and explore the breathtaking though largely untapped opportunities radio and television offer to critics.

BROADCAST CRITICISM

What criticism is broadcast by radio often masquerades as something else, perhaps as an interview which may give valuable information. The delightful opera quizzes heard during intermissions of the Metropolitan Opera Saturday afternoon broadcasts are another source of frequently first-rate criticism. One might wonder, though, whether much of what one hears is commentary rather than true criticism. Criticism usually relates to a specific event or performance, but commentary lacks such a reference or else starts with one and then moves away from it. As a result, commentary may be lacking, at least in part, in *actualité*, and tends to be freer, more casual and conversational, and less focused than true criticism.[1]

Criticism heard over radio, whether it be true criticism, commentary, or program notes, usually appears on the educational network or on stations specializing in classical music. Other commercial stations generally ignore music criticism, although the daily press, which caters to a mass public, prints it regularly. What can explain the difference?

The major reason in my opinion is that radio and TV broadcast everything in series, with only one show appearing at a time on a station or channel. A listener who doesn't like a program will probably change the station or channel or turn off the set. Since most broadcasters crave large audiences, they don't want this to happen. Therefore, they discourage true music criticism because it appeals to a smaller public, and they fear that even five minutes of it would make them lose listeners.

When criticism does appear over radio or television, would-be listeners must overcome two difficulties. First, they must tune in at a particular time to hear a program. (Videotape recorders, though, have solved the problem for those viewers willing to program them.) Then, since criticism is often immersed in the midst of a larger show—perhaps a general feature on the arts—hearing the criticism may require sitting through other material.

Newspapers, however, give readers easy access to any page at any moment. Some papers, too, give music criticism ample coverage because they feel a responsibility to report a broad spectrum of the news, and because they realize that even if only a small percentage of their readers focus on the music section, that group may be worth catering to. (Unfortunately, as we saw in chapter four, such favorable attitudes are becoming less common.)

Although their audiences were smaller than those of many commercial radio stations, classical music stations generally thrived because their advertisers appreciated the relatively high level of education and income of their public. Today, though, the declining audience for classical music is now putting a strain on American stations.[2] (Things may be better in Britain, however.[3]) The suicidal practices of some American classical stations aren't helping them, either. Instead of having their announcers read all advertisements, as was done in the past, some stations now use pre-recorded commercials similar to those found on other stations. Doing this may provide more money in the short run, but a garish commercial in the midst of classical music irritates listeners.[4] In addition, some stations, in a misguided attempt to make their offerings more appealing, are turning off listeners by programming many short, less challenging, and sometimes almost mindless pieces. After the demise of a New York City station, Edward Rothstein said in the *New York Times* that "WNCN was actually killed by the now common attitude that high culture must lower its standards and tastes to reach the greatest number of people."[5]

The criticism broadcast by a classical music station often differs significantly from what appears in the printed press. For instance, WFLN in Philadelphia tried to preview future events rather than review a past one, because its music director, Terry Peyton, felt that what takes place over radio doesn't last. (We may pick up yesterday's paper but not yesterday's radio program.) To help with previews, WFLN used guest speakers, including opera producers, directors, composers, singers, and well-known scholars such as H. C. Robbins Landon to describe Haydn, or Maynard Solomon to report on late Beethoven. Unfortunately, such criticism ended at WFLN about 1987, when new owners took over the station.[6]

Record reviews, which aren't after-the-fact events since a listener can still buy the recording, were the only real criticism on WFLN. Indeed, aside from commentary, record reviewing is probably the most popular form of music criticism on radio. One such program, "First Hearing," which appears on a number of stations, has a simple but effective format. After a moderator tells the title of a new recording, the radio audience and the panel of three critics hear the work. The critics then compare reactions, evaluate the performances, and may guess at the names of the performers. Only when their remarks are finished, does the moderator announce the performers and record company. Critics and radio audience thus match wits, though a critic familiar with current releases may have an advantage.

Some stations offered a greater variety of criticism than WFLN. For instance, WGMS-AM and FM in Rockville, Maryland, near Washington, D.C., had three critics review concerts and opening nights in that city and provide commentary on the arts. A critic also accompanied the National Symphony on tour and discussed the reviews the orchestra received while away. Unfortunately, when this station was sold near the close of 1988, the music criticism ended there too.[7]

WGMS kindly sent me transcriptions of some five-minute reviews by Paul Hume, reviews which resemble what is usually found in print athough the style is more conversational. Here is an example from February 16, 1984:

> Good afternoon. Let's take another look at a subject
> that keeps coming up from time to time. That is the matter

of the repertoire: the music that is played and sung in our concert halls and opera houses; AND—the music that is regularly neglected in those halls and houses.

This continually fascinating matter came forcibly to my mind several times in recent weeks because of music that has been heard in the Washington area lately or will be heard here in the immediate future; and it is the presence and the absence of this music that continues to intrigue me, and to raise certain vital questions. . . .

At no point does Hume use music to illustrate a point, even though that is one of radio's potentials. Consider how that might have helped his comments on July 4, 1984, about the American Vocal Ensemble singing British and American music:

And, in a way, it would be hard to think of any better singing of this music than these sixteen singers offered. Their gift for choral ensemble, for enunciation, and for intricate harmonic subtleties is an extraordinary achievement in a chorus that is now only in its third year. That I have a personal reservation about their insistence on employing what they have made the central factor in their tone production, a non-vibrato, or straight-toned texture is, to me a device that becomes very limiting in certain music of more recent vintage, particularly when a deep sense of emotional content is present in the words, as was the case in much of last night's concert.

Listeners who are unclear about how a tone with vibrato differs from one without, might appreciate a musical example. Ideally, the ensemble being reviewed would perform the excerpt, but at times this might be impractical. Recordings could be unavailable, or their use restricted by union or copyright regulations or broadcast fees, or the musicians might object to having a critic air a performance and then tear it to shreds.

Unfortunately, finding the right example adds to the preparation time for a review. Critics who are good pianists, however, can demonstrate a point at the keyboard—though obviously not vocal tone—but if they spoil a passage, a listener might write and ask how dare they review others when they can't play better themselves.

Using examples presents other problems, too. Illustrating an idea whenever it appears might become boring to a program's regular listeners, and choosing examples for such a heterogenous audience is hard, since what is perfect for the neophyte might seem obvious to the experienced listener. Besides, if each idea in a review must be accompanied by sound, a critic might have to omit a major point for lack of a good illustration.

Despite these difficulties, the use of sound and visual images suggests breathtaking possibilities for a criticism released from traditional boundaries. Written criticism is unlikely to disappear for it can say so much so quickly, but spoken criticism when used creatively could become a strong supplement.

Newspapers seem better than radio and TV for preserving a historic record of a region's musical events—a major function of criticism. A reader can scan a newspaper quickly and researchers can consult back issues for evidence about the past, whereas radio and television don't offer this service. Providing it wouldn't be impossible, however, for a nightly radio program on the arts could review concerts much like a newspaper and the program could be taped, transcribed, and indexed. The transcriptions and indexes could then be published in written form to furnish a permanent record as has been done with other programs.[8]

For instance, by perusing such an index, I found the reference to the following television report about Vladimir Horowitz performing in London. This example illustrates how American networks, when talking about music, usually present a feature story about a celebrity rather than true criticism.

> CBS EVENING NEWS WITH BOB SCHIEFFER 5/22/82
> (With Dan Rather substituting for Bob Schieffer)
>
> RATHER: The Russian-born pianist Vladimir Horowitz once said, "Without false modesty, I feel that, when I'm on the stage, I'm the king, the boss of the situation." Today in London, as Martha Teichner reports, a full concert hall agreed with him.
> (Audience applauding)
> VLADIMIR HOROWITZ: On the 22nd of May at 4:30 I will have to be my best.
> (Audience applauding)
> MARTHA TEICHNER: Today, at 4:30 in the afternoon, Vladimir Horowitz sat down at his piano and played a concert in London for the first time in 31 years.
> (Music, Horowitz playing)

MAN #1: I've never heard Horowitz, and he's probably the most wonderful pianist in the world I've come to listen to.

WOMAN: It's very hard to put it into words. It's like being able to taste a very rare wine.

MAN #2: I used to come to the Festival Hall as a little boy from the age of 12 almost twice a week, and I feel as though I'm here for the first time in my life. I'm tremendously excited.

(Music, Horowitz playing)

TEICHNER: Prince Charles invited Horowitz to play this benefit concert to raise money for the Royal Opera House. For the Prince of Wales, Horowitz played Schumann's *Scenes from Childhood* in honor of the birth of his first child, expected in July. (Music, Horowitz playing) When Horowitz played in London last, he was believed by many people to be the world's greatest pianist. So it is even now, when he is 77 years old.

JACK PFEIFFER (record producer): I've seen it in other musicians too as they grow older. They may grow older in their physical characteristics but musically, when they project themselves into the music, they become young again.

TEICHNER: Jack Pfeiffer has produced records for Horowitz for more than 30 years.

(Music, Horowitz playing)

PFEIFFER: He's like a—a racehorse, in a way. Once he gets ready, gets revved up to go on the stage, then he musters all of his physical capabilities, all of his psychological and musical capabilities, to do that performance.

(Music, Horowitz playing)

TEICHNER: The performances, so flamboyant in the early days, have changed.

HOROWITZ: I have no style because I change each time, and each day I play differently. Today I play differently than yesterday.

PFEIFFER: I think he gets better every day. As a pianist, I think he's as good as he ever was. But as a musician, he's much greater.

(Music, Horowitz playing final chords. Audience applauding)

TEICHNER: Martha Teichner, CBS News, London.[9]

CBS EVENING NEWS WITH BOB SCHIEFFER, broadcast over the CBS

This profile illustrates how serious music criticism is rarely found
on television. The only real criticism comes near the end, when
Teichner makes a brief point about the pianist's style of playing, but
it's a point which Horowitz seems to contradict immediately. To the
program's credit, however, it shows him performing, something
printed criticism can't do.

Television also has a marvelous ability to demonstrate how artists
look and move. A videotape can reveal that one performer's stage
presence is appealing, another's appalling, or disclose that one
conductor's beat is difficult to follow, another's clearer. Some
examples might appear in the equivalent of an essay rather than a
review. Audiences could enjoy the scores of avant-garde works which
use new and decorative forms of musical notation. Or a string quartet
could demonstrate how a subtle head nod or a movement of a bow arm
tells the other players how long to hold a note or what tempo to take.

Still, the need to maintain visual interest could lead to
superficiality. Displaying the regally dressed audience at opening
night of the opera is entertaining, but such images should supplement
genuine criticism, not supplant it. Indeed, at times the camera and
musical examples seem irrelevant to a review. Without lengthy
excerpts, which produce something other than criticism, the camera
and musical examples can't tell that the new sonata was derivative in
style, the tempo too slow, the pianist's technique sloppy, the violinist
out of tune, and the ensemble poor in the finale. Music criticism
should reflect upon what took place and should relegate any display of
sound or visual images to a secondary position.

Despite these concerns, the camera and musical examples have
much to offer music criticism when used discreetly. Since the spectacle
of television can overwhelm a review, radio may be the more natural
medium, but both media offer largely untapped resources for the
criticism of the future.

CRITICIZING THE MUSIC HEARD OVER RADIO AND TELEVISION

One might expect critics to love reviewing the music heard on
radio and television, since they can listen casually at home between

household chores without having to get dressed or go out. Still, this convenience alone doesn't seem to produce many reviews, for the press usually ignores radio programs, though it does better by television.

Consider what Virgil Thomson wrote in 1949 about Toscanini's broadcast of the first half of Verdi's *Aïda*. It's possible that his harsh words led to an improvement in the sound when the second half was broadcast.

Music
By VIRGIL THOMSON

AÏDA, opera with music by Giuseppe Verdi, text by Antonio Ghislanzoni, Acts I and II, broadcast from Studio 8-H, Radio City, yesterday evening with ARTURO TOSCANINI conducting the N.B.C. Symphony Orchestra. The cast:

Aïda	Herva Nelli
Amneris	Eva Gustavson
Priestess	Teresa Stitch Randall
Radames	Richard Tucker
Amonasro	Giuseppe Valdengo
Ramfis	Norman Scott
King of Egypt	Dennis Harbour
Messenger	Virginio Assandri
60-voice chorus	directed by Robert Shaw

Toscanini's *Aïda*

Once a year Arturo Toscanini, who conducts operas better than almost anybody else but who will not work with the Metropolitan, gives us the music of one by means of radio. Yesterday afternoon the first half of Verdi's *Aïda* was our fare, and next week the other half will be coming along. The N.B.C. Symphony Orchestra provides the instrumental support. Singers are listed above. The real star, of course, is the Maestro himself, showing us by means of music alone what dramatic animation means and how it need not at any point make war on clarity.

• • •

The Maestro, broadcasting, takes advantage of the fact that no distracting visual element or stage necessity is present to act as a brake. His music flows like running water, hasting o'er pebble and sand; and the sound of it is every bit as refreshing. His opera performances are limpid, lucid, expeditious. You hear the whole texture of the score better than you ever could in an opera house or from the broadcast of a full theatrical execution. They are a privilege, a pleasure, and, for all their distortion through speed, a model of pacing.

• • •

The faults of yesterday's *Aïda* lay on the vocal side. The singers were not poor singers, but neither was any one of them quite up to the occasion. They kept up with the Maestro's pace all right and mostly sang on (or near) the pitch. They had pleasant voices. They mostly wabbled a little, and they did not seem to have invariably a sure placement. What effect they gave in the hall I cannot imagine, since I could get no hint from the broadcast about the real volume of any of them. It sounded to me as if the soloists were too close to the microphone and the choral singers too far away.

Some engineering fault, moreover, either at the studio or in my machine (which is supposed to be a good one) made the voices seem to spread and blare and buzz. The Priestess, for instance, as sung by Teresa Stitch Randall, might easily have been two Teresa Stitch Randalls singing together. A double auditory image was present whenever she sang, also a huge and barnlike reverberation. This effect was engineering trickery, I am sure, because it came on and off with the temple music. It was not entirely pleasant to the ear or resembling, for Mrs. Randall's voice is in real life remarkable for its clarity of focus.

Engineering also played tricks on the scene between Amneris and Aïda by varying the volume in such a way (or possibly by not correctly adjusting it) that they seemed to be yards apart, though their conversation at this point is intimate. Who was responsible (engineers or artists) for the lack of vocal glamour in the two big arias, the tenor and soprano ones, I should not care to guess. Nor why the choral ensembles, all of them, lacked penetration in the soprano element. Perhaps it is thought not important, when the Maestro conducts, what the voices sound like. It is his show, not theirs. Well, his instruments sounded well yesterday and balanced brightly. I suspect that a change of acoustical set-up is needed for his opera broadcasts, if their vocal effects are to be a match for their instrumental perfection and for the brilliance of the Maestro's rocketlike readings.[10]

From *New York Herald Tribune,* 27 March 1949, © 1949, New York Herald Tribune

Although the sound and balance of broadcast music has probably improved greatly since Thomson wrote, what is heard over the air may still differ sharply from what is heard in the hall. Microphones and broadcast engineers introduce changes, and radio stations often reduce the dynamic range of their signals. Reviewing music heard over radio remains tricky, because the critic may not know whom to blame when the sound is poor.

Incidentally, the curious sentence at the end of the second paragraph is worth noting, even though it doesn't pertain to the topic of this chapter. Thomson says, "They [Toscanini's opera performances] are a privilege, a pleasure, and, for all their distortion through speed, a model of pacing." These almost self-contradictory last words may mean that although the relationships between tempos were excellent, the playing was generally too fast. That complaint is often made about Toscanini's conducting in his later years.

Although it should be easier to consider a station's programming than to judge the quality of its sound, critics largely ignored the subject in the past. Now, though, the pattern may be changing. When analyzing what went wrong with WNCN, two critics for the *New York Times*, Allan Kozinn and Edward Rothstein, also attacked the programming of New York City's only remaining commercial classical music station, WQXR, even though the station is owned by the New York Times corporation![11]

Unfortunately, despite the best efforts of the producers, televised concerts are plagued by a major problem which has no solution: The images on the screen often fail to fuse satisfactorily with the sound. Although a concert is a visual event, the televised pictures frequently seem superimposed upon the music and don't arise naturally from it. This clash can occur even when the screen shows the musicians playing the passage being heard or the audience listening to that passage. In a concert hall we can choose where and when to look, but what appears on a television screen is controlled and manipulated by a stranger, and may not mesh with our conception of the music. This loss of freedom disturbs many viewers.

Probably, the fewer the performers, the lesser the problem. Concerti often work well because the camera can focus on the soloist. The Metropolitan Opera's One Hundreth Anniversary celebration (October

22, 1983), which presented mostly arias and duets accompanied by orchestra, was memorable.

The difficulties become more severe when presenting larger groups. Since a static long shot of an orchestra soon becomes boring, long shots are usually broken up by close-ups.[12] But close-ups "think" for viewers instead of letting them choose where to look. The camera, as controlled by the director, makes them watch, say, the trombones, when they might prefer looking at the second violins or a larger portion of the orchestra. Besides, if the camera shifts from one solo instrument to another when the music does, the obvious mimicry of sound soon becomes tiresome. And when several melodic lines are playing simultaneously and the camera focuses on one, the choice may seem arbitrary. Some viewers are also irritated by another practice, having the camera concentrate on the conductor, which turns a performance of a Beethoven symphony into a star vehicle for the conductor.[13]

Yet Kirk Browning did just that when he televised Toscanini and the NBC orchestra, for Toscanini appeared in every shot. The technology of the time also required that the camera remain for a long time in one position before changing to another. Although Browning filmed programs differently later on, he thinks the approach worked when he filmed Toscanini. He says, "The maestro was one of those extraordinary people. The more you stayed on him, the better the picture."[14]

Later, Browning went to the other extreme and moved the camera continuously. He says:

> I think I do a little too much [zooming in], but if I'm going to err on any side, I'm going to err on the side of what I would call an active camera. In a way, you see, it's as though the camera were a committed member of the audience. It gives you a point of view about what's going on. If you sit too long on a frozen shot, with the camera totally passive, what you're doing stops being subjective. [15]

Some viewers thought that Browning's obsession with an active camera was distracting. Such a highly personal (subjective) interpretation of a concert maintains visual interest but presents one person's viewpoint which may clash with that of others. Edward Rothstein also noted about a Browning telecast, "In the Strauss work

[*Till Eulenspiegel*] the music's phrasing is often doing one thing while the camera is doing another."[16]

Approaches to filming the conductor differ in other ways, too. Browning says his Toscanini telecasts were the first to place cameras at the back of the stage so that the conductor could be seen full face. Browning's adept explanations and clear focus on the aesthetic questions pertinent to the filming of concerts and operas make him a logical figure to quote and discuss extensively. Despite the attention given to him, however, these pages make no pretense of giving a definitive evaluation of his work.

Browning is aware of the criticism of televised concerts and told Lucy A. Kraus:

> To a certain extent I agree with the critics. . . . I'm not absolutely sure that from a musical standpoint there is any way that television can represent a symphony orchestra in a completely satisfactory way. I think it's a compromise. You're always going to find people objecting to the metaphor, the detail, you pick. Sometimes we're more adroit than at other times in picking one.[17]

Earlier in the interview Browning said:

> What we are trying to do today in these concerts is to represent the *character* of the music. . . . If there is a fortissimo in the orchestra and everyone's playing, you have a certain aural energy. You can't represent that energy by shooting 110 people. By the time you get to a small screen, there's no energy left. So you get the *essence*—one timpani roll or one strong string accent—anything that represents the energy of the music. And, of course, it depends on the conductor. If he is particularly communicative, you anchor a lot on him. If he doesn't express much, you use less of him.[18]

Unfortunately, when the whole orchestra is playing loudly, photographing the timpani alone distorts the music, for it converts a tutti into a solo. At such moments either the visual image tampers with the music or the image lacks the intensity of the sound.

Kraus asked Browning how he made the music more interesting visually if a section repeats or the orchestral color is subdued. He replied:

> It's very tough. Sometimes it's dull. It's *just*
> *dull.* . . . You should not do too much Haydn and Mozart
> on television, because you cannot do it justice. Music of
> that period is very, very, hard to represent with images
> because it's not pictorial music. It's formal, structural
> music.[19]

Although experienced music lovers may enjoy an occasional
telecast if the camerawork isn't too distracting, most prefer hearing a
concert live from a good seat and choosing for themselves where to
look. (Fortunately, it's easier to turn off an irritating telecast than to
walk out on a concert.) Yet a telecast might be ideal for those less
experienced viewers who can't recognize which instrument is playing
and would appreciate having the camera follow the melodic line from
soloist to soloist. Besides, those unfamiliar with conductors, or would-
be conductors studying baton technique, might enjoy a telecast which
focuses on the conductor.

Still, videotapes of filmed concerts quickly lose appeal upon
repeated viewings, for the visual images become boring and restrict
the ear and the imagination. It's true that repeated hearings of a
recording can have the same dulling effect, but with recordings the
reverse often happens, and the enjoyment increases with greater
familiarity with the music.

A far better case can be made for opera on television than for
concerts, since opera was designed with visual display in mind. A
good telecast of an opera makes a fine show and may even satisfy
those who would prefer being in the opera house. An added attraction
for many is that the show is free and and can be watched at home.
Although television miniaturizes the grandiose display which is
characteristic of live opera,[20] the audience may feel more involved
because the camera brings it closer to the principals during intimate
exchanges.

Opera telecasts are made in two ways, either by filming in a studio
or at a live opera performance. Each has its own merits and demerits.
Studio productions let directors place cameras wherever they please
without obstructing vision and allow for greater flexibility in casting.
For instance, when Peter Herman Adler filmed *Salome* in 1954 for the
NBC Opera Television Theatre, Elaine Malbin was excellent visually
and vocally in the title role even though she could never perform the
part in an opera house. Irving Kolodin observes, "Needless to say,

Miss Malbin doesn't have a Salome voice, nor was it necessary. The number and proximity of the microphones scattered about the studio kept her audible at almost all times."[21]

In that production one person acted the part of John the Baptist and another sang it. A dancer similar in appearance to Miss Malbin also substituted for her in the Dance of the Seven Veils. Making such a change would be awkward in the theatre or on live television. The endless possibilities along these lines are limited only by the feelings of a public which might want to see a great singer regardless of how that person looked.

Studio productions permit retakes of scenes that went poorly and often have better makeup, lighting, and even acting than "live" ones. ("Live" appears in quotes because the videotapes are often broadcast long after the performance.) The makeup which works in the hall becomes garish on television, and the grand gestures which convey emotion to a three-thousand seat house seem old-fashioned and hammy on the small screen. A "live" production also reveals which singers gaze too intently at the conductor or prompter.[22]

Preparing a studio production is usually more time consuming and costly, however. The opera is no longer bound by the restrictions of a proscenium theatre, and so the director must restage the work completely and create new sets and costumes. Nevertheless, the unsatisfactory results of filming "live" restricted its use for years, until improvements in quality and its lower (though still considerable) cost now make it the more popular method.[23]

There are other arguments for "live" performances, too. Many singers thrive on the interaction with a real audience and perform better with one than in the colder environment of the studio. "Live" productions can also film two performances of the same production and choose the best scenes. Doing this may increase the cost, however, since some unions charge more when two performances are televised.[24]

"Live" televised opera can have a variety of camera work styles, as was the case for televised concerts. Kirk Browning, for instance, prefers to alternate among six cameras, four down front and two higher up in the side boxes. Two of the front ones are at the singer's eyeline at the extreme left and right sides of the stage, and the other two are on either side of the conductor and slightly lower to avoid interfering with the audience's sightlines. These camera positions let

Browning photograph the singers low from the side, which he prefers.[25]

European directors often shoot singers from above (along with lots of floor), but Browning finds this demeaning to the performers. Sometimes, though, the stage director or set designer makes a special request, as happened when Zefferelli asked Browning to place a camera in a center box to show the sets for *La Bohème* head on. Browning complied, though doing this would normally not be one of his priorities.[26]

Various techniques are used to cut from one shot to the other. The camera may shift from a soloist to a close-up of another performer to show that person's reaction to what is being sung. The split-screen image has also been borrowed from film and television for duets in which the singers stand far apart, so that the images of both faces can be presented simultaneously. This device is particularly useful for ensembles without dramatic action during which the performers project their innermost thoughts and feelings. In certain cases these techniques even make televised opera better than live.

Scenes with few participants are easiest to photograph, because large scenes suffer from the apparent arbitrariness of the camerawork—the difficulty which plagues televised concerts. For instance, when the stage is filled with a chorus, soloists, and an entering procession, the choice of what to show may seem as capricious as it is in a filmed orchestral concert. A static shot best conveys the relationship between the changing procession and the other performers, but this soon becomes visually dull. Close-ups avoid the monotony of a static shot but destroy the grandeur of the scene and may confuse viewers about what is happening onstage. A knowledge of these and other camera techniques helps a critic understand a telecast's style (or lack of one) and may explain why one telecast succeeds and another fails.

Except when reviewing televised concerts and operas, music criticism has treated radio and television cautiously as if afraid of them. Yet if critics would overcome their shyness and make better use of these media, particularly by broadcasting more criticism, their words might reach those younger listeners who favor radio and television over the printed press. The results would be beneficial for everyone.

Epilogue

Coping with the 1990s:

The Public and the Press in a Time of Change

Few readers of music criticism realize how much critics, editors, and publishers care about their opinions. In fact, newspapers sometimes commission surveys to find out what readers think about an issue. They can't do this about every question, however, and when they are mistaken about what the public wants the results can be unfortunate. For instance, an editor or publisher might cut back on the amount of music criticism printed in the mistaken belief that only a handful read it. To avoid such disasters, wise readers make their wishes known.

Writing a letter to a critic is one way to do this. A letter needn't be one of complaint, for critics and editors welcome other mail including thanks for a job well done and word about what people like to read. When a reader has a gripe, however, it's usually best to write directly to the critic, preferably in a friendly manner. That might bring about a dialogue which clears the air.

A letter of complaint comes most appropriately from a disinterested reader rather than from a friend or relative of the person who was panned. The classic example of what not to do is Harry Truman's letter attacking Paul Hume's review of Margaret Truman's vocal recital. The letter accomplished nothing for Margaret but made Hume famous. Of course, a review that is inaccurate on a purely factual level may deserve a polite response from anyone.

Whether one should challenge a critic's judgment is questionable, however. Simply disagreeing with the critic's assessment is usually a poor excuse for making a fuss, since a review may be worthwhile even if its final verdict is debatable. Remember that criticism flourishes best where there are many reviewers. All may be decent critics even if their

191

opinions clash at times, provided their descriptions are precise and their conclusions are backed by clear-cut reasons. The reasons are often more important than the value judgment itself which may simply reflect the critic's taste.

At times, though, a reader may still feel the need to complain. If writing to a critic at that time would be awkward, or if a letter hasn't produced a satisfactory response, it may then be appropriate to write to an editor. Nobody should do that, however, without giving it considerable thought beforehand, for one can cause much harm. Some worthwhile critics were probably fired because of such actions, while others were left feeling inhibited and less effective, or else so unhappy that they changed jobs.

The usual purpose in filing a complaint should be to help the critic improve in some weak area, perhaps in the quality of writing, or the understanding of music, or ethical behavior. Only rarely should one ask for a critic's dismissal, though it's proper to ask for the reassignment of a staff reporter with little musical background who serves as a music critic.

Often, when a problem extends beyond the scope of a single review, it's hard to tell whether the fault lies with the critic, editor, or publisher. When those higher up set destructive policies, a critic may be helpless. If space is cut or record reviews are eliminated, if concert reviews appear at illogical or inconsistent intervals after the event, if features and previews are favored over reviews, if displaying interesting pictures becomes a higher priority than providing articles with real content, if the Sunday music page becomes a wasteland inhabited by only two or three padded essays and profiles, or if the size of the music staff is cut, then someone in the administrative chain above the critic is probably at fault.

At such times, readers should complain loudly and (preferably) swiftly to bring about improvement. Granted, it's often hard to know to whom to complain, since papers and journals have many types of administrative structure. For instance, an editor usually chooses what to review and allocates the available space, but on some papers a critic makes these decisions. When a reader doesn't know who is in charge, a call or letter to the paper or journal might provide the answer.

Here are some issues to consider regarding the decisions usually made by an editor: When choosing what to review, does the paper maintain a reasonable balance between events in the community and what happens elsewhere? Or does the paper senselessly review the

Metropolitan Opera and ignore a nearby company? Do reviews and essays receive sufficient space, or do profiles, interviews, and advance publicity crowd them out? Is the criticism of popular music and rock flourishing while that of classical music languishes?

Part of the communication process may involve educating an editor, publisher, or broadcaster about what is needed, whether it be more space for criticism, better pay for critics in order to get good ones, or what to look for when hiring a new one. What seems obvious to a reader may not be apparent to those higher up.

Here are some other ways that readers could improve music criticism: An individual or group might organize a round table or series of round tables on some aspect of criticism, and then persuade a local radio station or educational television channel to broadcast the events. (These media should be encouraged to carry more criticism in any case.) One might also urge regional magazines and newsletters to include music criticism or expand what they have. Another approach might be to raise funds to send a local music critic, or would-be critics, to a conference or workshop on criticism. (Tact may be needed, though, to avoid offending those critics who might bristle at the suggestion that their writing needs improvement.) With a little imagination and a good brainstorming session, other ideas may come to mind.

These reflections are particularly pertinent now because of the crisis affecting classical music in the United States, and the curious response of the press to what is happening. The art of classical music is in decline and its audience is graying, partly because rock and other forms of popular music are attracting younger people more than classical music. These changes threaten the very existence of music criticism, since if classical music declines, so must the criticism that talks about it. Other institutions and individuals are at risk, too, including orchestras and music schools who may lose their financial stability and musicians who may lose their jobs.

With so much change in the air, music criticism should be at its liveliest. Critics should be devoting essay after essay to the topic, while seeking the opinions of musicians, scholars, and the public on what to do about the crisis. Those seeking answers should also study how classical music functions in Europe where things are better.

Some of this inquiry and discussion is taking place but not enough, largely because of the unfortunate behavior of the daily press. With remarkably bad timing, many newspapers have cut the space for classical music and reduced the number of classical music critics. Although reporting about popular music, jazz, and sometimes ethnic music now often appears on the music page, reducing the space for classical music is disastrous, particularly when a major story is unfolding. When something loses popularity, however, newspapers automatically cut its space without considering whether this is the time to make an exception.

Although publishers and editors are probably the chief villains, some blame must fall on those critics who go about business as usual and largely ignore the crisis. (After all, what good is music criticism if it slights the major issue confronting music today?) Many music lovers are guilty, too, for complacently accepting what is happening in the daily press.

Because music criticism is so dependent upon the music it studies, it makes sense to ask here what has brought about this decline. Is the music education in the public schools (or the lack of it) partly at fault? Have cutbacks in school funding hindered the development of a love of music in many Americans? Have the leading performers, composers, and teachers contributed to the problem by not paying enough attention to music in the public schools? Or has the relativistic attitude of public school music education, which often embraces all kinds of music without regard to their value, helped bring about the present situation?

A related factor is the growing interest in popular culture among scholars and others. (Marching bands, for instance, which are so important in many public schools, are an aspect of popular culture.) Underlying the study of popular culture, at least in some circles, is the assumption that each aspect of it is worthy of attention regardless of artistic merit. Here, too, one might ask whether a relativistic frame of mind contributes to the problem by suggesting that classical music is no more deserving of attention than any other kind of music.

Is the loss of interest by younger people in classical music a symptom of a growing anti-intellectualism in the United States? Does this disinterest stem from the curious way that today's middle- and upper-class American youth often copy the language, music, and style of the poorer classes and the ghetto?

Are the stilted format and etiquette of the classical concert turning off younger listeners? Are they bothered, for example, by not being allowed to applaud between movements of a piece? (Not only didn't this rule apply when many of the works were initially performed, but it makes little sense for those whose first movements seem to demand applause.)

Are ticket prices for classical programs too high for young people? (It must be admitted, though, that those for rock concerts aren't cheap, either.) Or does the frequent need to subscribe to a series keep the younger audience away? Many of its members can't lay out the cash for a subscription or commit themselves to a series of programs.

The most important question, however, may be why the public largely ignores today's new music. Some composers, of course, have found an audience, but none has the appeal of a Debussy, Ravel, Strauss, Stravinsky, or Puccini. The problem is complex with no simple answers. Does the public's attitude reflect its dislike of the difficult and seemingly incomprehensible music so often found today (though less than ten or twenty years ago), music that is favored by the groups giving grants and prizes and by the prestigious universities hiring composers? Does the enormous potential of the new and ever-changing electronic technologies and instruments overwhelm composers and made it difficult for them to develop coherent and meaningful styles? Does the variety of possibilities available today—including resources from folk and ethnic music, jazz and popular music, and the vast heritage of Western art music—add to the confusion for composers? Or does the multiplicity of new styles bewilder the public and leave it apathetic? (Minimalism, which is easy to follow, is the only new style to attract a large audience.) In the seeming absence of new compositions of quality, has the public tired of an art that increasingly relies on works from the past?

Granted, everything isn't as bad as these questions suggest. Many major orchestras and performance groups are still thriving, concert life remains active in large cities, and the growth of regional opera companies throughout the United States is a bright spot. New composers and performers are coming forth, regardless of whether they find audiences. It's also possible to push the panic button too hard. We are in a period of major change from which the art of classical music could emerge strengthened and revitalized, though undoubtedly changed.

Still, each of the questions asked above and others like them could serve as the basis for a more intense debate than we are now experiencing. The press should be filled with articles on the topic by critics, community figures, musicians, music lovers, students, and other young people. Radio and television should sponsor round tables or even a major symposium with participants from a broad range of society, perhaps with financial support from a foundation.

Whatever the final outcome, music criticism will be changed by this turmoil. If the decline of classical music continues, smaller papers will intensify their search for critics who can review all kinds of music—classical, jazz, popular, ethnic, or rock. Although part-timers may still cover classical concerts, only large papers will use full-time ones for that purpose. As a result, classical music journals catering to the general public may increase in importance and circulation in order to satisfy readers slighted by the daily press.

The nature of reviews may also change so that they talk in the future as much about the cultural and sociological background as about the music. This style of writing, which is not unknown today, caters to readers with little technical knowledge of classical music. Critics may also seek other ways to communicate to those sensitive to music but lacking experience with classical music. The outcome could be beneficial, too, if more articles about classical music were directed toward the fans of rock, for some of them might even learn to appreciate Beethoven.

Whatever happens, with so much at stake music criticism should be at its most vibrant. Everyone—the public, the press, and the music world—should try to raise its energy level. The result could be one of the great periods in the history of music criticism, a period whose lively discussion could assist the art of music.

Appendix

Questionnaire to Critics

In order to learn more about the current practice of music criticism, I sent a questionnaire to the 246 American and Canadian critics who belonged to the Music Critics Association in 1980. (The organization is now called the Music Critics Association of North America.) Although this list may not have provided a statistically valid sampling of music critics, it was still useful because the organization's members had a broad range of experience and held a variety of jobs. Some positions were in radio and television, but the overwhelming majority were with newspapers and journals, including major papers with large circulations and obscure ones with fewer readers. Most criticism was of classical music.

One hundred and forty critics returned a completed form; 6 declined the opportunity because they were no longer practicing criticism, and exactly 100 of the 140 signed their names.

After the questionnaire comes an analysis of the responses.

QUESTIONNAIRE

My address
March 27, 1980

To the members of the Music Critics Association:

It would be greatly appreciated if you could take a little time to complete this questionnaire to help me gather information for a book I am writing on music criticism. My mailing list consists of the membership of the Music Critics Association to which I belong.

Specific details would be welcome if you have the time. Otherwise please do what you can. For extra space you may use the back of this questionnaire or attach another sheet of paper.
Many, many thanks!

Sincerely yours,

Robert D. Schick

Name (Optional)—Nothing will be printed which would betray an individual's identity.

1. Do your writings always receive a by-line? If not:
    a. Which kinds do not?
    b. Does your place of employment have a stated general policy on giving by-lines? If so, please describe briefly.
2. Do you review other arts or take on journalistic tasks other than music criticism? If so, which ones? Is this done voluntarily, or only out of necessity?
3. Must you review music of a type distasteful to you—e.g., rock concerts for those not liking them? If so, which kinds and how often?
4. Does contemporary music receive sufficient space in your newspaper or magazine, etc? Is there any other field neglected? If either is the case could you please describe and say why?
5. What types of reviews, etc., get the most feedback from your readers or listeners? Please mention any interesting patterns of response.

6. a. Have pressures ever been exerted upon you which threatened your integrity as a critic? If so, please describe.
   b. Has an editor, publisher, director, etc., ever tried to influence the number of positive or negative reviews you write?
7. If your paper, magazine, radio or TV station has any unusual or innovative column or feature about music, please describe it.

* * *

Please check one:

1. Is your work as a critic basically _____ part-time, _____ full-time?
2. Do you have _____ 1 or 2 main employers, _____ work free-lance?
3. Do you work for a _____ newspaper, _____ magazine, _____ other? (Please describe.)
4. If you work for a newspaper, is its circulation _____ below 50,000, _____ below 100,000, _____ below 250,000, _____ above 250,000?
5. Was your education primarily in music _____, or another field _____? If the latter:
    a. Which one?
    b. Did you get your training _____, on the job _____, or elsewhere? (Please describe.)
6. (Please check all that apply.) Do you write or deliver _____ concert reviews, _____ record reviews, _____ interviews, _____ essays, _____ publicity announcements, _____ program notes, _____ record liner notes, _____ other (please specify)?

ANALYSIS OF THE RESPONSES

Section One

Question One

In reply to the first question, 104 said their writings always received a by-line; 15, in effect, said "Almost always," even though this was not an official choice; 18 said "No," and 3 left it blank. The works without by-lines were chiefly rewrites of publicity releases about concerts and music series, as well as other routine announcements. One critic, though, mentioned ghostwriting a book. Concert reviews almost always received a by-line. Several writers said that when a shorter piece appears on the same page as one that is by-lined, it sometimes has no name. Here are two specific comments:

1. Occasionally they squeeze too much on the page and there is no room for the name. Not done in a premeditated fashion.
2. [To merit a by-line] a piece must either be opinionated or require enterprising research or exceptional writing.

The last part of the question, "Does your place of employment have a stated general policy on giving by-lines? If so, please describe briefly," elicited two observations worth reporting:

1. If our copy is changed, and we don't wish to have our by-line appear, we may request that.
2. By-lines may *not* be used over a writer's objection.

Question Two

To the first part of question two, "Do you review other arts or take on journalistic tasks other than music criticism?" 94 said "Yes," (two-thirds of the replies); 45 said "No," and 1 left it blank. Some were bothered because I didn't define music criticism. When counting answers, I recorded profiles, interviews with musicians, and reviews of opera movies as music criticism but excluded reviews of musical theatre. Of the 94 whose work involved more than music, 59 did this voluntarily, 6 only out of necessity, 11 indicated that both categories applied (some people liked certain assignments but not others), and 18 either left the question blank or wrote answers that were unclear or hard to categorize.

One person who covered other fields only out of necessity said:

> My feeling . . . is that work is simply organized poorly at the top. Specializing is discouraged in the interest of "freshness"—although writing done from this base often is produced in a panic of ignorance.

Here are the fields mentioned by the 94 who did more than music criticism, along with the number who checked each category. Since some critics listed more than one area, the totals exceed the number of critics.

JOURNALISM

feature: 10
all stories (general, varied): 7
news: 3
editing: 3
columnist: 2
city desk
interviews, profiles, stories about people, celebrity appearances: 6

editorial writer
news editing & page layout
obituaries
politics
public service editor
society
special sections

THE ARTS

dance: 27
theatre & theatre arts: 27

wine: 2
architecture

musical theatre: 5
visual arts: 10
film: 9
book reviewing & literature: 8
all arts (general culture scene,
  recreation, etc.): 19

arts politics
fiction
food
pop reviews
profiles related to arts

OTHER

travel features: 3
education & pedagogy: 3
Chinese culture
gay politics

gunnery
radio: 2
TV
other media

Question Three

The third question, "Must you review music of a type distasteful to you—e.g., rock concerts for those not liking them?" drew 14 positive responses plus 3 replies saying "Yes," for earlier in their careers. Nobody had to cover such programs often, however, except for one person who had to review a rock or pop concert weekly. One hundred and thirteen people said "No," 5 submitted blank answers or comments which could not be categorized, and 5 rejected the question. Here are two examples showing what that last phrase means:

1. Music is music, whether rock or classic. Each is to
    be reviewed on its own merits.
2. If I were to consider an entire type of music
    distasteful, I would not belong in this business.

Two other replies are worth repeating. One respondent said:

I have guilt pangs for not being able to enjoy distasteful items like rock concerts and bad "big band" jazz groups and marching bands. These are especially frustrating to review (on the occasions when I have done so), not because I feel that I lack expertise, but because I am so obviously feeling pain when everyone else is having pleasure. Thus I feel like a Malvolio. And at such moments I wonder if musical criticism is really the pertinent thing; perhaps I should be reviewing the crowd rather than the performance. I rather admire Pauline Kael in her film criticism when, finding herself at a bad movie, she is able to observe the pleasure of the people around her in the audience and thus turn a negative occasion into a positive one.

Another person made an unexpected observation at the end of the following passage: :

I review virtually all popular music concerts in this area, and several dozen art music concerts/recitals per year. Certain styles of music—e.g., "heavy metal" rock, disco, electronic avant-garde music—do not appeal to me; nor do certain performers. On the other hand, those styles/performers have been known to pleasantly surprise me.

Not to be cagey, but my enjoyment of performances depends on variables of mood, timing and workload.

The types of music some disliked reviewing, including the replies of the last two writers, are listed below. Some individuals gave several examples, others none.

rock: 6

heavy metal rock: 2

popular music: 5

country & western

marching bands

"big band" jazz groups

disco

opera

Bruckner

electronic avant-garde

certain "serious" compositions

Question Four

Answering the first part of question four, "Does contemporary music receive sufficient space in your newspaper, magazine, etc.?" proved difficult for many because I didn't define "contemporary." A few also asked who determines what is sufficient. Sixty-eight replied "Yes"; 43 said "No"; 3 said "Perhaps" ("Yes and No"); 7 said the critic chooses what to review; 9 said as much as there is, implying that there wasn't much around; and 10 left the question blank. Two kinds of subjective answers told as much about the writers as about the situation. One group was rather accepting of situations which neglected contemporary music, while the other said that one could never get enough for one always wants more.

Some found the question irrelevant because contemporary music had nothing to do with the specialties of their journals. Free-lance critics claimed they had to consider what would appeal to their market. Limitations of space or staff kept others from reviewing all that they wished, and a small number who felt unqualified to review contemporary music avoided it. Two had editors who thought the public wasn't interested. Here are some specific replies:

1. I think so, but Eric Salzman might not.
2. If by contemporary music you mean Charles Wuorinen or Luigi Dallipiccola, no one here even knows they exist.
3. Heavy orientation of press and concert world to standard repertoire. Extreme conservatism of general music public.
4. No, but that's a reflection of the city itself.
5. It's not considered of interest by the senior critic.
6. [From an individual in a rural city:] We don't do much with so-called avant-garde because we don't have all that much locally and wires [wire services], etc., don't provide a lot of national.

To the second part of the question, "Is any other field neglected?" 36 said "Yes," 44 said "No," 7 said the critic chooses what to review, and 53 left the question blank. (Sixty of the respondents (43 percent) indicated in at least one part of this question that some area received inadequate attention.) The question continues, "If either is the case could you please describe and say why?" Two comments pertain to both parts of the question:

1. Music and the arts in general are not deemed newsworthy and take a back seat to virtually all other types of news or feature writing.
2. It's simply a case of editors more concerned with their social ties than with keeping abreast of trends—both serious and popular—in music.

An interesting assortment of neglected fields was mentioned. Jazz (8) led the list, with one writer noting, "especially new or experimental," and another, "especially by local musicians." The other fields were as follows:

NEGLECTED FIELDS

early (pre-Baroque) music: 3	church music: 2
essays: 2	folk music: 2
amateur performances	ballads
classical guitar	classical music
ethnic music	pop music
record reviews	out-of-state events
concerts not in standard halls	music in the schools

Question Five

The fifth question asks, "What types of reviews, etc., get the most feedback from your readers or listeners? Please mention any interesting patterns of response." Though it elicited a variety of answers, three striking types emerged, plus a fourth minor one:

1. Forty-three wrote that negative reviews brought the most replies. In three cases organized campaigns attacking the critic followed the writing of such reviews.
2. Twenty-two said that those involving local performers produced many letters, often from friends or family.
3. Fourteen said reviews of big-name performers or artists with a following aroused readers.
4. Five noted that opera reviews brought forth much reaction. Another critic also mentioned light opera in this regard.

The last three categories frequently overlapped with the first, for it was often a negative review of a local performer, famous artist, or opera that goaded readers into sending letters. Here are some replies telling what brought forth responses:

1. Negative opinions of beloved performers.
2. The more unpleasant reviews get the most letters to the editor.
3. Negative reviews about cult figures like _____.
4. Negative reviews of _____ based artists result in letters; good writing and long essays on _____ artists result in many conversations. [The reviewer works in the city whose name I omitted.]
5. Unfavorable reviews of living legends.
6. Reviews which find shortcomings in local performers, eliciting indignant responses from parents and other relatives and friends.
7. Naturally adverse criticism. The local symphony is most sensitive to adverse criticism.
8. I get response—always *positive*—when a poor performance is deemed so in my reviews. Readers appear to appreciate objective appraisals if the appraisals are well substantiated.

9. Generally speaking, the bigger the audience the more chance of response from the reader. The local opera people will think you should be more considerate of the tremendous amount of labor involved in putting anything on; the teen-agers will not appreciate reading that their idol is inept and especially, musically; the older crowd doesn't like to hear that Liberace is more interested in the money than the music. It depends on whose ox is being gored.

10. Rock reviews, pieces on local political-musical problems (e.g., power struggles in musical groups).

11. Rock music, because the fans tend to identify with and fantasize over many of the acts.

12. Historical recordings.

13. Reviews of anything religious. Some readers take exception to the most tame comment.

14. Feature interviews with personalities in the arts.

15. Pop reviews.

16. Contemporary—a very vocal and ambitious minority.

17. Reviews of college student concerts and productions—students and faculty seem quite genuinely interested in an outside view of their work.

18. Usually think pieces or, especially, controversial subjects (exposés).

19. Opera and vocal concerts. Positive reviews tend to get as much feedback as negative.

20. Opera reviews mostly from opinionated fans with whom there is no arguing.

21. Reviews by stringers—resentment over getting number two critic.

22. Self-interest. These will come after, say, a column of flute LP reviews, from flutists who hope you get to their records next time.

23. I don't know—except that if you pull a boner, you hear about it!

Question Six

The first part of question six asks, "Have pressures ever been exerted upon you which threatened your integrity as a critic? If so, please describe." Forty-two said "Yes"; 94 said "No," and 4 left it blank. Here are some responses from those who answered "Yes."

1. There are always pressures.
2. Occasional problems resulting from being simultaneously a practicing musician and a critic. [Another person reported, though, that this was not a difficulty.]
3. Just the subtle insidious corruption of being part of a musical community.
4. Not successfully.
5. From local member of _____ [a performing group] recommending that I be fired. Editor stood up for me strongly.
6. Sure. Everyone attempts to influence you—except the editors, who are impartial.
7. Indirect pressure to give favorable [review] to person considered interesting by editor.
8. I have had reviews which were unfavorable to the establishment cut extensively or not printed.
9. Yes. I try to avoid reviewing friends—occasionally it's unavoidable—which is touchy.
10. Letters to editor, two delegations, questioning my qualifications, when criticism was adverse. No real threat, however.
11. Several times a particular press person at a major record company took exception for my "bad" reviews. Once [this individual] asked, "Why were you the ONLY critic that didn't like this record?"
12. Time and space limitations.
13. Not by the paper. Individuals have tried to influence me or draw me out at concerts.

14. Stylistically, I've been told to keep my humor.
15. Friendships with artists, etc.
16. The manager of a local orchestra has tried to influence my editors.
17. [A local group] arrived in a body to try to persuade editor to fire me.
18. One opera house paid all of my expenses . . . for a review.
19. Once. A small record company sent me records several years old and hinted it would be worth my while if I reviewed them. I did not.
20. Dissatisfied readers, musicians, etc., have complained and threatened to have me fired.
21. Boosters want to enlist me for public relations campaigns.
22. During the last regime, the editor tried to cut back the quantity of reviews in favor of feature stories, personality and trend stories.
23. A pianist disgruntled over a less than enthusiastic review mounted a campaign to get me fired. He failed.
24. "Please go easy on _____" says editor. I have never complied. I am still employed.
25. At my former job, in_____, my publisher ordered that I be kept from reviewing important opening night [performances] . . . following my negative review of _____ which he attended. That, in large part, was the reason I moved here.
26. Not as a critic. As an *editor*, yes—from advertisers, mostly.

After recounting a horror tale of various kinds of gross interference, one writer concludes more optimistically:

27. In many ways the pressure I receive, from both
     inside and outside the organization, is the result of
     a local tradition that just because something
     happened it was automatically great. That, I hope,
     is changing—as are critical standards in this town
     generally. If I sometimes feel depressed over the
     negative aspects of my particular position, I can at
     the same time take quite a bit of heart in that.
     Especially since I believe that in the last _____
     years I have had a lot to do with that.

In order to protect my informants, I deemed it wiser to rewrite the
final two cases rather than to quote them directly: (28) An editor, who
belonged to an organization's board of directors, wrote an apology for
the critic's negative review of that group. (29) A critic was threatened
with lawsuits on several occasions and once underwent litigation over
a review. The editors always supported the critic.

The second part of question six asks, "Has an editor, publisher,
director, etc., ever tried to influence the number of positive or negative
reviews you write?" (Some replies to the first part pertain here, too.) I
raised the issue because Peter Pastreich of the San Francisco
Symphony told the Carnegie Hall Conference that editors encourage
critics to write negative reviews because they sell more papers than
positive ones. Though this seemed far-fetched, I took the opportunity
to check on the facts.

Twenty people said "Yes"; 113 said "No"; and 7 left the question
blank. None supported Pastreich's position, though some suggested the
reverse, that positive reviews were favored. Here are some comments,
mostly from those who said "Yes":

1. [From an editor] Our policy is to use our limited
    space as much as possible for positive reviews,
    since we always have more than we can publish.
2. Never directly—paper has a general policy of
    politeness.

3. Publisher sometimes tries to get features supporting his friends.
4. Yes, but rarely.
5. Not successfully.
6. Once or twice when I've been very negative—otherwise, no.
7. I'm sure we are all pressured by groups with vested interest in getting a positive review of their performance.
8. My editors never did. I was considered the "expert."
9. Continually.
10. Not directly; it would be much easier to write only positive reviews.
11. One skunk killed a negative paragraph about a friend of his; the rest of the review was printed.
12. Once.
13. No. But positive reviews sometimes get better exposure (not always).
14. Very seldom, and then early on in my career only.
15. Yes—unsuccessfully.
16. On a previous paper—result, I quit.
17. A magazine I worked at allowed the managing editor to exert his personal tastes on all stories and reviews, so he often edited out information he did not personally agree with.
18. [One individual who said "No," added] On more than one occasion, though, I have been asked to tone down my negative reviews a bit by my entertainment editor—whenever several negative letters have been received. This is merely a gesture.
19. No, but I'm careful.

I thought it best not to quote example (20) directly. A critic said that a radio station once refused to broadcast a somewhat negative review because the local paper had just raved about the same program.

As a change of pace, here is an encouraging reply to end this section:

> 21.   No, and they resist efforts of others to influence
>   what I write.

Question Seven

The seventh question, "If your paper, magazine, radio or TV station has any unusual or innovative column or feature about music, please describe it," drew 118 blank responses and 22 answers. Here are some replies, with only one comment about their feasibility or degree of innovation:

1.   Technical information concerning the sections of the orchestra.
2.   I have been specializing in musical instruments columns where an artist discusses his or her approach to playing an instrument.
3.   Weekly column "Sounding Board" deals in editorial way with the business side of the arts: funding, government support and legislation, volunteerism, board structures, education.
4.   My column—"Tales of Tessitura"—was originally written for people who hate opera.
5.   A series of articles in which local music figures discussed their favorite works and recordings.
6.   New music column; TV column re classical telecasts.
7.   My "Overtones" program on twentieth-century music. I interview locals as well as "well-known" composers and performers.
8.   Five-minute, two times daily program on the arts.

9. The _____ orchestra has been searching from among its guest-conductors this season for a permanent conductor. I have been doing an ongoing series of interviews with these guest-conductors in conjunction with this search.
10. One half of a page is devoted to classical music analysis each Saturday.
11. All the critics (classical music and dance, rock music, art and architecture, theater and film, food, etc.) must use "star" system to evaluate performance, i.e.,

****—excellent
***—good
**—fair
*—poor

[The stars precede the reviews.]

(This last procedure is most prevalent in film reviewing, though it is sometimes found elsewhere. For instance, the *National Newspaper Index*, which covers the *Christian Science Monitor, Los Angeles Times, New York Times, Wall Street Journal* and the *Washington Post*, gave a summary grade to each concert review listing for 1982 and surrounding years. (The index has since abandoned the practice.) The results were confusing, however, because critics often use a double standard and treat a younger performer more gently than a senior one. As a result, a famed artist might receive a C+ or B- and someone greatly inferior a higher grade. This problem suggests that concert reviews don't lend themselves to such easy summaries.)

I thought it best to summarize example (12). One paper gave critics greater freedom than usual about what to write, which let them choose some less-than-usual topics, including concerts of student compositions, lecture-recitals, and bootleg LPs.

Section Two

The second half of the questionnaire asked for data about the profession that was generally more objective and impersonal than what was found above.

Question One

The first question asks, "Is your work as a critic basically _____ part-time, _____ full-time?" In reply, 81 said their work was basically part-time; 54 said full-time, and 5 left it blank. These answers are significant because they suggest that a majority of the profession work only part-time as critics.

Question Two

Question two asks, "Do you have _____ 1 or 2 main employers, _____ work free-lance?" Eighty-seven said they had one or two main employers; 50 said they worked free-lance, and 9 left it blank. The number exceeds 140 because 6 people checked both boxes. Some of the 87 who had one or two main employers must have worked only part-time, since question one indicates that only 54 worked full-time.

Question Three

The answers to the third question reveal that 118 worked for newspapers, 30 for magazines, 8 for radio, 1 for TV, 3 for news bureaus, and 2 for newsletters. Five left it blank and 4 said "other" without giving further clues. Here, too, the number exceeds 140 because some checked multiple answers.

Question Four

Here are the answers that people gave when asked about the circulation of their newspapers:

Below 50,000:   25
Below 100,000:   16
Below 250,000:   32
About 250,000:   1
Above 250,000:   38
Blank: 28

Although the category of "About 250,000" wasn't in the questionnaire, one person added it. Some of those who didn't reply probably worked only for magazines.

Question Five

The first part of question five begins: "Was your education primarily in music _____, or another field _____? If the latter: a. Which one?" Seventy-two said their education was "primarily in music"; 51 said in "another field"; 14 said "both"; and 3 left it blank. (Some who said "both" studied music and the other subject(s) at different times. For me to count a reply as "both," however, the study of music had to be formal and matriculated.)

Here are the subjects mentioned under "both":

BOTH

Music & journalism: 4   Music & Chinese studies
Music & English: 3   Music & engineering
Music & literature   Music & history
Music, dance, & English   Music & biology
Music & philosophy & history

When preparing the list of other fields, if a reply stated both liberal arts and a major, I listed the answer under the major. The number of subjects given below is less than the number of people who checked "another field" (51), since some respondents didn't name the subject.

OTHER FIELDS

Journalism: 8	American history
Journalism & political science	American studies
History: 4	Art
Drama: 2	Biology
English: 10	Chemistry
English major & journalism minor	Classics
English & French	French
English & history	Government
English literature: 3	Liberal Arts
English major & music minor: 2	Naval science
English literature & library science	Psychology

The last part of question five was directed to those whose education was not in music. The question reads as follows: "b. Did you get your training _____ on the job or _____ elsewhere (please describe)?" Unfortunately, although I meant training in *music*, some thought I meant training in *journalism*, and the results were too confusing to tabulate. They were reassuring, however, in one respect, for nobody mentioned starting musical training *after* becoming a critic. Some of the critics were self-taught; others studied privately, often for extensive periods; two had played in orchestras; and one performed professionally before becoming a critic.

Question Six

The instructions for question six say, "Please check all that apply." The question asks: "Do you write or deliver _____ concert reviews, _____ record reviews, _____ interviews, _____ essays, _____ publicity announcements, _____ program notes, _____ record liner notes, _____ other (please specify)?" (Although program and record liner notes are not music criticism by my definition, they are closely related, and I wished to discover how many critics wrote them.) Here are the answers:

WHAT CRITICS DID

Concert reviews: 131
Record reviews: 87
Interviews: 106
Essays: 89

Publicity announcements: 44
Program notes: 46
Record liner notes: 31
Other: 22

A breakdown of the comments under "Other" now follows. (Two people listed more than one item.)

OTHER

Features: 7
Profiles: 2
Columns covering any topic of interest: 5
Weekly opinion column chiefly about the business side of the arts
Musical history & condensed biographies of composers, singers, dancers & musicians

Scholarly articles
Reviews of music books: 2
Radio lectures on lives of composers
News stories about musical events: 4

Notes

Preface

[1]Oscar Thompson, *Practical Musical Criticism* (New York: M. Witmark and Sons, 1934; reprint, New York: Da Capo Press, 1979).

[2]Monroe C. Beardsley, *Aesthetics: Problems in the Philosophy of Criticism* (New York: Harcourt, Brace, and World, 1958), 4.

[3]The following table lists the conferences on music criticism which I attended, along with the shorter names (in parentheses) under which they sometimes appear in the notes:

DATE	CONFERENCE NAME
Aug. 7–16, 1974	Institute on Reviewing Piano Performance and Literature (Maryland institute), University of Maryland, College Park, MD
Aug 4–12, 1978	Institute on Contemporary Music, Tanglewood, Lenox, MA (I attended for only a few days.)
May 8–11, 1979	International Conference on Music Criticism (Carnegie Hall conference), New York, NY
June 8–17, 1979	Institute on Contemporary Experimental Music (experimental music institute), New York, NY (I was present for only the first seven days.)
Nov 3, 1979	Panel Discussion on Music Criticism (New York round table), which I organized and moderated. Annual meeting of the American Musicological Society, New York, NY
June 19–20, 1980	Seminar on Music Criticism and the Business of Music, held as part of the annual meeting of the American Symphony Orchestra League, New York, NY
June 2–11, 1983	Symposium on Recorded Music (symposium on recordings), New York, NY (The first four days overlapped with the annual meeting of the Music Critics Association of North America.)

Mar 28–29, 1987	Symposium on Music Criticism in America's Press (Washington Symposium), Washington, DC
May 27–30, 1988	Annual Meeting of the Music Critics Association of North America (1988 MCANA meeting), Charleston, SC
June 14–17, 1990	Annual Meeting of the Music Critics Association of North America (1990 MCANA meeting), Berkeley, CA
Nov 9, 1990	Round table discussion on "The Responsibility of the Press Toward Ethnic Music" (Oakland round table), which I organized and moderated. Annual meeting of the Society for Ethnomusicology, Oakland, CA
May 19–24, 1991	Annual Meeting of the Music Critics Association of North America, New York, NY
Oct 29–Nov 1, 1992	Annual Meeting of the Music Critics Association of North America (1992 MCANA meeting), Chicago, IL
Feb 22–28, 1994	Musical Life in Philadelphia, Philadelphia, PA (I attended only two evenings.)
Mar 3–6, 1995	Musical Life in Philadelphia, Philadelphia, PA

Although I couldn't be present at the June 15–18, 1994, Dallas, Texas, meeting of the Music Critics Association of North America, (1994 MCANA meeting), I have a tape recording of a panel discussion on the "Role of the Contemporary Critic."

The Music Critics Association of North America, Inc. (MCANA)—7 Pine Court, Westfield, NJ 07090; telephone: 908-233-8468—sponsored or co-sponsored all of these conferences except for the New York and Oakland round tables.

[4]David Hume, "Of the Standard of Taste," reprinted in *Aesthetics: A Critical Anthology*, George Dickie and R. J. Sclafani, eds. (New York: St. Martin's Press, 1977), 600.

Chapter One: Some Basic Issues

[1]Georges Bizet, untitled essay in *La Revue Nationale et Étrangère*, 3 August 1867, quoted in Winton Dean, *Bizet* (London: J. M. Dent, 1948), 279.

[2]*Harvard Dictionary of Music*, 2d ed., s.v. "Music criticism."

[3]Leon Plantinga made this point on November 3, 1979, during the Panel Discussion on Music Criticism (New York round table), which was held in New York City at the annual meeting of the American Musicological Society.

[4]Robert Palmer, "Critic's Notebook: Jazz Festival: A Ben Hur Mentality," *New York Times,* 1 July 1982.

[5]John Russell, review of *Art in the Third Reich,* by Berthold Hinz, *New York Times,* 3 April 1980.

[6]Ibid.

[7]Monroe C. Beardsley, *Aesthetics: Problems in the Philosophy of Criticism* (New York: Harcourt, Brace, and World, 1958), 567–71.

[8]St. Augustine, *St. Augustine's Confessions,* trans. William Watts, *Loeb Classical Library* (New York: G. P. Putnam's Sons, 1925), vol. 2, bk. 10, chap. 33, pp. 167–69.

[9]*Dwight's Journal of Music* 39 (18 January 1879): 14.

[10]Mina Curtiss, *Bizet and His World* (New York: Alfred A. Knopf, 1958), 396.

[11]This was published by his son, Daniel Halévy, in *Revue de Musicologie* 68 (November 1938): 130–31. Quoted in Curtiss, *Bizet and His World,* 395.

[12]Curtiss, *Bizet and His World*; Dean, *Bizet*; Nicolas Slonimsky, *Lexicon of Musical Invective,* 2d ed. (New York: Coleman-Ross, 1965).

[13]Curtiss, *Bizet and His World,* 410, 414, 420–21, 424; Dean, *Bizet,* 114.

[14]Curtiss, *Bizet and His World,* 395.

[15]Ibid., 415.

[16]Dean, *Bizet,* 51–52.

[17]Ibid., 52.

[18]Curtiss, *Bizet and His World,* 320, 394.

[19]Pierre Berton, *Souvenirs de la vie de théâtre* (Paris, 1913), 259 ff., quoted in Curtiss, *Bizet and His World,* 394.

[20]This opinion was expressed by some unnamed judges at the Academie des Beaux-Arts in Paris about an early opera of Bizet's, *La Guzla de l'Émir*, which was probably written about 1861 but was never performed and is now lost. Quoted in Dean, *Bizet*, 56, with background material provided on 23 and 55.

[21]Curtiss, *Bizet and His World*, 211.

[22]Paul de Saint-Victor, review of *Carmen*, in *Moniteur Universel*, March 1875; quoted in Slonimsky, *Lexicon*, 63–64.

[23]Meyerbeer: Dean, *Bizet*, 224; Verdi: Donald Jay Grout, *A Short History of Opera*, one-volume edition (New York: Columbia University Press, 1947), 349–50.

[24]Quoted in Charles Pigot, *Georges Bizet et son oeuvre* (Paris, 1886; 2d ed. with additions, Paris, 1911), 43; quoted in Curtiss, *Bizet and His World*, 121.

[25]Dean, *Bizet*, 59.

[26]Ibid., 48–51.

[27]Ibid., 217.

[28]Ibid., 113.

[29]Curtiss, *Bizet and His World*, 389; Dean, *Bizet*, 112.

[30]Curtiss, *Bizet and His World*, 397.

[31]*Le Siècle*, 8 March 1875; quoted in Curtiss, *Bizet and His World*, 404.

[32]Georges Bizet, untitled essay in *La Revue Nationale et Étrangère*, 3 August 1867; quoted in Dean, *Bizet*, 278.

Chapter Two: The Function of Music Criticism

[1]Oscar Thompson, *Practical Musical Criticism* (New York: M. Witmark and Sons, 1934), 29.

[2]M. D. Calvocoressi, *The Principles and Methods of Musical Criticism*, 2d ed. (London: Oxford University Press, 1931), 28.

[3]Monroe C. Beardsley, *Aesthetics: Problems in the Philosophy of Criticism* (New York: Harcourt, Brace, and World, 1958), 9.

[4]Robert J. Matthews, "Describing and Interpreting a Work of Art," *Journal of Aesthetics and Art Criticism* 36, no. 1 (fall 1977): 5–14.

[5]V. Radanovic, "Theory and Criticism with Reference to Creativity in Music," *International Review of the Aesthetics and Sociology of Music* 2, no. 2 (1971): 278.

[6]John Rockwell told this to the Institute on Contemporary Experimental Music (experimental music institute), which was held in New York City from June 8–17, 1979.

[7]*The New Grove Dictionary of Music and Musicians*, s.v. "Bach, Johann Sebastian," p. 794, by Christoph Wolff.

[8]Winton Dean, "Critic and Composer," *Opera* 3, no. 3 (March 1952): 160.

[9]Henry Edward Krehbiel, *New York Tribune*, 24 November 1920, quoted in Barbara Mueser, "The Criticism of New Music in New York: 1919–1929" (Ph.D. dissertation, The City University of New York, 1975), 62.

[10]Barbara Mueser, "Criticism of New Music," 62.

[11]Ibid., 8.

[12]Ibid., 12–13.

[13]Ibid., 36–41.

[14]Virgil Thomson, *The State of Music* (New York: William Morrow, 1939), 117.

[15]Thompson, *Practical Musical Criticism*, 31–33.

[16]Benjamin Britten, "Variations on a Critical Theme," *Opera* 3, no. 3 (March 1952): 144.

[17]Harold C. Schonberg, "Music: Szell Leads the Philharmonic," *New York Times*, 29 October 1965.

[18]Leon Plantinga, review of *The Musical World of Robert Schumann: A Selection from Schumann's Own Writings*, ed. and trans. Henry Pleasants, *Journal of the American Musicological Society* 18, no. 3 (fall 1965): 417.

[19]Hans W. Heinsheimer, "A Music Publisher's View of Reviewing," *Notes* 26, no. 2 (December 1969): 229.

[20]Kurt Stone, "The Art of Reviewing Music," *Notes* 26, no. 2 (December 1969): 231.

[21]I am indebted to Michael Saffle for pointing this out.

[22]Donal Henahan, "No Improvement in Concert Bad Manners," *New York Times*, 7 May 1976.

[23]Tom Johnson, "Artists Meet at Niblock's Loft," *New York Village Voice*, 9 May 1977, 64.

[24]Leighton Kerner, "The Last Platitudes of the '70s," *New York Village Voice*, 16 April 1979.

[25]Virgil Thomson, "Voice Forum," *New York Herald Tribune*, 1 December 1946; reprinted in Virgil Thomson, *The Art of Judging Music* (New York: Praeger, 1955), 94–97.

[26]Donal Henahan, "Playing the Angles on the Piano," *New York Times*, 30 April 1976.

[27] Zofia Lissa, "The Precarious Art of Music Criticism," *The World of Music* 14, no. 3 (1972): 34.

[28]Daniel Webster, "Curtis is ready to move backward," *Philadelphia Inquirer*, 6 March 1977, sec. 1, p. l.

[29]Alan Rich, *Careers and Opportunities in Music* (New York: E. P. Dutton, 1964), 193.

[30]Michael Steinberg pointed this out at the International Conference on Music Criticism (Carnegie Hall Conference), which was held in New York City from May 8–11, 1979.

[31]Harold C. Schonberg, "On Trills and Other Ornaments," *New York Times*, 3 June 1979, sec 2, p. 19; Frederick Neumann, *Ornamentation in Baroque and Post-Baroque Music* (Princeton: Princeton University Press, 1978).

[32]Andrew Porter, *Music of Three Seasons* (New York: Farrar, Straus, & Giroux, 1978), xiv.

[33]Tom Johnson, "New Forms for New Music," *New York Village Voice*, 4 September 1978, 102.

[34]Calvocoressi, *Principles and Methods*, 171–72. Calvocoressi quotes from Ernest Newman, *A Musical Critic's Holiday* (New York: Alfred A. Knopf, 1925), but the page number given for the excerpt, 207, is wrong.

[35]Ernest Newman, *A Musical Critic's Holiday*, 281.

[36]John Rockwell, "The Pop Life: Two disks with an appeal for teen-agers," *New York Times*, 28 September 1979.

[37]Robert Freeman stated this during a music honors convocation at the School of Music, West Chester University, West Chester, PA, on May 7, 1985.

[38]Thompson, *Practical Musical Criticism*, 33.

[39]Henry Kamm, "Maazel Departure the Climax of Drama in Vienna," *New York Times*, 27 May 1984, sec. 1, p. 64.

[40]Shirley Fleming, "Alfred Frankenstein 1906–1981," *High Fidelity* 31, no. 10 (October 1981): 75.

[41]The Information Services Office of Louis Harris and Associates (630 Fifth Avenue, New York, NY 10111) sent me a copy of their "Arts Bibliography," which lists twenty-three surveys conducted by their now defunct subsidiary, the National Research Council of the Arts, Inc. Most took place in the early and mid-1970s, though two are from the 1980s. None is specifically concerned with the power of the

critic, nor is any exclusively about music. The reports are still available, usually for a fee, from addresses listed in the "Arts Bibliography."

I have seen summaries of all of these reports but have seen only one in its entirety, a 1973 survey on "Americans and the Arts" which is reproduced in *The Harris Survey Yearbook of Public Opinion 1973: A Compendium of Current American Attitudes* (New York: Louis Harris and Associates, 1976), 437–504.

In *Criticizing the Critics* (New York: Hastings House, 1979), John W. English discusses some of the Harris surveys made in 1970, 1973, 1974, and 1975 on pp. 73–74, 88, and 117.

Newspapers sometimes commission studies of their readers' interests in music and the other arts to help them decide what to print. I wrote to two papers which had authorized such surveys, but neither would let me see the results on the grounds that the information was private and might help its competitors if published.

Judith Lynne Hanna conducted a panel discussion on "The Impact of the Critic," using participants from dance, theatre, film, music, and the visual arts. Her report on the panel, "The Impact of the Critic: Comments from the Critic and the Criticized," is found in *Social Science and the Arts*: 1984, ed. John Robinson (Lanham, MD University Press of America, 1985), 141–62.

Her paper also discusses three other surveys:

1. A study of all of the arts, commissioned by the National Endowment for the Arts

2. A survey of theatre, commissioned by the Marketing Department of the John F. Kennedy Center for the Performing Arts in Washington, DC

3. A survey of Off and Off-Off Broadway theatre-goers in New York City

[42]Hilda Baumol, William J. Baumol, and Edward Wolff, "A Study on the Influence of Music Critics," (Mimeographed, c. 1980). A report sponsored by the National Endowment for the Humanities through the agency of the Carnegie Hall Corporation.

[43]Ibid., 16.

[44]Ibid., 21.

[45]Ibid., 31.

[46]Ibid., 3–4.

[47]Joan Peyser, *Bernstein: A Biography* (New York: Beech Tree Books/William Morrow, 1987), 240–42.

[48]Ibid., 301–6, 369–71.

[49]Britten, "Variations," 145.

[50]Patrick J. Smith, introduction to "The Futility of Music Criticism" by Derek Cooke, *Musical Newsletter* 2, no. 1 (January 1972): 7.

[51]Robert Palmer and John Rockwell made this point at the experimental music institute.

[52]Virgil Thomson, "Taste in Music," in Virgil Thomson, *The Musical Scene* (New York: Alfred A. Knopf, 1945), xiii.

[53]Harold C. Schonberg, "A Lifetime of Listening," *New York Times*, 8 February 1981, sec. 6, p. 38; a similar quotation appears in Ruby Mercer, "Editorial Comment," *Opera Canada* 13, no. 1 (spring 1972): 2.

[54]Ernest Newman, *A Musical Critics Holiday*, 268.

[55]Gary Graffman states this in Dave Helland and Bob Doerschuk, "Gary Graffman: Classical Eclecticist," *Contemporary Keyboard* 4 (December 1978): 44.

Chapter Three: The Qualifications and Training of a Critic

[1]John Ardoin, "A Critic Looks at Criticism," *Catalyst*, spring 1976, 9.

[2]Ibid.

[3]Andrew Porter, preface to *Music of Three Seasons* (New York: Farrar, Straus, & Giroux), p. xii.

[4]*The New Grove Dictionary of Music and Musicians*, 6th ed., s.v. "Newman, Ernest."

[5]George Bernard Shaw, preface to *Immaturity* (London: Constable & Co, 1930), particularly p. xxxi; preface to *London Music in 1888–89*; reprinted in *G.B.S. on Music* (Harmondsworth, Middlesex: Penguin Books, 1962).

[6] Porter, preface to *Music of Three Seasons*, xi–xii.

[7]Harold C. Schonberg, "A Lifetime of Listening," *New York Times*, 8 February 1981, magazine section.

[8]Bernard Rosenberg and Deena Rosenberg, "A Music Critic Speaks: An Interview with Michael Steinberg," *Musical Newsletter* 6, no. 4 (fall 1976): 9.

[9]When I was first introduced to Jay Harrison of the *New York Herald Tribune* during a concert intermission, he told me that nobody discusses the program with him before he writes the review.

[10]What happened to Graham actually occurred to me when I was writing for *Musical Courier*. An answer to my questionnaire to critics also is pertinent. When asked, "Have pressures ever been exerted upon you which threatened your integrity as a critic?" one respondent said, "Individuals have tried to influence me or draw me out at concerts."

[11]Rosenberg and Rosenberg, "A Music Critic Speaks," 13.

[12]Michael Nyman mentioned this at the Institute on Contemporary Experimental Music (experimental music institute), held June 8–17, 1979, in New York City.

[13]George Bernard Shaw discusses the need to understand the business of music in "How to Become a Musical Critic," reprinted in George Bernard Shaw, *How to Become a Musical Critic*, edited by Dan H. Laurence (New York: Hill and Wang, 1961), pp. 5–6. (First published in The *Scottish Musical Monthly*, December 1894.)

The panelists at the International Conference on Music Criticism (Carnegie Hall conference), which was held in New York City from May 8–11, 1979, felt that critics should be able to answer questions like these:

- How do concert managements select their artists, orchestras their soloists, and record companies their performers?
- What other business considerations affect the making of recordings, including the choice of works to record?
- What power do boards of directors of performing groups (both local and national) wield over the music we hear?
- Who are these board members and what are their viewpoints?

Critics who hope to improve the musical scene must also know what things cost and who has the real power. They should also understand the labor-relations practices of musical groups, and how government support and legislation affect music. The answers to such questions vary from country to country and region to region. In Europe, for instance, where government arts councils and radio station orchestras are powerful, many answers will differ from those in the United States.

[14]"Composer and Critic: Two Views of Their Responsibility to the Art of Music and Its Public," *Newsletter: Institute for Studies in American Music* 10, no. 2 (May 1981): 1, 10.

[15]Shaw, "How to Become a Musical Critic," 2. He also holds that a critic must avoid applying standards that are pedantic or irrelevant to the music being reviewed.

[16]Several speakers discussed reference books and on-line data bases helpful to critics at the annual meeting of the Music Critics Association of North America, Chicago, IL, 30 October 1992.

[17]At the Symposium on Music Criticism in America's Press, Nancy Malitz described how a kindly editor taught her what she needed about journalism. The symposium was held on March 28–29, 1987, in Washington, DC.

[18] Byron Belt talks about the problem of critics falling asleep at concerts in "Critic at Large: Why Music Critics?" *Music Journal* 34, no. 2 (February 1976): 8.

[19]Michael Steinberg mentions Virgil Thomson's problems in Rosenberg and Rosenberg, "An Interview," 16.

[20]Virgil Thomson, *Virgil Thomson* (New York: Alfred A. Knopf, 1966), 334.

[21]Shaw wants critics to identify the distinctive traits of performers in *How to Become a Musical Critic*, 4.

[22]Barbara Mueser, "The Criticism of New Music in New York: 1919–1929" (Ph.D. dissertation, The City University of New York, 1975), 105–6.

[23]Michael Meckna, "Copland, Sessions, and Modern Music: The Rise of the Composer-Critic in America," *American Music* 3, no. 2 (summer 1985): 204.

[24]Jaroslav Vogel, *Leos Janácek,* rev. and ed. Karel Janovicky (New York: W. W. Norton, 1981), 147, 223–25.

[25]Max Graf, *Composer and Critic: Two Hundred Years of Musical Criticism* (New York: W. W. Norton, 1946), 275–78; Ernest Newman, *A Musical Critic's Holiday* (New York: Alfred A. Knopf, 1925), 194–95.

Chapter Four: Music Criticism and Journalism

[1]The replies to my questionnaire to critics provided the information about the employment of critics. In the Appendix see the replies to *Section One,* Question Two, and *Section Two,* Question One.

[2]Walter Fox, my colleague at West Chester University, told me this.

[3]George Bernard Shaw, "Stanford on the Critics," in *G. B. S. on Music* (Harmondsworth, Middlesex: Penguin Books, 1962), 187–88.

[4]Three editors at the Symposium on Music Criticism in America's Press (Washington symposium), held in Washington, DC, on March 28–29, 1987, made suggestions about how to hire a qualified music critic. J. Ford Huffman, the managing editor of the Features and Graphics division of Gannett News Service, would place want ads in trade journals and let people in music schools know about the opening. He would consider people with academic or newspaper experience. Huffman wants somebody who can write well, cover a fire if the theatre catches on fire, and write for every reader.

Jennie R. Buckner, the managing editor of the *San Jose Mercury News,* would publicize the job opening by informing the Music Critics Association of North America, and by placing an ad in *Editor and Publisher* magazine. She would consider all journalists and not just those who write for newspapers. Buckner would require that the person know the subject well and would ask for help in judging this, possibly even from someone not on the paper. In order to find a person who writes wonderfully, she would insist on a tryout so she could see the raw copy, since some people look good because their editors make them. In addition, the person chosen must care about making writing accessible to the lay person.

David Cooper, the third editor, would use a different approach and ask friends for recommendations. He noted, too, that whatever the position he is hiring for, he wants somebody who has a passion to do the work.

During the ensuing discussion, Robert Freeman, director of the Eastman School of Music, suggested informing the College Music Society so that its newsletter could notify musicians of the vacancy.

[5]On June 16, 1994, at the annual meeting of the Music Critics Association in Dallas, TX (1994 MCANA meeting), William Littler

discussed how he participated in France in an unsuccessful attempt to establish such criteria.

[6]Nancy Malitz made this point at the Washington symposium.

[7]Michael Walsh said this at the Washington symposium.

[8]Ned Rorem, *Critical Affairs: A Composer's Journal* (New York: George Braziller, 1970), chap. 12; Benjamin Britten, "Variations on a Critical Theme," *Opera* 3, no. 3 (March 1952): 144–46.

[9]Letter from François Olivier to the editor, published as "You Be the Critic: Come on, Maureen, Learn Your Viols," *Montreal Gazette*, 12 October 1979, 52.

[10]This point was made at the Washington symposium.

[11]Jerome Wigler, and others, "Michael's Reviews Struck a Discordant Note," *News of Delaware County* (Pennsylvania), 27 August 1981, 19.

[12]Davyd Booth, "Critiquing the Critics: One Musician's View," *Seven Arts*, November 1993, 14.

[13]"The Critic: Hero or Villain? A Conversation at the Eastman School of Music," *Rochester Review*, spring–summer 1982, 7–11.

[14]Virgil Thomson, *Virgil Thomson* (New York: Alfred A. Knopf, 1966), 324–25.

[15]Harold C. Schonberg mentioned this at the International Conference on Music Criticism (Carnegie Hall conference), held in New York City on May 8–11, 1979.

[16]Olga Samaroff, "The Performer as Critic," in *Music and Criticism: A Symposium*, ed. Richard F. French (Port Washington, NY: Kennikat Press, 1969), 83–86; John Rockwell, "Music: Bucquet Returns: Her Piano Program Teams Xenakis and Stockhausen Pieces with Bach," *New York Times*, 23 October 1975.

[17]B. H. Haggin, "Music Criticism Today," *Commentary* 46, no. 4 (October 1968): 71.

[18]Michael Steinberg, "Abbado, Cleveland Orchestra," *Boston Globe*, Saturday, 10 February 1973, 11.

[19]Samaroff, "Performer as Critic," 88.

[20]Ibid., 87.

[21]Samuel Lipman, "A Constitution for Critics," *Music Journal* 35, no. 9 (November 1977): 11.

[22]*The New Grove's Dictionary of Music and Musicians*, 6th ed., s.v. "Criticism," by Winton Dean.

[23]Max Graf, *Composer and Critic: Two Hundred Years of Musical Criticism* (New York: W. W. Norton, 1946), 173–74.

[24]Ernest Newman, "A Third Open Letter to a Young Musical Critic, on the Subject of Libel," in *A Musical Motley* (New York: Alfred A. Knopf, 1925), 142–43.

[25]Andrew Porter, preface to *Music of Three Seasons* (New York: Farrar, Straus, & Giroux), p. ix.

[26]Scot Haller, "Creators on Creating: Eudora Welty," *Saturday Review*, June 1981, 46.

[27]Porter, preface to *Music of Three Seasons*, p. ix.

[28]Ibid., p. x.

[29]Harold C. Schonberg mentioned this at the Institute on Reviewing Piano Performance and Literature (Maryland institute), held at the University of Maryland, College Park, MD, on August 7–16, 1974.

[30]David Cairns made this point at the Carnegie Hall conference.

[31]Graf, *Composer and Critic*, 115.

[32]My friend, Michael Rosse, who had lived in Bombay, told me this.

[33]Michael C. Tusa, review of *Writings on Music*, by Carl Maria von Weber, *Nineteenth Century Music* 6, no. 3 (spring 1983): 273.

[34]Olin Downes, "Stravinsky Introduces His Concerto; Mengelberg Conducts Schubert," *New York Times*, 6 February 1925.

[35]Oscar Thompson, *Practical Musical Criticism* (New York: M. Witmark and Sons, 1934), 9.

[36]Daniel Schorr made this point at the Washington symposium.

[37]Edward Rothstein brought up this concern at the annual meeting of the Music Critics Association (1992 MCANA meeting), Chicago, IL, on October 29, 1992.

[38]Allan Shields, "Critic Past, Critic Present," *Music Educators Journal* 58, no. 4 (December 1971): 27.

[39]Nicholas Kenyon, "Personal questions: Music: Nicholas Kenyon on a symposium exploring Mozart's piano concertos," *Observer* (London), Sunday, 26 November 1989.

[40]Harold C. Schonberg, "A Lifetime of Listening," *New York Times*, 8 February 1981, sec. 6, p. 40.

[41]Eric Salzman reported this on November 3, 1979, in New York City at the Panel Discussion on Music Criticism (New York round table), held at the annual meeting of the American Musicological Society. He also wrote to me on June 5, 1980, to clarify the details.

[42]William Littler mentioned this at the Carnegie Hall conference.

[43]Thomson, *Virgil Thomson*, 321.

[44]George Bernard Shaw, *How To Become a Musical Critic*, ed. Dan H. Laurence (New York: Hill and Wang: 1961), 178–83.

[45]Max Graf, *Composer and Critic*, 28–29.

[46]Schonberg, "Lifetime of Listening," 40.

[47]Mina Curtiss, *Bizet and His World* (New York: Alfred A. Knopf, 1958), 394.

[48]Alan Walker, *Franz Liszt, v.1: The Virtuoso Years 1811–1847* (New York: Alfred A. Knopf, 1983), 164.

[49]Henry F. Chorley, *Modern German Music*, v.2 (New York: Da Capo, 1973), 66–67.

[50]Gilbert Chase, review of *The Principles and Methods of Musical Criticism*, by M. D. Calvocoressi, *Notes* 26, no. 2 (December 1969): 237–41; Ernest Newman, "A Syndicate of Musical Critics," in Ernest Newman, *A Musical Motley* (New York: Alfred A. Knopf, 1925), 227; additional comments by Newman are quoted in "The Temptations of Saint Kritikus," *Musical America* 56 (10 February 1936): 13; Virgil Thomson, *Virgil Thomson*, 81.

[51]Edward Downes, "The Taste Makers: Critics and Criticism," in Paul Henry Lang, ed., *One Hundred Years of Music in America* (New York: G. Schirmer, 1961), 241–42.

[52]This point was made at the Carnegie Hall conference.

[53]The *Philadelphia Evening Bulletin* paid for its own concert tickets when I worked for it.

[54]Samaroff, "Performer as Critic," 82–83.

[55]Harold C. Schonberg stated this at the Maryland institute.

[56]For instance, at the *New York Herald Tribune*, Geoffrey Parsons tried to confer with Virgil Thomson before making changes in Thomson's Sunday essays. This matter is described in John Vinton, "The Art of Gentlemanly Discourse: Geoffrey Parsons to Virgil Thomson," in John Vinton, *Essays After a Dictionary* (Lewisburg, PA: Bucknell University Press, 1977), 56–59.

[57]Hard feelings about this matter were rampant at the annual meeting of the Music Critics Association (1988 MCANA meeting), held in Charleston, SC, on May 27–30, 1988.

[58]Samuel Singer, *The Student Journalist and Reviewing the Performing Arts* (New York: Richards Rosen Press, 1974), 22.

[59]This point was made at the Institute on Contemporary Music, held at Tanglewood in Lenox, MA, on August 4–12, 1978.

[60]Robert Schick, "Curtis Stages 3 Operas," *Philadelphia Evening Bulletin*, 19 October 1974.

[61]Richard Freed made the remark about grammar at the 1988 MCANA meeting.

[62]Jennie R. Buckner made this last point at the Washington symposium.

[63]Daniel Schorr told this at the Washington symposium.

[64]I learned these guidelines largely by watching what is printed. Harold C. Schonberg also mentioned (4) and (5) at the Carnegie Hall conference and Isaac Stern mentioned (6) at the Washington symposium.

[65]Edward Rothstein discussed this matter at the 1994 MCANA meeting. See also Alex Ross, "The Debut: Grand Rite of Passage Now Passé," *New York Times*, 19 May 1993.

[66]Virgil Thomson, *Virgil Thomson*, 329–30.

[67]Ruth King, "Who Are the Record Critics?" *Music Journal* 35, no. 9 (November 1977): 14.

[68]A point made at the Carnegie Hall conference.

[69]Andrew Porter, preface to *Music of Three Seasons*, xiii.

[70]James Wierzbicki reported this at the Washington symposium.

[71]Television producer Clemente D'Alessio said this when we spoke on July 18, 1984.

[72]Charlotte Greenspan, "Performers and Instruments," *Nineteenth Century Music* 3, no. 1 (July 1979): 72–75; Geza Revesz, *The Psychology of a Musical Prodigy: Erwin Nyiregyházi* (Reprint of 1925 edition, New York: Johnson Reprint, 1970); Harold C. Schonberg, "The Case of the Vanishing Pianist," *New York Times*, sec. 2, pp. 15–16.

[73]James T. Oestreich, "For Rudolf Bing at 88, Operatic Drama Lingers," *New York Times*, Sunday, 11 March 1990, sec. 2, p. 1.

[74]Thomas Willis said this at the Carnegie Hall conference.

[75]The situation seems brighter in England. See John Rockwell, "Britain's Usually Staid Classical-Music Broadcasters Cause a Bit of a Ripple," *New York Times*, 6 January 1993.

[76]Scott Cantrell stated this at the 1994 MCANA meeting.

[77]Paul Hertelendy made this point at the 1994 MCANA meeting.

[78]This matter was discussed at the annual meeting of the Music Critics Association held in New York, NY, on May 19–24, 1991.

[79]Ibid.

[80]Ibid.

[81]Nancy Malitz made these points at the 1992 MCANA meeting.

[82]Allan Kozinn, "The World of Richard Strauss, Murky and Not So Honorable," *New York Times*, 25 August 1992. Kozinn's review and the *Times'* reaction to it were discussed at the 1992 MCANA meeting.
[83]"Editors' Note," *New York Times*, 26 August 1992, sec. A, p. 2.

Chapter Five: The Principles Behind Value Judgments

[1]Samuel Beckett, *Waiting for Godot* (New York: Grove Press, 1970), 48b.

[2]James S. Ackerman in James S. Ackerman and Rhys Carpenter, *Art and Archaeology* (Englewood Cliffs, NJ: Prentice-Hall, 1963), 145–56.

[3]John M. Robertson, *New Essays towards a Critical Method* (London and New York: John Lane, 1897); Robertson's ideas are discussed in M. D. Calvocoressi, *The Principles and Methods of Musical Criticism*, 2d ed. (London: Oxford University Press, 1931), 36, but Calvocoressi does not give the page number for Robertson's book.

[4]Monroe C. Beardsley, *Aesthetics: Problems in the Philosophy of Criticism* (New York: Harcourt, Brace and World, 1958), 44–45.

[5]George Bernard Shaw, "Stanford on the Critics," in *G. B. S. on Music* (Harmondsworth, Middlesex: Penguin Books, 1962), 185.

[6]Anatole France, *La Vie litteraire* (On Life and Letters), vol. 1, preface, trans. A. W. Evans (Freeport, NY: Books for Libraries Press, 1971), vii–viii.

[7]Paul Rosenfeld, *Musical Chronicle* (New York: Harcourt, Brace, 1923), 131.

[8]Barbara Mueser, "The Criticism of New Music in New York: 1919–1929" (Ph.D. dissertation, The City University of New York, 1975), 143.

[9]Beardsley, *Aesthetics*, 524–43.

[10]Ibid., 531.

[11]George Dickie, "The Myth of the Aesthetic Attitude," *American Philosophical Quarterly* 1, no. 1 (January 1964): 56–66.

[12]Monroe C. Beardsley, *Aesthetics: Problems in the Philosophy of Criticism*, 2d ed. (Indianapolis: Hackett, 1981), lxi.

[13]John Dewey, *Art as Experience* (New York: Minton, Balch, 1934), 42–43.

[14]See Beardsley, *Aesthetics*, either edition, 471–72.

[15]Dewey, *Art as Experience*, 37–38.

[16]Leonard B. Meyer, *Emotion and Meaning in Music* (Chicago: University of Chicago Press, 1956), 60–73.

[17]Allan Kozinn, "The 'Unfashionably Romantic' Music of John Corigliano," *New York Times*, 27 April 1980, sec. 2, p. 19.

[18]John Rockwell spoke at Haverford College, Haverford, PA, on March 6, 1986.

[19]Meyer, *Emotion and Meaning*, 27.

[20]Immanuel Kant, *Critique of Judgment*, 2d ed., trans. J. H. Bernard, (London: Macmillan, 1914), #1, p. 45n; quoted in Monroe C. Beardsley, *Aesthetics from Classical Greece to the Present* (New York: Macmillan, 1966), 212.

[21]Monroe C. Beardsley, *Aesthetics from Classical Greece to the Present*, 180.

[22]Ibid., 214.

[23]Deborah Jowitt, *Dance Beat* (New York and Basel: Marcel Dekker, 1977), 176.

[24]Alan Rich, "On the Firing Line," *Opera News* 35, no. 11 (9 January 1971): 10.

[25]Antony Flew, *A Dictionary of Philosophy* (New York: St. Martin's Press, 1979), s. v. "Relativism."

[26]*The New Encyclopaedia Britannica*, 15th ed., s. v. "Relativism, ethical."

[27]Flew, *Dictionary of Philosophy*, s. v. "Relativism."

[28]Cleanth Brooks, *The Well Wrought Urn* (New York: Reynal and Hitchcock, 1947), 231.

[29]Bruno Nettl, *Theory and Method in Ethnomusicology* (New York: The Free Press of Glencoe, 1964), 10–11.

[30]Beardsley, *Aesthetics: Problems in the Philosophy of Criticism*, either edition, 494–95. For an example of genre criticism, see Edith Borroff, "Entertainment Vindicated," *The American Music Teacher* 28, no. 3 (January 1979): 17.

[31]Beardsley, *Aesthetics: Problems in the Philosophy of Criticism*, either edition, 486.

[32]Ibid., 205–09.

[33]Leonard B. Meyer made this point from the floor during a round-table discussion on music criticism which took place at the annual meeting of the American Musicological Society (New York City, November 3, 1979).

[34]Meyer, *Emotion and Meaning*, 32.

[35]Mina Curtiss, *Bizet and His World* (New York: Alfred A. Knopf, 1958), 438.

[36]Kozinn, "John Corigliano."

[37]Michael Tippett, "Some Categories of Judgement in Modern Music," *Soundings* 1, no. 1 (1970): 3.

[38]Calvocoressi, *Principles and Methods,* 106.

[39]Maynard Solomon, "Charles Ives: Some Questions of Veracity," *Journal of the American Musicological Society* 40, no. 3 (fall 1987): 460.

[40]Monroe C. Beardsley, *Aesthetics: Problems in the Philosophy of Criticism,* either edition, 460.

[41]Readers desiring further suggestions about how to evaluate music should consult Arnold Schoenberg, "Criteria for the Evaluation of Music," in Arnold Schoenberg, *Style and Idea,* ed. Leonard Stein (New York: St. Martin's Press, 1975); and Virgil Thomson, "The Art of Judging Music," in Virgil Thomson, *The Art of Judging Music* (New York: Alfred A. Knopf, 1948).

Chapter Six: The Concert and Opera Review

[1]Allan Kozinn, "Piano: Mark Anderson," *New York Times,* 5 March 1988.

[2]Will Crutchfield, "A 'Figaro' With Early Instruments," *New York Times,* 20 June 1989.

[3]Walter Legge, "Hugo Wolf," in Elisabeth Schwarzkopf, *On and Off the Record: A Memoir of Walter Legge* (New York: Scribner's, 1982), 35; first published in *Manchester Guardian,* February 1936.

[4]John Rockwell, "Schiff's Central European Assortment," *New York Times,* 22 October 1989.

[5]Oscar Thompson, *Practical Musical Criticism* (New York: M. Witmark and Sons, 1934), 29.

[6]Bernard Holland, "Recital: _____ Piano Debut," *New York Times,* 1 March 1982.

[7]Nicolas Slonimsky, *Lexicon of Musical Invective,* 2d ed. (New York: Coleman-Ross, 1965).

[8]Daniel Webster, "Phila. Orchestra Tests Carnegie Hall's New Sound," *Philadelphia Inquirer,* 2 November 1989.

[9]Patrick J. Smith, "American Criticism: The Porter Experience," *Nineteenth Century Music* 2, no. 3 (March 1979): 256.

[10]Michael Kennedy, "Roaring brawl and lyric musing: Michael Kennedy on two extraordinary new compositions," *Sunday Telegraph* (London), 26 November 1989.

[11]Michael Steinberg, "Harbison debuts 'Five Songs,' " *Boston Evening Globe*, 2 March 1973.

[12]Rodney Milnes, "Le Grand Macabre: Festival Hall," *Financial Times* (London), 1 November 1989.

[13]Virgil Thomson, "Fairy Tale about Music," *New York Herald Tribune*, 13 January 1945.

[14]Peter Heyworth, "Terror Town on the Downs: Peter Heyworth on Tippett's new opera and serious Rossini," *Observer* (London), Sunday, 8 July 1990.

Chapter Seven: Writing the Concert and Opera Review

[1]In 1971 I heard Martin Bernheimer of the *Los Angeles Times* tell his class on music criticism at UCLA: "Avoid technical language you can't manage."

[2]Andrew Porter, "Musical Events: Island Symphony," *The New Yorker*, 30 October 1978, 148.

[3]Edward Rothstein, "Esther Lives in Modern Musical Terms: Hugo Weisgall's 10th opera has its world premiere at City Opera," *New York Times*, 11 October 1993, sec. C, p. 11.

[4]Harold C. Schonberg stated this at the Symposium on Music Criticism in America's Press (Washington symposium), which took place in Washington, DC, on March 28–29, 1987.

[5]Michael Steinberg, "Jochum conducts Boston Symphony," *Boston Globe*, 27 January 1973, 12.

[6]Artur Rubinstein, Eastman Theatre, Rochester, NY, 23 February 1959, 8:15 P.M.; Birgit Nilsson, Royce Hall, UCLA, Los Angeles, CA, 31 March 1971, 8:30 P.M.

[7]Hector Berlioz, *Evenings with the Orchestra*, trans. Jacques Barzun (New York: Alfred A. Knopf, 1969), "Seventh Evening," 76–98.

[8]Pennsylvania Opera Theatre, June 1, 7, and 8, 1985, at the Walnut St. Theatre, Philadelphia, PA.

[9]Philadelphia Lyric Opera Company, May 27 and 29, 1975, at the Academy of Music, Philadelphia, PA; director: James deBlasis; scenery and costume designer: Henry Heymann.

[10]John Rockwell, "When France Goes Into a Straussian Trance," *New York Times*, 21 April 1994.

[11]Most or all of the participants in the International Conference on Music Criticism (Carnegie Hall conference) agreed with this point. The conference was held in New York City on May 8–11, 1979.

[12]Joseph Spencer stated this at the annual meeting of the Music Critics Association (1990 MCANA meeting), which was held in Berkeley, CA, on June 14–17, 1990.

[13]Monroe C. Beardsley, *Aesthetics: Problems in the Philosophy of Criticism* (New York: Harcourt, Brace, and World, 1958), 21–24.

[14]Martin Bernheimer made this point in 1971 during his class on music criticism at UCLA.

[15]James Goodfriend, "Going on Record: Objective Music Criticism," *Stereo Review* 22, no. 1 (January 1969): 48.

Chapter Eight: Intentions, Program Music, and the Expression Theory

[1]William Mann, "RPO/Gardelli, Festival Hall," *Times* (London), 7 June 1973.

[2]Monroe C. Beardsley, *Aesthetics: Problems in the Philosophy of Criticism* (New York: Harcourt, Brace & World, 1958), 17–29.

[3]Eduard Hanslick, *The Beautiful in Music*, 7th ed., 1885, trans. Gustav Cohen (Indianapolis: Liberal Arts Press, 1957), 59.

[4]Beardsley, *Aesthetics*, 29.

[5]Carritt's statement is indirectly quoted in Alan Tormey, *The Concept of Expression* (Princeton: Princeton University Press, 1971), 127.

[6]Beardsley, *Aesthetics*, 320.

[7]Hanslick, *Beautiful in Music*, 50.

[8]Eduard Hanslick, *Music Criticisms* 1846–99, trans. and ed. Henry Pleasants (Baltimore: Penguin Books, 1950), 92.

[9]For further information about program music, see the brilliant tenth chapter in Carl Dahlhaus, *Esthetics of Music*, trans. William W. Austin (Cambridge: Cambridge University Press, 1982). Monroe C. Beardsley's lucid description presents a different emphasis in *Aesthetics: Problems in the Philosophy of Criticism* (348–52), as does Hanslick in *The Beautiful in Music*.

For the expression theory, Beardsley (325–32) and Hanslick are both good. Particularly recommended, though, is Alan Tormey, *The Concept of Expression*, especially chapters 4 and 5. For a different viewpoint, see Guy Sircello, *Mind and Art* (Princeton: Princeton University Press, 1972).

Chapter Nine: The Record Review

[1]David Ranada, "The Case for Minimal Miking in Recording," *Stereo Review* 46, no. 10 (October 1981): 56–58; Andrew Kazdin, "The Case for Multiple Miking in Recording," *Stereo Review* 46, no. 11 (November 1981): 64–66; Bruce Bartlett, "Microphoning," *Stereo Review* 46, no. 10 (October 1981): 50–55.

[2]Erich Leinsdorf, *Cadenza: A Musical Career* (Boston: Houghton Mifflin, 1976), 168–70.

[3]David Hamilton, "Misremembering Bayreuth," *High Fidelity* 32, no. 4 (April 1982): 58.

[4]James Oestreich said this at the Symposium on Recorded Music (symposium on recordings) held in New York City from June 2–11, 1983.

[5]Ruth King, "Who Are the Record Critics?" *Music Journal* 35, no. 9 (November 1977): 16.

[6]David Hall and David Hamilton spoke at the symposium on recordings.

[7]This topic was discussed at the International Conference on Music Criticism (Carnegie Hall conference) held in New York City from May 8–11, 1979.

[8]King, "Who are the Record Critics?" 14.

[9]James Goodfriend made this point at the symposium on recordings.

[10]Tim Page, "Glenn Gould Interviewed by Tim Page," *The Piano Quarterly*, no. 115 (fall 1981), 18.

[11]Samuel H. Carter, Thomas Frost, Andrew Kazdin, Paul Myers, Howard H. Scott, "Recording Gould: A Retake Here, a Splice There, a Myth Everywhere," *High Fidelity* 33, no. 2 (February 1983): 55.

[12]Leinsdorf, *Cadenza*, 132–33.

[13]Andrew Kazdin stated this at the symposium on recordings.

[14]Hall spoke at the symposium on recordings.

[15]Carter Harmon, one of the producers of CRI, reported this at the symposium on recordings. Fred Scott, the company's business manager, confirmed that this information was still up to date when we spoke by phone on July 23, 1993.

[16]My information on legal questions regarding pirated recordings comes from the symposium on recordings; *Circular R99: Highlights of the New Copyright Law* (Washington, D.C.: Copyright Office, Library of Congress, n.d.); and Sidney Shemel and M. William Krasilovsky, *This Business of Music*, rev. ed. (New York: Billboard, 1977), ch. 12.

[17]John Canarina, "Will the Real Colin Wilson Please Stand Up?" *High Fidelity* 31, no. 8 (August 1981): 48. A series of letters to the editor continued the discussion in the same magazine: 31, no. 11 (November 1981): 8; 31, no. 12 (December 1981): 4; 32, no. 2 (February 1982): 4.

[18]Peter G. Davis, "Gems from a Trove of Vocalism," *New York Times*, 3 August 1980, sec. 2, p. 20.

[19]Steven Smolian, "Caruso—Legendary Performer," *Association for Recorded Sound Collections—Journal* 8, nos. 2–3 (1976): 106.

[20]Davis, "Gems," sec. 2, p. 20; Steven Smolian, "Standards for the Review of Discographic Works," *Association for Recorded Sound Collections—Journal* 7, no. 3 (1976): 49–50.

[21]Harold C. Schonberg, "Player Piano Nights: Masters Return," *New York Times*, 16 July 1982, sec. C, p. 3.

[22]Irving Kolodin and Max Wilcox spoke on this subject at the symposium on recordings.

[23]Thomas Frost stated this at the symposium on recordings.

Chapter Ten: Reviewing Ethnic Concerts and Recordings

An earlier and considerably shorter version of this chapter was read on April 13, 1984, at the Newark, NJ, campus of Rutgers University during the annual meeting of the Mid-Atlantic Chapter of the Society for Ethnomusicology (MACSEM).

[1]Oscar Thompson, *Practical Musical Criticism* (New York: M. Witmark and Sons, 1934), 28.

[2]John Rockwell, "Music: India's Best Woman Singer," *New York Times*, 21 October 1977.

[3]Paul Hertelendy made this remark during the session on "The Responsibility of the Press Toward Ethnic Music" (Oakland round

table). This discussion, which I organized and moderated, took place on November 9, 1990, in Oakland, California, at the annual meeting of the Society for Ethnomusicology (SEM). The session was recorded and I made a transcription of the tape. The program listing and abstract read as follows:

SEM Round Table: What is the Responsibility of the Press
Toward Ethnic Music?

Chair: Robert D. Schick (West Chester University)
Participants:
    Robert Browning (World Music Institute)
    David Gere (*Oakland Tribune*)
    Paul Hertelendy (*San Jose Mercury News*)
    Gertrude Robinson (Loyola Marymount University)
    Karl Signell (University of Maryland, Baltimore County)
    Ricardo Trimillos (University of Hawaii)

ABSTRACT

Although performances of ethnic music are increasing in number in this country, their coverage in the daily press is often unsatisfactory. The panel will consider why this is so, along with ways of improving conditions, so that the press can help ethnomusicology. There will be no formal papers. After opening with a five-minute talk by each participant, the panel will debate the issues, followed by questions from the floor. The topics to be discussed will include the following:

    1) the role of the press in educating the public about ethnic music, including the space given to reviews, previews, and essays;

    2) the selection and training of critics for this job. Should ethnomusicologists also be reviewers?

    3) what a review should include;

    4) the problems faced by critics when reviewing a performance;

    5) how the profession of ethnomusicology can help the press do a better job.

[4]David Gere made this observation at the Oakland round table.
[5]Ricardo Trimillos made this point at the Oakland round table.

[6]Paul Hertelendy pointed this out at the Oakland round table.

[7]*The American College Dictionary* (New York: Random House, 1966), s. v. "Acculturation."

[8]Robert Palmer, "Pop: Peter, Paul, Mary," *New York Times*, 22 October 1980.

[9]Tom Johnson, "Zenska Pesna Sing as One," *New York Village Voice*, 27 February 1978.

[10]Paul Lashmar, "Record Releases: World Music," *Observer* (London), 12 August 1990.

[11]Paul Griffiths, "Nihon Ongaku Shudan: Queen Elizabeth Hall," *Times* (London), 16 September 1978.

[12]Robert Browning surveyed these critics in preparation for the Oakland round table, where he delivered his report.

[13]At the Oakland round table David Gere described an example of such manipulation.

[14]Ricardo Trimillos pointed this out at the Oakland round table.

[15]Gertrude Robinson stated this at the Oakland round table.

Chapter Eleven: Radio and Television Criticism

[1]Donald Lee of National Public Radio explained to me the difference between true criticism and commentary on May 22, 1986.

[2]For a discussion of the pressures on classical music stations today, see Seth Mydans, "Los Angeles Journal: In a Quest for Profit, Beethoven Is Ousted," *New York Times*, 20 September 1989; two letters replying to that article are printed in "Letters: On Radio, Beethoven Isn't About to Roll Over," *New York Times*, 6 October 1989.

[3]John Rockwell, "Britain's Usually Staid Classical-Music Broadcasters Cause a Bit of a Ripple," *New York Times*, 6 January 1993.

[4]Allan Kozinn, "Music Notes," *New York Times*, 16 November 1992.

[5]Edward Rothstein, "Classical View: WNCN Met the Enemy. Guess Who?" *New York Times*, 2 January 1994.

[6]Terry Peyton spoke to me on July 30, 1984, and again on August 21, 1991.

[7]Two employees of radio station WGMS in Rockville, Maryland, kindly provided this information—John Chester and Mary Kading in 1984, and Mary Kading again in 1990.

[8]For example, the *CBS News Index 1982* (Sanford, NC: Microfilming Corporation of America, 1983). Transcripts of the broadcasts listed in the index are available on microfiche from the publisher.

[9]CBS Evening News with Bob Schieffer, 22 May 1982; listed on p. 542 of the *CBS News Index 1982* (Sanford, NC: Microfilming Corporation of America, 1983) as "Vladimir Horowitz plays benefit concert in London. My 22: P13."

[10]Virgil Thomson, "Toscanini's Aïda," *New York Herald Tribune*, 27 March 1949.

[11]Allan Kozinn, "Critic's Notebook: Marked Diminuendo In Classical Radio," *New York Times,* 22 December 1993; Edward Rothstein, "Classical View: WNCN Met the Enemy. Guess Who?" *New York Times*, 2 January 1994. Letters to the editor on this and related topics appeared in the *New York Times* on 10 October 1993, 24 December 1993, and 15 January 1994.

[12]Television producer Clemente D'Alessio made this point when we spoke on July 18, 1984.

[13]Steven A. Herman discusses this in a letter to Donal Henahan, quoted in Donal Henahan, "Music View: Must Symphony Concerts and Television Be Incompatible?" *New York Times*, 20 February 1983.

[14]Jack Kuney, "Calling the Shots at the Metropolitan Opera: Kirk Browning Interviewed by Jack Kuney," *Television Quarterly* 20, no. 4 (1984): 77.

[15]Ibid., 79.

[16]Edward Rothstein, "Concert Telecasts Can Be an Art Form," *New York Times*, 2 Mar 1984. The camerawork was by Kirk Browning in a "Live from Lincoln Center" telecast of the New York Philharmonic under Zubin Mehta.

[17]Lucy A. Kraus, "He Calls the Shots on Those 'Live from' Programs," *New York Times*, 29 April 1979, sec. D, p. 35.

[18]Ibid., sec. D, p. 34.

[19]Ibid., sec. D, p. 35.

[20]John Rockwell, "The Impact of TV on Opera," *New York Times*, 25 January 1981, sec. D, p. 1.

[21]Irving Kolodin, " 'Salome' on NBC-TV, League of Composers," *Saturday Review*, 22 May 1954, 30.

[22]John J. O'Connor, "Tchaikovsky's 'Queen of Spades,' "*New York Times*, 9 April 1984.

[23]Rockwell, "Impact of TV," sec. D, p. 19.

[24]Miriam Lewin of the Opera Company of Philadelphia told me this in 1984.

[25]Kuney, "Calling the Shots," 78–79.

[26]Ibid.

Bibliography

This bibliography does not list articles or reviews from newspapers. The chapter notes include many such examples as well as additional references from books and journals.

Adorno, Theodor W. *Introduction to the Sociology of Music.* Translated by E. B. Ashton. New York: The Seabury Press, 1976.

Allen, Warren Dwight. *Philosophies of Music History.* New York: American Book Company, 1939.

Ardoin, John. "A Critic Looks at Criticism." *Catalyst* (spring 1976): 8–9.

Ashley, Paul, with Camden M. Hall. *Say It Safely: Legal Limits in Publishing, Radio, and Television*, 5th ed. Seattle: University of Washington Press, 1976.

Bach, Karl Philipp Emanuel. *Essay on the True Art of Playing Keyboard Instruments.* Translated and edited by W. J. Mitchell. New York: W. W. Norton, 1949.

Badura-Skoda, Eva, and Paul Badura-Skoda. *Interpreting Mozart on the Keyboard.* Translated by L. Black. New York: St. Martin's Press, 1962.

Baumol, Hilda, William J. Baumol, and Edward Wolff. "A Study on the Influence of Music Critics." Mimeographed, c. 1980. A report sponsored by the National Endowment for the Humanities through the agency of the Carnegie Hall Corporation.

Beardsley, Monroe C. *Aesthetics from Classical Greece to the Present: A Short History.* New York: Macmillan, 1966.

———. *Aesthetics: Problems in the Philosophy of Criticism.* New York: Harcourt, Brace, and World, 1958; 2d ed., Indianapolis: Hackett, 1981. The two editions are identical in all respects except that the second edition also contains a postscript numbered in lower-case Roman numerals.

Belt, Byron. "Critic at Large: Why Music Critics?" *Music Journal* 34, no. 2 (February 1976): 8.

Borroff, Edith. "Entertainment Vindicated." *The American Music Teacher* 18, no. 3 (March 1979): 12–17.

Britten, Benjamin. "Variations on a Critical Theme." *Opera* 3, no. 3 (March 1952): 144–46.

Bullough, Edward. "Psychical Distance as a Factor in Art and an Aesthetic Principle." *In Aesthetics: A Critical Anthology*, edited by George Dickie and R. J. Sclafani. New York: St. Martin's Press, 1977. (Other anthologies often include this article in incomplete form.) First published in *British Journal of Psychology* 5 (1912): 87–98.

Burns, Richard. "A University Course in Historical Sound Recordings." *Association for Recorded Sound Collections—Journal* 5, no. 1 (1973): 4–25.

Caldwell, John. Review of *Anatomy of Musical Criticism*, by Alan Walker. *Music and Letters* 48, no. 3 (July 1967): 265–66.

Calvocoressi, M. D. *The Principles and Methods of Musical Criticism*, 2d ed. London: Oxford University Press, 1931.

Chase, Gilbert. Review of *The Principles and Methods of Musical Criticism*, by M. D. Calvocoressi. *Notes* 26, no. 2 (December 1969): 237–41.

Clark, Kenneth. "Critics of Opera and the Amateur." *Opera* 3, no. 3 (March 1952): 149–54.

Clarke, Henry Leland. "Composers Reviewing Composers." *Notes* 26, no. 2 (December 1969): 221–25.

Cole, Hugo. "Critics and Composers." *Composer* (London), no. 47 (spring 1973): 1–5.

"Composer and Critic: Two Views of Their Responsibility to the Art of Music and Its Public." *Newsletter: Institute for Studies in American Music* 10, no. 2 (May 1981): 1.

Cone, Edward T. "The Authority of Music Criticism." *Journal of the American Musicological Society* 34, no. 1 (spring 1981): 1–18.

Cooke, Deryck. "The Futility of Music Criticism." *Musical Newsletter* 2, no. 1 (January 1972): 7–9.

"The Critic: Hero or Villain? A Conversation at the Eastman School of Music." *Rochester Review*, spring–summer 1982, 7–11.

Critical Issues. (Formerly *Newsletter of the Music Critic's Association, Inc.*) Music Critic's Association of North America, Inc., 7 Pine Court, Westfield, NJ 07090, U.S.A.

"Critics compare opinions. Martin Bernheimer and others." *Music and Artists* 5, no. 1 (February–March 1972): 14–15.

Dahlhaus, Carl. *Esthetics of Music*. Translated by William W. Austin. Cambridge: Cambridge University Press, 1982.

Dart, Thurston. *The Interpretation of Music*. London: Hutchison, 1954.

Dean, Winton. "Critic and Composer." *Opera* 3, no. 3 (March 1952): 154–61.

———. *The New Grove Dictionary of Music and Musicians*, 6th ed. S.v. "Criticism."

Debussy, Claude. *Monsieur Croche the Dilettante Hater*. In *Three Classics in the Aesthetic of Music*. New York: Dover, 1962.

Dewey, John. *Art as Experience*. New York: Minton, Balch, 1934.

Dickie, George. "The Myth of the Aesthetic Attitude." *American Philosophical Quarterly* 1, no. 1 (January 1964): 56–66.

Donington, Robert. *Baroque Music, Style and Performance: A Handbook*. New York: W. W. Norton, 1982.

———. *The Interpretation of Early Music*. London: Faber and Faber, 1963.

Dorian, Frederick. *The History of Music in Performance*. New York: W. W. Norton, 1942.

Downes, Edward. "The Taste Makers: Critics and Criticism." In *One Hundred Years of Music in America*, edited by Paul Henry Lang. New York: G. Schirmer, 1961.

Downes, Olin. "Be Your Own Music Critic." In *Be Your Own Music Critic*, edited by Robert E. Simon, Jr. Garden City, NY: Doubleday, Doran, 1941.

Ehle, Robert C. "Music as Revelation." *The American Music Teacher* 28, no. 6 (June–July 1979): 28.

French, Richard F., ed. *Music and Criticism: A Symposium*. Port Washington, NY: Kennikat Press, 1969.

———. "On Reviewing Music." *Notes* 26, no. 2 (December 1969): 213–20.

Fuller, David. Review of *Ornamentation in Baroque and Post-Baroque Music: With Special Emphasis on J. S. Bach*, by Frederick Neumann. *Journal of the American Musicological Society* 33, no. 2 (summer 1980): 394–402.

Gilman, Lawrence. "Taste in Music." *Musical Quarterly* 3, no. 1 (January 1917): 1–8.

Goldstein, Norm, ed. *The Associated Press Stylebook and Libel Manual*. Reading, MA: Addison-Wesley, 1992.

Graf, Max. *Composer and Critic: Two Hundred Years of Musical Criticism.* New York: W. W. Norton, 1946.

Gray, Maxine Cushing, ed. *The Art of Criticism: Twenty Articles Reprinted from "Northwest Arts."* Seattle: Northwest Arts (Box 97, Seattle, WA 98125), 1984.

Gray, Michael H. "Discography: Its Prospects and Problems." *Notes* 35, no. 3 (March 1979): 578–92.

Griffith, A. C. "Historical Transcriptions: Problems in the Transfer of Historical Recordings to L.P." *Association for Recorded Sound Collections—Journal* 8, no. 1 (1976): 28–32.

Hanslick, Eduard. *Music Criticisms 1846–99*, rev. ed. Translated and edited by Henry Pleasants. Baltimore: Penguin, 1963.

————. *Vom Musikalisch-Schönen*, Leipzig: R. Weigel, 1854. Seventh edition, 1891, translated by Gustav Cohen under the title, *The Beautiful in Music.* Indianapolis: Bobbs-Merrill, 1957. Eighth edition, 1891, translated by Geoffrey Payzant under the title, *On the Musically Beautiful.* Indianapolis: Hackett, 1986.

Harewood, Earl of. "Comment." *Opera* 3, no. 3 (March 1952): 132–36.

Heinsheimer, Hans W. "A Music Publisher's View on Reviewing." *Notes* 26, no. 2 (December 1969): 226–30.

Hume, David. "Of the Standard of Taste." In *Aesthetics: A Critical Anthology*, edited by George Dickie and R. J. Sclafani. New York: St. Martin's Press, 1977. First published in 1757.

Hunt, Todd. *Reviewing for the Mass Media.* Philadelphia: Chilton, 1972.

Jacobs, Arthur. *The International Cyclopedia of Music and Musicians*, 10th ed. S.v. "Criticism, Musical."

Jones, Samuel. "Towards a Philosophy of Music Criticism." *Symphony News* 27, no. 1 (February 1976): 11.

Koffka, Kurt. "Problems in the Psychology of Art." In *Art: A Bryn Mawr Symposium.* Bryn Mawr, PA: Bryn Mawr College, 1940.

Kolodin, Irving, ed. *The Critical Composer: The Musical Writings of Berlioz, Wagner, Schumann, Tchaikovsky, and Others.* Port Washington, N.Y.: Kennikat, 1969.

Leichentritt, Hugo, revised by John Reeves White. *Harvard Dictionary of Music*, 2d ed. S.v. "Music Criticism."

Lipman, Samuel. " A Constitution for Critics." *Music Journal* 35, no. 9 (November 1977): 8–11.

Lissa, Zofia. "The Precarious Art of Music Criticism." *World of Music* 14, no. 3 (1972): 20–38.

Loewenstein, F. E. "Bernard Shaw, Music Critic." In *Hinrichsen's Musical Year Book,* v. 6, 1949–50, edited by Max Hinrichsen, 147–52. London: Hinrichsen Edition Limited, n.d.

Malitz, Nancy. "About Face: How Trends in Taste and Technology Affect the Role of the Music Critic in the Daily Newspaper." *Criticus Musicus* 1, no. 1 (spring 1993): 36–44.

Matthews, Robert J. "Describing and Interpreting a Work of Art." *Journal of Aesthetics and Art Criticism* 36, no. 1 (fall 1977): 5–14.

McLean, Eric. "Hanslick Had It Better." *World of Music* 14, no. 3 (1972): 3–18.

Meyer, Leonard B. *Emotion and Meaning in Music.* Chicago: University of Chicago Press, 1956.

———. *Music, the Arts, and Ideas.* Chicago: University of Chicago Press, 1967.

Mihelcic, Pavel. "Musical Criticism and Modern Music." Excerpted in *International Review of the Aesthetics and Sociology of Music* 2, no. 2 (1971): 280.

Mozart, J. G. Leopold. *A Treatise on the Fundamental Principles of Violin Playing.* Translated by E. Knocker. London: Oxford University Press, 1948.

Mueser, Barbara. "The Criticism of New Music in New York: 1919–1929." Ph.D. diss., The City University of New York, 1975.

Myers, Rollo. "The Possibilities of Musical Criticism." *Musical Quarterly* 14, no. 3 (July 1928): 387–96.

Neumann, Frederick. *Ornamentation in Baroque and Post-Baroque Music: With Special Emphasis on J. S. Bach.* Princeton: Princeton University Press, 1978.

New Music and Its Criticism. Bilthoven, Netherlands: Foundation Gaudeamus, P. O. Box 30, n.d.

Newman, Ernest. *A Musical Critic's Holiday.* New York: Alfred A. Knopf, 1925.

———. *A Musical Motley.* New York: Alfred A. Knopf, 1925.

———. "A 'Physiology' of Criticism." In *From the World of Music,* edited by Felix Aprahamian. New York: Coward-McCann, 1957.

———. "A Postscript to *A Musical Critic's Holiday.*" *Musical Times* 66, no. 992 (1 October): 881–84; no. 993 (1 November): 977–81; no. 994 (1 December 1925): 1076–79.

Newman, William S. *Beethoven on Beethoven: Playing His Piano Music His Way.* New York: W. W. Norton, 1988.

Parakilas, James P. "Music for the People: George Bernard Shaw's Musical Socialism." *Musical Newsletter* 7, no. 1 (winter 1977): 21–28.

Porter, Andrew. *A Musical Season.* New York: Viking Press, 1974.

———. *Music of Three Seasons.* New York: Farrar, Straus, & Giroux, 1978.

Porter, James. "Documentary Recordings in Ethnomusicology: Theoretical and Methodological Problems." *Association for Recorded Sound Collections—Journal* 6, no. 2 (1974): 3–16.

Prieberg, Fred K. "The Critic Is Superfluous Today." *World of Music* 14, no. 3 (1972): 39–52.

Quantz, Johann Joachim. *On Playing the Flute,* 2d ed. Translated by Edward R. Reilly. New York: Schirmer Books, 1985.

Radovanovic, Vladan. "Theory and Criticism with Reference to Creativity in Music." *International Review of the Aesthetics and Sociology of Music* 2, no. 2 (1971): 275–80.

Review of the Arts: Film and Television. New Canaan, CT: Newsbank.

Ringer, Alexander. "Music Taste and the Industrial Syndrome." *International Review of the Aesthetics and Sociology of Music* 5, no. 1 (June 1974): 139–53.

Rockwell, John. "On Music Criticism as a Career." *Newsletter of the Music Critics Association, Inc.* 18, no. 1 (November 1979): 6–7. Address of newsletter: Music Critics Association of North America, Inc., 7 Pine Court, Westfield, NJ 07090, U.S.A.

"The Role of the Music Critic." *Central Opera Service Bulletin* 14 (April 1972): 20–21.

Rosen, Charles. "The Proper Study of Music." *Perspectives of New Music* 1, no. 1 (fall 1962): 80–88.

Rosenberg, Bernard, and Deena Rosenberg. "A Music Critic Speaks: An Interview with Michael Steinberg." *Musical Newsletter* 6, no. 4 (fall 1976): 9–18.

Salzman, Eric. "The Revolution in Music." In *New American Review,* No. 6, 76–96. New York: The New American Library, 1969.

Schoenberg, Arnold. "Criteria for the Evaluation of Music." In Arnold Schoenberg, *Style and Idea,* 2d ed., edited by Leonard Stein. New York: St. Martin's Press, 1975.

Scholes, Percy A. *The Oxford Companion to Music,* 10th ed. S.v. "Criticism of Music."

Schonberg, Harold C. *Facing the Music.* New York: Summit Books, 1981.

Schumann, Robert. *On Music and Musicians.* Edited by Konrad Wolff. Translated by Paul Rosenfeld. New York: McGraw-Hill, 1946.

Sedak, Eva. "Some Problems in Contemporary Musical Criticism." *International Review of Music Aesthetics and Sociology* 1, no. 2 (December 1970): 169–78.

Sessions, Roger. *The Musical Experience of Composer, Performer, Listener.* Princeton: Princeton University Press, 1950.

Sharpe, Robert. "The Critical Consensus." *Music Review* 35, no. 1 (February–May 1974): 58–62.

Shaw, George Bernard. "How to Become a Musical Critic." In George Bernard Shaw, *How to Become a Musical Critic*, edited by Dan H. Laurence. New York: Hill and Wang, 1961. (First published in the *Scottish Musical Monthly*, December 1894.)

———. *Music in London 1890–94: Criticisms Contributed Week by Week to the World.* London: Constable, 1931.

———. "Stanford on the Critics." In *G. B. S. on Music*, pp. 184–89. Harmondsworth, Middlesex: Penguin Books, 1962. (First published in the *World*, 13 June 1894.)

Shields, Allan. "Critic Past, Critic Present." *Music Educators Journal* 58, no. 4 (December 1971): 27.

Singer, Samuel L. *The Student Journalist and Reviewing the Performing Arts.* New York: Richards Rosen, 1974.

Sircello, Guy. *Mind and Art.* Princeton: Princeton University Press, 1972.

Slonimsky, Nicolas. *Lexicon of Musical Invective*, 2d ed. New York: Coleman Ross, 1965.

Smith, Patrick J. "American Criticism: The Porter Experience." *Nineteenth Century Music* 2, no. 3 (March 1979): 254–63.

Smolian, Steven. "Standards for the Review of Discographic Works." *Association for Recorded Sound Collections—Journal* 7, no. 3 (1976): 47–55.

Stein, Erwin. "The Critic's Position." *Opera* 3, no. 3 (March 1952): 146–48.

Steinberg, Michael. Review of *Music of Three Seasons: 1974–1977*, by Andrew Porter. *Notes* 35, no. 4 (June 1979): 874–76.

Stone, Kurt. "The Art of Reviewing Music." *Notes* 26, no. 2 (December 1969): 231–36.

Strunk, William Jr., and E. B. White. *The Elements of Style*, 3d ed. New York: Macmillan, 1979.

"The Temptations of Saint Kriticus." *Musical America* 56 (10 February 1936): 13.

Thompson, Oscar. *Practical Musical Criticism.* New York: M. Witmark & Sons, 1934. Reprint, New York: Da Capo, 1979.

Thomson, Virgil. "The Art of Judging Music." In *The Art of Judging Music.* New York: Alfred A. Knopf, 1948.

———. *Music Right and Left.* New York: Henry Holt, 1951.

———. *The Musical Scene.* New York: Alfred A. Knopf, 1945.

———. *The State of Music.* New York: William Morrow, 1939.

Tormey, Alan. *The Concept of Expression.* Princeton: Princeton University Press, 1971.

Vermeulen, Ernst. "Congress on 'New Music and Criticism' in Rotterdam." *Sonorum Speculum* 44 (autumn 1970): 12–22.

Vinton, John. "The Art of Gentlemanly Discourse: Geoffrey Parsons to Virgil Thomson." In John Vinton, *Essays After a Dictionary.* Lewisburg, PA: Bucknell University Press, 1977.

Wellek, Rene. "Aesthetics and Criticism." In *The Philosophy of Kant and Our Modern World*, edited by Charles W. Hendel. New York: Liberal Arts Press, 1957.

Westrup, Sir Jack. *An Introduction to Musical History.* London: Hutchinson, 1955.

Zinsser, William. *On Writing Well*, 2d ed. New York: Harper & Row, 1980.

About the Author

Robert D. Schick was born in 1929 in New York City where he attended the High School of Music and Art. He holds a bachelor's degree from Swarthmore College, a master's with a major in music composition from Columbia University, and a Doctor of Musical Arts with a major in piano performance and pedagogy from the Eastman School of Music. He has also audited classes in ethnomusicology at several universities.

His training in music criticism began in high school when he elected a class in journalism. Later he served as a part-time music critic, briefly for *Musical America* in the fall of 1955, for *Musical Courier* in 1956–57, and from February 1974 through April 1975 for the *Philadelphia Evening Bulletin*.

His chief piano teacher was the noted pedagogue, Isabelle Vengerova, with whom he studied for ten years. His book about her method, *The Vengerova System of Piano Playing*, was published by Penn State Press in 1982. While at Eastman he also studied piano with Cecile Genhart.

Since 1959 he has been a college professor, first at Chatham College and since 1961 at West Chester University. He has taught piano, vocal accompanying, music criticism, aesthetics, introductory courses in non-Western music, and music theory. He also performs regularly as an accompanist, chamber musician, and solo pianist.

Index

The index begins with chapter one and covers all that follows except for the postscript to chapter seven, the appendix, and the bibliography.